DATE DUE

MAR 2 1 2008	
JUL 0 5 2008	
OCT 25 2008	
11~14	

HOUSE LUST

HOUSE LUST

AMERICA'S OBSESSION WITH OUR HOMES

Daniel McGinn

CURRENCY   DOUBLEDAY

NEW YORK   LONDON   TORONTO   SYDNEY   AUCKLAND

A CURRENCY BOOK PUBLISHED BY DOUBLEDAY

Published in the United States by Doubleday, an imprint of The Doubleday Broadway
Publishing Group, a division of Random House, Inc., New York.
www.currencybooks.com

Book design by Nancy Campana

Library of Congress Cataloging-in-Publication Data
McGinn, Daniel F.
    House lust : America's obsession with our homes / by Daniel McGinn. — 1st ed.
       p. cm.
    1. Home—United States—Psychological aspects. 2. Homeowners—United States—
Psychology. 3. Home ownership—United States. I. Title.
HQ536.M413 2007
155.9'4—dc22   2007027746

ISBN: 978-0-385-51929-8

PRINTED IN THE UNITED STATES OF AMERICA

SPECIAL SALES
Currency Books are available at special discounts for bulk purchases for sales promotions
or premiums. Special editions, including personalized covers, excerpts of existing books,
and corporate imprints, can be created in large quantities for special needs. For more
information, write to Special Markets, Currency Books, specialmarkets@randomhouse.com.

10   9   8   7   6   5   4   3   2   1

First Edition

To Amy

CONTENTS

INTRODUCTION

Rachael Brownell is a financial analyst with three kids, but every so often she and some friends get together for a girls' night out. They'll wipe off the baby drool, dab on some makeup, don high heels, and head to an Irish pub near their homes in Bellingham, Washington. They'll drink mojitos and maybe flirt a little with the cute bartender. And as the night unfolds, the women's conversations grow deeply personal. What do they *really* think of being a mom? What do they *really* think of their marriages? And inevitably, the talk turns to another topic that's close to their heart: their houses.

"Real estate falls into that category of intimate things—'What do you *really* think of your house?'" Brownell says.

Outwardly, Brownell's gang has no reason for discontent. Each has a kitchen with the granite countertops, stainless-steel appliances, and hardwood floors that have become the standard markers of suburban success. And yet . . . for each of these women, something is missing. One woman confides that while her house is perfectly adequate, she longs to move to something larger, with a master bedroom farther away from her children's rooms. Brownell, who recently moved into an airy, high-ceilinged, built-from-scratch home, admits that she has longings, too. "My house is really pretty, with plenty of room, but it just doesn't do it for me," she says. "My artistic imagination isn't lit up by it—it's too much 'practical' and not enough 'dreamy.' It's a little soulless."

Her longing for something different is why, at home the next day, Brownell is likely to be online, cruising real estate Web sites. She's not actually shopping for a home—she's just seeing what's out there. The hours she spends on sites like Realtor.com are a voyeuristic hobby that's not much different from her friends' devotion to magazines like *Martha Stewart Living*. But Brownell is only half joking when she calls her online house habit "a sad addiction"—and she's not at all kidding when she admits to clicking on these sites nearly every day. Her husband can take solace: At least she's not cruising Match.com.

Down the coast in San Diego, Susie Sincock has a different way of satisfying her interest in other people's homes: She watches hour after hour of HGTV. Sincock, a twenty-nine-year-old mother of three, says shows like *House Hunters* (which follows couples, documentary-style, as they shop for homes) are among the few kinds of programs she and her husband, Andy, enjoy watching together. In the last year Susie has watched at least 100 episodes. When the Sincocks watch, they tend to do play-by-play: "That tile is hideous," or "The backyard is atrocious—don't buy that one!" Lately they've begun watching a newer show called *Flip This House*, in which investors buy beat-up homes and do quick renovations before selling them for big profits. Susie and Andy rent, but debating what they like (and don't like) about these TV houses has helped them prepare for the day when they'll buy. "It's a good way to communicate and dream together," she says.

Across the country in Philadelphia, Nicole and Marc Lombardi's home fixation is a far more active pursuit. In late 2006 the couple bought a 1925 home in need of serious updating. So they routinely come home from work and head straight for their toolbox, spending evenings and weekends ripping down drywall, replacing fixtures, and getting quotes for professional help. Their typical weekend might include three separate trips to Lowe's or Home Depot. Nicole says they have a master plan for fixing up each room—and executing it could take ten or fifteen years. Young couples have always bought fixer-uppers, but Nicole, thirty, sees her friends far more engaged in this activity than their parents or grandparents. "It used to be that if you needed a new sink, you went to the hardware store and bought one," she says. "Now you can spend hours and hours online, picking out the style of faucet, the kind of metal. You don't have to be a professional to do it, and there's this world of possibilities." The Lombardis love looking at their made-over spaces, and they show off before-and-after renovation photos as aggressively as some new parents tout baby pictures.

Over the last few years, a lot of us would have been happy to take a look. Everywhere you turned Americans were talking about, valuing, scheming over, envying, shopping for, refinancing, or just plain ogling homes. The writer Daphne Merkin has described this widespread yearning as "Real Estate Lust," "a condition whose symptoms include a compulsive scanning of real estate ads and incessant discussions of who paid what for how much, as well as a fascination with the size and shape—down to the number of bedrooms, closets and bathroom windows—of apartments and houses that belong to people other than ourselves." *Washington Post* columnist Eugene Robinson diagnoses the condition as the moment when "a house or an apartment becomes not just a place of shelter or an emblem of status or even a considered investment, but an obsession that haunts us no less intensely than Vladimir Nabokov's nymphet Lolita tortured the imagination of poor, sick Humbert."

To my ear, "Real Estate Lust" sounds too economic, too transaction-oriented. It's too focused on profits and losses, and doesn't capture all the complicated, nonfinancial emotions that come into play when we think about our homes. Most of us aren't in love with the game of real estate—we're obsessed with the trophy at the end. So I prefer a simpler coinage: House Lust.

Rachael Brownell, Andy and Susie Sincock, and Nicole and Marc Lombardi suffer from it. Maybe you do, too. As comedian Jeff Foxworthy might put it, if you can instantly identify whether a countertop is made of Argentine Balmoral or Giallo Imperial granite, you may have House Lust. If you've visited the Web site Zillow, which estimates home values, and plugged in the addresses of friends, co-workers, and exes to see how much their houses are worth, there's a good chance you have House Lust. If, upon hearing that a friend has bought a new home, you can't resist asking its square footage, the lot size, and the year it was built, it's very possible that you have House Lust.

This syndrome is not altogether new. Homes and real estate have always had a peculiar hold on the American psyche. Our founding fathers considered land ownership a prerequisite to voting. A generation later, their pioneer descendants settled the West, drawn largely by an irresistible lure: cheap (or even free) land. We still tell our children the story of the Three Little Pigs (the moral: Build the sturdiest house you can), and spend rainy afternoons marching pieces around Monopoly boards (the lesson: The key to profits is location, location, location). And for decades, many people have had a Sunday-morning ritual that has nothing to do with church: Over coffee they read the real estate listings, even if they've no intention of buying or selling a home.

But in the last generation this fascination turned to an all-consuming pastime. "Before the last decades of the twentieth century, it is striking that there was relatively little public discussion of home prices," writes Yale economist Robert Shiller, who scoured a century's worth of newspapers to better understand real estate's role in the American psyche. But as prices rose sharply in the late 1990s, many of us began to chatter incessantly about our houses. In recent years if you went to a dinner party in San Francisco, Boston, or Miami, the housing market almost certainly came up somewhere between the first cocktail and the last bite of dessert. This banter has become so ubiquitous that commentator Michael Kinsley has even proposed a system that would utilize it for predicting home price movements—one he calls the Dinner Party Index.

Much of this chatter focused on the question that forms the undercurrent of every boom: How long can the good times last? You don't need an economics degree to realize that home values can't continually appreciate at 20 percent a year, as they did in parts of the country during the first years of the twenty-first century. In retrospect, there's little doubt that people's obsessions with homes weren't just a side effect of the boom. The ways in which their obsessions manifested themselves actually helped drive the boom higher, as home values were pushed upward by frenzied buyers, would-be flippers, and overblown renovations. Sure enough, by late 2005 it was clear that the housing market had peaked, and the boom was over. In 2006, FOR SALE signs began languishing in yards of homes that not long ago inspired bidding wars. Home prices in many regions began falling. Soon it became painfully apparent that many people had stretched too far to buy homes that were too expensive. Foreclosure rates began to soar. Mortgage companies began to fail. As this book went to press late in the summer of 2007, analysts were predicting that home prices would fall nationwide for the first calendar year since the Great Depression.

For a time, the housing bust felt like the all-too-predictable coda to the irrational exuberance of the boom. But suddenly, as real estate woes sent financial markets reeling and threatened to send the economy into recession, the bursting of this bubble felt far more ominous. As the Federal Reserve and the White House took steps to reassure the markets, the housing bust claimed status, for a few news cycles at least, as a full-blown national crisis.

During this boom and the ensuing bust, newspapers and magazines devoted acres of space to covering it. Much of this discussion focused on examining the economic forces that drove the cycle—and debating who deserves blame for letting America's home-philia get so out of hand. Should Alan Greenspan's Federal Reserve have let interest rates remain so low for so long? Should lenders have given so many loans to millions of high-risk "sub-prime" borrowers? Should real estate agents have encouraged buyers to aggressively overbid for homes in hot markets? Was it really wise that so many Americans came to regard it as perfectly normal to borrow against the equity in their homes to pay off a credit card or fund a trip to DisneyWorld?

Those questions interest me, but they're not the subject of this book. Instead, my aim is to explore the behavior and psychology that drove the boom—and how those behaviors and psychology helped contribute to the bust that followed. How did home renovations come to routinely turn families' lives upside down? Why do thousands of us now watch reality shows about home flipping or house hunting? Why did so many people decide to start investing in real estate, or quit good jobs to seek a fortune selling houses? How did House Lust become so contagious?

When historians look back on the first years of twenty-first-century American life, the housing boom will be a secondary story, a distant background note to 9/11 and the War on Terror. But against this history, the country's mania for homes has provided a buoyant counterweight. Far from Fallujah, we've watched with keen interest as our friends and neighbors engaged in hand-to-hand combat for houses. And in many neighborhoods, if you'd judged the nation's interests by its backyard-barbecue conversation—settings where subjects like war, death, and politics are risky conversational gambits—a lot of people find homes to be more compelling than any geopolitical struggle. "At the end of the day, what the house down the street sold for has a more important impact on people's lives than religion or politics," says Greg Spring, an executive at a Los Angeles firm that creates real estate television shows.

Some people might mock that view as shallow or even blasphemous, but he's got a point. Early in my reporting for this book, I met with a homebuilder to arrange to spend time with people buying houses in a nascent subdivision. Before he agreed, the executive asked me a simple question: "You aren't going to make fun of our homeowners, are you?" I stammered a bit. I suspected some of the behaviors I was likely to encounter during my reporting might be both revealing and funny. But ultimately, I didn't write this book to make fun of people afflicted with House Lust. I'm laughing with them, not at them, for a simple reason: I'm one of them.

Since childhood I've felt a profound connection with the homes in which I've lived. I grew up in a center-hall colonial built in 1929. My family owned it from the time I was two until I was twenty-two, and I knew it so well I could navigate it in pitch blackness. My parents used that home's appreciation to help pay my college tuition, and when they sold it, I cried. Today I live in a Cape Cod–style home in Massachusetts to which I've grown equally attached. I've spent long weekends on do-it-yourself improvements, and then experienced that unique mix of joy and horror as my home was ripped naked and rebuilt by a professional, using far more borrowed money than I'd intended to spend. During the real estate boom, my wife and I watched in amazement as our home soared in value, though it left us, for a time at least, in a disconcerting position: At the market's peak, we wondered whether we could still afford to buy the house we lived in if we didn't already own it. And as home values have fallen, we've wondered if our home improvements may have been *over-improvements*—and we worry how well they'd pay off if we had to sell our home. As I traveled the country reporting on the boom and bust, I met a lot of people experiencing the same feeling.

And I'm not just interested in my own home—I'm interested in yours, too. I periodically drop by open houses in my town, pretending to be looking "for a friend" while I poke through closets and inspect the master bath. Over playdates and at picnics I'm known to steer conversations to house gossip: Why is that ranch on Mill Road languishing on the market? Do you think that remodel on Fisher Street really makes sense now that home prices are falling? I remain a complete sucker for shows like *This Old House*, *Extreme Makeover: Home Edition*, and *Designed to Sell*. My Web browser "favorites" contains a link to our local tax-assessment database—and if I've been in your house, I've probably looked up the price you paid for it and the square footage, just out of curiosity. In keeping with biblical admonitions, I do not covet my neighbor's wife. But if coveting a "5BR, 3.5BA immac Col, gran/cherry kit, lg MBR on priv 2 acres" is a sin, I'm afraid I have some explaining to do.

In *Beauty Junkies*, her examination of America's plastic surgery obsession, Alex Kuczynski admits that after spending far too much time around the cosmetically enhanced, she developed a bizarre habit: using Adobe Photoshop to edit photos of her relatives' faces, illustrating (for her own amusement) what she'd do if they let her play amateur surgeon. While I don't use architectural software, I do the same mental exercise with the homes I visit, visualizing how I'd move the walls to improve the layout, how I'd redo the kitchen, or deciding which side of the house is best suited for an addition.

In my job as a reporter at *Newsweek*, I've met dozens of people who share my obsession. I wrote about a couple in a suburb of Boston who offered $700,000 to buy a home that they hadn't even been inside. They were so worried about losing out on a property in such a desirable neighborhood that when they couldn't find the Realtor to show them inside quickly enough, they phoned in a bid from the curb. I met many people who felt no anxiety about taking on variable-rate, interest-only mortgages to stretch to buy the homes of their dreams. "If all my friends are doing the same thing," they said, "how risky can it be?" In Virginia I spoke with homeowners at a new subdivision who'd embarked on an arms race involving backyard decks. Each one was building ever more lavish structures, trying to outdo his neighbors, to the point that some of these decks cost up to $200,000 and took a team of bricklayers months to create. I met no shortage of real estate agents and architects who complained that clients have become so overinvested in home-related decisions, their fields have begun to involve psychiatry and couples counseling. Along the way I met plenty of real estate agents and home flippers whose zeal for real estate was making them rich. And even as we realized the boom couldn't last, it was as if we couldn't help ourselves.

There's no single explanation for what causes House Lust, but after interviewing several hundred people throughout the boom—buyers, sellers, builders, brokers, architects, and sociologists among them—I have identified five primary drivers. Economics underlie several of them, but beyond dollars and cents, each describes a psychological shift in the way we think about our houses.

The High-five Effect. I'm not a huge sports fan, but if the Patriots make a late-season play-off run, I'll start watching. People can't help jumping on the bandwagon, donning a championship jersey and enjoying the vicarious thrill that comes from cheering on a winner. The phenomenon isn't much different when it comes to houses. From 2001 to 2006, the average U.S. home rose in value by 56 percent. In some of the hottest regions prices doubled over that period, while in a few white-hot markets values jumped 40 percent in a single year. And with the homeownership rate at record levels—it rose from 44 percent in 1940 to 69 percent in 2006—more people than ever had a rooting interest. Sure, there are places that have missed out on this boom. If you live in Detroit or Cleveland, you're far less likely to suffer House Lust than people in hot spots like San Jose or Bethesda. But prices rose sharply in a broad swath of the country, so millions of us have had a reason to high-five and celebrate our sense that our houses were quietly making us rich.

Our House *Is* Our Retirement Plan. For most of the twentieth century, houses were the most important asset for middle-class families. In the early days of the twenty-first, homes grew even more important. In 2005, for the first time since the Great Depression, the nation's savings rate dipped below zero, meaning the average American was spending more than he earned. Families were doing this, some economists reckoned, because they figured the rising value of their home was providing all the savings they needed. And as home prices soared, people began pulling money out of homes to fund other spending—a behavior that helped revive the economy from its 2001 recession and the economic hit of 9/11. In a world of disappearing pension coverage and shrinking 401(k) matches, Americans feel more reliant on their homes to provide for their economic future than ever before. To further torture my sports metaphor, not only have Americans begun jumping on a winning team's bandwagon, but they've also been betting on it—heavily. And as anyone who's ever thrown a few bucks in a March Madness pool knows, the more money you have riding on the game, the more closely you watch.

We Used to Play the Market. During the Boom We Began Playing Our Houses. A generation or two ago, the average family took out a thirty-year mortgage, which they intended to pay off someday. There were no home equity lines of credit, refinancing was unusual, and whatever wealth a homeowner built up in the house stayed there until it was sold. No more. In the early 2000s it was easy to find people who refinanced every year or two, often cashing in equity to fund renovations or even vacations. Instead of bragging about golf handicaps, some people bragged about the interest rates on their mortgages. In markets where prices rose sharply, some people cashed out their profits entirely by selling their house and relocating somewhere cheaper. In the corporate world, chief financial officers earn big money for figuring out how a company should best utilize its assets—paying dividends to shareholders or issuing bonds to raise capital. Thanks to the revolution in home finance, today many homeowners operate like mini-CFOs, deciding just how much of their wealth to keep in their houses. As home prices went down and interest rates on exotic mortgages went up, many of these neophyte financiers undoubtedly wish they'd been more conservative. It's an emotion shared by the people who became irrationally exuberant for tech stocks a decade earlier—and a remorse that's all too common when boom times come to an end.

It's So Easy to Peek in the Window. With so much riding on our houses, it's only natural that many of us became obsessed by what they're worth—and while we're looking up the value of our own home, what's the harm if we gather some market intelligence on the homes of our friends and neighbors? Finding this information has never been easier. Unlike what's in someone's bank or brokerage accounts, information on real estate transactions has always been open to public scrutiny, usually in dusty courthouse files or tax assessors' offices. But in the Internet age, you can learn lots about your neighbors' homes without leaving your desk. Thanks to Web sites like Zillow and PropertyShark, voyeurs can now conduct these explorations on a national scale. Gossip columns (and even the *Wall Street Journal*) now routinely report on what properties celebrities are buying and selling. And HGTV, which a decade ago was a tiny channel airing mostly arts-and-crafts shows, now airs a nightly lineup of programs that highlight the real-life drama of real people buying and selling homes for profit. Yale's Shiller cites media "amplification" as a key driver of most booms, and in the same way that the cable channel CNBC and now-defunct tech magazines like the *Industry Standard* helped hype stock investing during the 1990s, channels like HGTV and Web sites like Zillow stoked Americans' appetite for peering into one another's homes in the 2000s.

You Are Where You Live. At my children's former preschool each spring, just before Father's Day, the kids drew posters describing their dad. The poster lists his favorite food, his favorite TV show, his age, and his job. On this last category, the kids are a little murky. "He talks on the phone." "He does computer." "He makes money." Their cluelessness is understandable: Today so many upper-middle-class job titles are vague amalgams ("network interface IT enabler") that it's become hard to talk about our work, or size people up based on their professions. (At a recent dinner party, when I asked a woman with one of these jobs what she actually did, she apologetically shot me down: "I could tell you more about it, but you won't understand it and it's not that interesting.") As so many of the jobs that help pay megamortgages on nice homes have evolved into such narrow, incomprehensible niches, addresses have become a substitute for occupation when making status judgments. Humans, like all animals, have an innate need to size one another up. Since we can't do it by sniffing (at least most of the time), and as jobs have become less useful status markers, instead we send signals by where we live—a piece of information that communicates socioeconomic rank as clearly as shoulder stripes denote status in the military.

In America, homeownership has always been treated as a virtue. But even before the boom receded, House Lust had a dark side. For an extreme—and tragic—case, look no further than the Upper East Side of Manhattan, to the East Sixty-second Street town house owned by Nicholas Bartha. The sixty-six-year-old doctor lived there for twenty years, and the beloved home was also his only significant asset. In July of 2006, after a five-year divorce battle that was going to force him to sell the house, Bartha sent his former wife an e-mail. "I always told you I will only leave the house if I am dead," he typed, then cut a gas line and blew up the $6.4 million home. The doctor died a few days later, but by then the public's interest had shifted to something more important than life or death: the value of the now-vacant lot, which eventually sold for $8.3 million.

Beyond headline-making incidents like that are quieter stories of people who felt left out of our great national house party. Troy Wolverton is a thirty-five-year-old newspaper reporter in San Jose, married, one child. In 2003 he and his wife began looking at homes in San Francisco. Determined to spend no more than $600,000, they traipsed through tiny two-bedroom, one-bath houses, often in neighborhoods that weren't as nice as the one in which they rented. Late that fall they saw a home listed at $520,000, and submitted a bid of $600,000. Theirs was one of twenty-four offers for the house—and it wasn't even in the top half of bids. In all, they lost out on four homes before giving up, but their story is hardly extreme; in San Francisco, you don't have to look hard to find people who bid on a dozen homes before winning the right to carry each other over the threshold. "We got pretty frustrated, not only because we kept getting outbid, but because our real estate agent was really pushing us to take on a less conservative mortgage that would have enabled us to bid more," says Wolverton, who was reluctant to take out the adjustable-rate, interest-only loan that, for a time, became the usual route to homeownership in high-priced markets. As a result, his family is still renting.

In retrospect, Wolverton's fiscal restraint may look unusually wise. By 2007 newspapers were filled with heart-wrenching stories of people facing foreclosure and of families who could no longer make their house payments once their variable-rate mortgages reset. It was becoming all too clear that House Lust had caused many Americans to make disastrous decisions. As this book went to press, the airwaves were filled with debates about whether those hit hardest deserve a bailout and discussions about whether new regulations might prevent others from suffering the same fate. Those debates will drag on, but in the meantime, their stories may serve as cautionary tales to help keep people's enthusiasm in check when the bust turns into a boom again someday.

In the pages ahead, I tell stories of a group of people who became fixated on homes. The aim is not to give a comprehensive economic analysis of the boom and bust. If you're hoping for a Roger Lowenstein–style dissection of the rise and fall of the housing market, you will be disappointed. And while I'm offering disclaimers, let me offer one more: This book focuses on an admittedly skewed sample of Americans. There are examples of house-crazed people at every income level, but it tends to be wealthier homeowners who obsess the most about the value of their homes—and who have the disposable income to turn this passion into a more active pursuit by buying trophy homes, vacation homes, or investment properties. As a result, the majority of the people in the pages ahead are upper-middle-class, and some are flat-out rich. As someone who works in a city with very high housing costs, I'm very aware of the problems of homelessness and the lack of affordable housing. These issues are, alas, topics for another book.

Instead, in the chapters that follow I'll explore the ways in which the boom transformed a certain group of Americans into real estate junkies. During many months of reporting, I spent time with people smitten with the ideal of building a new home from scratch—one unsullied by previous residents, where the buyers can choose every cabinet knob and bathe in a virginal Jacuzzi tub. I encountered people so convinced that homes are the route to riches, they've bought rental properties, sight unseen, in faraway states over the Internet. (In an extreme case of laughing with them, not at them, I'll relate how I took this plunge myself, by buying a rental property in Idaho via e-mail.) I watched as husbands and wives argued over whether a plasma television *really* constitutes a home improvement. (For the record, I side with the husband, as long as he remembers me at Super Bowl time.) And I spent time in the field studying an oft-misunderstood species whose numbers have been multiplying at an astonishing rate—yes, I'm talking about the super-gregarious primate known as the North American Realtor—and I'll describe how I joined their ranks, too, by enrolling in real estate school. I also met plenty of people for whom the old-fashioned American Dream of homeownership has been replaced by a new fantasy befitting an affluent age: buying a second (or even a third) home, a place where they can get away from it all—when they're not cleaning out the gutters.

The people in the pages ahead all exhibit classic symptoms of House Lust—a condition that I believe will last well after the commotion surrounding the current boom and bust cycle are distant memories. (I'll have more to say on that subject in the Epilogue.) As far as I can tell, House Lust is chronic. It can be managed, but like any addiction, there's no real cure.

CHAPTER ONE

MINE'S BIGGER THAN YOURS: POTOMAC, MARYLAND

How Square Footage Became the New Scorecard

As you walk in the front door of Steven and Tammy Goldberg's house, you can't help but stop and gasp at the foyer, with its 22-foot ceiling and dual staircases—one curving up the right side of the room, the other up the left. A massive chandelier hangs overhead. Polished tile-work sits underfoot. Peer between the stairs from the front doorway and you'll catch a glimpse of the family room, another two-story space with a fireplace that climbs to the ceiling. The first time people walk in the Goldbergs' doorway, they utter a near-universal reaction: "Wow."

That single syllable, above all else, is what sells homes in the Goldbergs' neighborhood in Potomac, Maryland. "As soon as you open that door, you do the 'Wow' thing," says Rouhi Forghani, the sales manager at this development, called Potomac View. "In this community, needs are secondary. The first priority is to have a home where everybody opens the door and says, 'Wow,' so you can brag to your coworkers and friends, and you can throw a party and impress people."

And if the staircases don't impress them, the size sure will. The Goldbergs' newly built house, one of forty-six that will someday fill this neighborhood, started out at 6,000 square feet. But then they finished the basement, bringing the total to around 9,000 square feet. Beyond the dual-staircase foyer, this home has a back stairway, four bedrooms, and . . . let's see . . . how many bathrooms?

"Four upstairs, one on the first floor—that's five—one in the basement—no, two in the basement. So, seven. Right?" Tammy Goldberg says. We're sitting in Potomac View's model home with Pat Kirby, project manager for Toll Brothers, the company building this subdivision.

"Six and a half baths," Kirby says, correcting her. "The first floor is a half bath."

"Oh, wait, I have two half baths," says Goldberg, who's lived in the house just a couple of months.

"Two half baths, right," the project manager says.

"So I have four full—five full—and two halves," Goldberg says, still sounding a little unsure. "One in the basement, and four upstairs. Five full."

"Six full and two halves," the project manager says, suddenly sounding a little confused himself. "You have two in the basement."

"No," Goldberg corrects him. "I only have one full bath in the basement. It's a half and a full in the basement. So five full and two halves." It's taken nearly twenty seconds to reconcile how many bathrooms there are in the house, and Goldberg chuckles at the ridiculousness of it. "We don't use all our bathrooms, that's for sure."

As recently as 1950, one-third of American homes lacked complete indoor plumbing. Today in places like Potomac, asking a homeowner how many bathrooms are in her house can provoke something reminiscent of a vintage Abbott and Costello routine. If a house hunter checked the Potomac listings for the summer of 2006, he'd find that among the 259 single-family homes on the market, more than half—160—had five or more bedrooms, and 148 had four or more bathrooms.

The bathrooms aren't the only things that have multiplied—all around the house the space is getting bigger. And not just at the Goldbergs'. In 1950 the average American home measured just

983 square feet—meaning you could fit nine of them inside the Goldberg home. But over time the average has crept steadily upward—and by 2005, according to census data, the average newly built U.S. home measured 2,434 square feet. One in five new homes now has a three-car garage, double the percentage of fifteen years ago. One in four has three or more bathrooms. Nearly 40 percent have four or more bedrooms. When it comes to American homes, the only thing that's decreased in recent years is the size of the plots of land on which they're built and the size of the families who live inside.

Finger-wagging moralists decry these "trophy homes" as studies in excess, and critics say our fondness for them is nothing short of demented. You're probably familiar with this line of criticism: In the last fifteen years, our cars have morphed into gas-guzzling SUVs, our bodies have Big Gulped their way to epidemic obesity, and our homes have puffed up into flabby, aesthetically lacking edifices, structures that are far too oversize to be classified as "shelter"—and too often financed with jumbo mortgages that threaten to crush us. Heating and cooling these megahomes contributes to global warming—and so does cutting down trees to build them. Surely there must be a better way to live.

As someone who's afflicted with House Lust—and someone who's increased the size of my home by 25 percent since I bought it—I have a slightly more forgiving view. It's true that oversize homes are partly about showing off. Homes have always been a status symbol, and the ways we denote status are constantly shifting. Once upon a time the richest man in the village was the one with the chubby wife, whose ample posterior was a sign that he was wealthy enough to feed his family well. Today the richest man on the block (who, in these egalitarian times, may be earning less than his wife) probably has a thin wife and a gargantuan house. As the times change, so do the markers of achievement.

But beyond the quest for status, there is a complicated mix of factors driving us to live large, all of which I'll be exploring in the pages ahead.

Some of them are economic. Young couples have always been told to "buy the most house you can afford." But we've been living in an era of extremely low interest rates: The average thirty-year mortgage stayed below 7 percent between 2002 and 2007, and it hadn't hit double digits in seventeen years. Along with those low rates, underwriting standards grew remarkably lax during the good times, with lenders offering to lend more than 100 percent of a home's value and not even requiring income verfication. Together those factors meant that "the most home you can afford" might be absurdly large. Mortgage interest remains one of the last great tax deductions, so one can argue that the U.S. government *wants* us to borrow big to supersize our houses, and so borrow we do. And in the early 2000s, a time when the stock market seemed to move mostly sideways, people felt even more justified in investing as much money as possible in a house, since home values seemed to go nowhere but up. If you know Google stock is poised to rise, are you going to buy 100 shares or 1,000 shares? Likewise, in the hot housing market of the early twenty-first century, many buyers felt the smart strategy was to buy as many shares of housing as they could, which left a lot of people living in really big homes.

Another set of forces driving our embrace of bigger homes stems from the supply side: They're what builders want to sell us. As land prices have escalated, builders say it's become all but impossible to put small homes on expensive lots, and, generally speaking, bigger homes deliver bigger profits. New kinds of building products (like "laminated veneer lumber" and wooden I-beams) have made it easy for carpenters to build houses with palatial interior spaces. We used to admire the soaring ceilings of European cathedrals; now we can enjoy the same neck-cramping view looking up in our family rooms.

The final factor that's driven our quest for larger homes is a newfound fascination with measuring our spaces. Builders have always thought of homes in terms of square footage, but the metric didn't have quite the hold on the public consciousness in years past as it does now. Today, in some neighborhoods, finding someone who doesn't know the square footage of her house can be as hard as finding a *Playboy* centerfold who doesn't know her bust size. It's a cliché that when it comes to real estate, the three things that matter are location, location, location. But beyond being trite, that line is also becoming a fallacy. These days many people are willing to move far from the city, compromising their location to get more space. In the twenty-first-century location still matters. But for many buyers square footage matters more.

In a sense our changing notions of what constitutes a really big home aren't that different from the way other everyday objects have been upsized, downsized, and resized in recent years. Before Starbucks hit the scene, if you'd ordered a small coffee you probably walked out of the diner with an eight-ounce beverage. By 2002 the industry-wide measure of a "small" beverage had increased to twelve ounces—and instead of complaining about that inflation, more buyers complained that the twenty-ounce large wasn't big enough. In the fashion industry, "vanity sizing" has led to a similar inflation in clothing sizes. Today the average 155-pound American female wears a size twelve, even though a few years ago the same-size woman would have worn a sixteen—and to accommodate ever-thinner supermodel types, high-fashion brands now sell "subzero" clothing sizes that use negative numbers. In salaries, the *New York Times* has reported, $200,000 is the new $100,000—a threshold that signifies entry into an upper-class club. What's happened to homes isn't much different from these other resizings. Nowadays 3,200 square feet is the new 2,000.

At the top of the market, the results of this surge of space are residences in which visitors might require MapQuest to navigate their way from room to room. Some of these houses are so spread out that if you shout "Dinner" from the kitchen, you face long odds of actually luring anyone to the meal—which, if they do come, can be eaten in the dining room, the eat-in kitchen, at the breakfast bar, or in the outdoor dining area.

Even those of us who don't aspire to live in these sorts of houses are being affected by them, like it or not. Amenities that were once found only in rich people's homes have a way of trickling down to the masses, so a glimpse inside these tricked-out spaces can illustrate the kinds of features we'll simply *have* to have in our homes someday soon, regardless of size.

One manifestation of an obsession is when somebody wants more and more of something, whether it's Beanie Babies, Krispy Kreme doughnuts, or plastic surgery. And in real estate, what many of us want more of is space. How did it become perfectly normal for affluent Americans to live in 5,000-square-foot homes? How, exactly, do we use all this square footage? And despite all the criticism heaped on these homes and their owners, is there anything really wrong with this lifestyle—or are the complaints mostly just sour-grapes commentary from people who can't afford an oversize home? To answer these questions, I spent time in Potomac, a Washington suburb known for having some of the largest homes on the East Coast, and I also visited extremely large (and extremely small) homes elsewhere in the nation.

To get a better sense of why America's houses have been growing even faster than its waistlines, it makes sense to start by exploring the platonic ideal of a really nice home. To do so, I visited the New American Home, which the country's homebuilders construct at a site near their annual convention each year.

The project's origins are humble. The first New American Home, built outside Houston and opened to the public on January 21, 1984, contained just three bedrooms and two and a half baths in 1,500 square feet. The exterior featured lavish landscaping and a private patio, but the interior design was modest. Aside from a tiny powder room and laundry, the first floor was one open room featuring a kitchen, living area, and dining space. Upstairs the focal point was the master suite, featuring a large, windowed bathroom with a raised whirlpool tub in the center. It was, according to the promotional material, "the kind of place a young couple could dream about coming home to."

But dreams change. By 1988 the show house was 2,400 square

feet. Only one year later it had jumped to 5,400 square feet. By 1996 it swelled to 7,385 square feet. The size doesn't increase every year, but from 1995 to 2006 the builders didn't construct any New American Home smaller than 3,100 square feet. And the 2006 version, surrounded by spotlights in a field twelve miles from the Orlando convention center, turned out to be its biggest ever.

Behind the stucco facade, visitors encounter a home measuring 10,023 square feet. There are three staircases (plus an elevator), six baths, five fireplaces, and nine flat-screen TVs. Over-the-top features abound. Off the garage lies a small bathroom with no toilet, just a urinal. Upstairs is the requisite home theater, a billiards parlor, and a spa with a built-in massage table. Outside are upstairs and downstairs covered patios, each with built-in grills and bars, overlooking an infinity edge pool containing four little islands of palm trees. The home's upstairs laundry is the size of a 1970s kitchen, but with so much cabinetry and granite counters you know you're not in the Carter era. On the floor plan there are no hallways. In a house this big they're called galleries, and they're not intended just for passing between rooms. Instead, galleries are meant to be minimuseums where the owner can hang his art collection.

The overall aesthetic reminds me of the large, open homes used on reality TV shows. As I wander around, I keep waiting for the Bachelor to emerge to hand me a rose.

This is my first time in a New American Home. But I'm surrounded by real estate writers and builders who've been visiting these show homes for years. "At least it doesn't look like it was decorated for a South American drug kingpin, like last year," says one woman, exploring the master suite. Asked what he thinks, one gentleman pauses. "Ornate?" he says, trying to find a polite way to say, "Not for me." One builder, who lives in a home nearly this large himself, points out that despite all the space, the family room isn't very big. So much of the home's entertainment spaces are on outdoor patios, he says, it'd be hard to throw a party on a rainy or chilly day.

But we put aside this nitpicking to ogle the remaining features. The kitchen features twin Sub-Zero refrigerators and five different faucets—two on normal sinks, one pot filler over the stove, one for the built-in pasta cooker, and one set over a small trough sink that's in the middle of the massive kitchen island, so far from the edge that a six-foot man has to stretch to reach it. Other guests and I ponder, What could anyone do with this all-but-unreachable sink? Finally we ask an assistant to the architect. She shrugs, then suggests it'd be a great spot to keep wine bottles on ice (presumably when both Sub-Zeros are full). She offers to get the architect to show me around further, but she doesn't know where he is right now. She apologizes. "It can be really hard to find somebody in a 10,000-square-foot house."

After this convention ends, the Orlando Home would go on the market for $4.2 million. That's pricey, but it's a far cry from what the superrich spend on their homes—like the 66,000-square-foot compound that Bill Gates built on the banks of Lake Washington, near Seattle. The Gates home boasts a 1,000-square-foot dining room, a pool with an underground music system, and, of course, computerized everything. By some estimates it's worth $100 million.

To get a better sense of what constitutes a *really* high-end home, I should examine a billionaire's residence. Unfortunately, the Gateses haven't invited me to visit. However, I happen to live not far from a home being built for a billionaire. So one day I drop by for a house tour.

In 1972 Jim Davis spent $100,000 to buy a tiny Boston shoe company called New Balance. At the time it had just six employees who made thirty pairs of sneakers a day. But then the jogging craze hit, and *Runner's World* magazine rated New Balance the best shoe on the market. Sales took off. Today the company is still privately held by the Davis family, and by one estimate they're worth $1.6 billion.

In early 2006 Jim and his wife, Anne, lived in a 6,112-square-foot home in Newton, Massachusetts, that the local tax assessor valued at $2.9 million. But a mile and a half away the couple was building a home that, by local standards, is pretty impressive. A few years earlier the Davises had bought an existing home on two acres that had previously been occupied by a religious order. A team of architects had spent months figuring out how to renovate it, but ultimately decided it'd be easier to tear it down and start over. The architects drew up plans for a stately new residence. Its size, including the mostly finished basement: 29,000 square feet.

On the day I stop by the basic structure is complete, and the construction crew is a few months away from completing the interior details. In the front hallway, workers are lying on their backs atop scaffolding, crafting delicate plaster molding up near the ceiling. Beyond the large foyer lies the two-story family room, with two balconies. Toward the left side of the first floor are two large kitchens, one for the family and one for the staff. The staff kitchen is by no means shabby—twin refrigerators, fancy tile backsplashes, a huge commercial stove. But the family kitchen is massive, with an island so big that, like Australia, it might be better classified as a continent. Throughout the house luxurious touches abound, like in the library, which has a secret panel leading to a staircase that spirals down to the wine cellar.

As I walk around with the construction manager, what's striking is that while the proportions are grand, the basic set of rooms isn't wildly different from what you'd find in a normal suburban home. Yes, the first floor has its service kitchen, a craft room, and a warren of storage spaces near the garage, but most of the space is devoted to the foyer, living room, kitchen, and dining room—the standard setup for a normal-size home. Unlike robber baron–era mansions, modern-day megahomes don't feature dozens of bedrooms or entirely new kinds of rooms—they mostly just take the rooms you'd find in a normal house and make them really, really big.

Upstairs, on the second floor, the two children's rooms and the guest room are each the size of nice hotel rooms, and the master bedroom has an entrance rotunda and a living room–size sitting area. The master bath is large, but it's nothing you don't see every month in *Architectural Digest*.

On the third floor are staff quarters and storage; in the basement there's the requisite bar, media room, billiards room (the Davises call it the "club room"), and enough heating and cooling equipment to run a small office building. Sure, there are quirks befitting a billionaire (and his architect), such as the requirement that the house have no visible radiators or ducts. (The home has radiant heat, and conditioned air circulates through tiny seams in ceiling beams.) But when you're spending this kind of money, you can afford to be idiosyncratic.

Building a home this size creates special challenges. If you're overseeing the tile installation, for example, you can't tell the tile guy to go work in the bathroom. With seven bathrooms, you need to be more precise. So during construction, every room in the house has a number on its wall, which the workers use to refer to it. (The master bath is room 208.) Simply getting the crew of fifty-five workers to the job every morning presents a problem, since there isn't enough parking for all those pickup trucks. The contractors' solution was to set up a satellite parking location across town and run shuttle buses to get workers to and from the job each morning.

Figuring out how much a home this size will be worth when it's completed is an interesting exercise, since there isn't anything comparable in the entire town. But for Elizabeth Dromey, the city's tax assessor, it's no idle question: Even before the house is complete she has to calculate the Davises' property tax bill. I tell Dromey I've heard buzz that the Davises spent more than $30 million on the project. "Cost does not equal value," Dromey says, but clearly this will be a valuable home. In early 2006 the assessor's office listed it as only 35 percent complete, but even without a certificate of occupancy, Dromey estimated its value at $6.286 million—meaning that even though it's uninhabitable, it's the fifth-most-valuable home in Newton. By the time it's finished the house will assess at $11 million, more than any home has ever sold for in Newton. It was hard settling on that number, she admits, but she did find one comparable property that helped guide her: a large home a few towns away owned by the CEO of Reebok.

The Davis home may sound expensive, but on a national scale it's not even at the top of the market. New York apartments now routinely top $25 million. In Palm Beach, Donald Trump aims to sell an estate for $100 million. The *Wall Street Journal*'s term for these highest-end residences is "hyperestates," which they define as those costing more than $30 million. In early 2006 there were about sixty such properties for sale in the United States, including twenty in Manhattan and a dozen in Los Angeles. So while it's twelve times the size of the average newly built home and more than three times the size of the Goldbergs' home in Potomac, the Davis home—at least by some measures—looks downright modest.

Driving through Potomac one day, Tammy Goldberg came across a sign by a developer advertising "mansions." At home that night she asked her husband: In the twenty-first century, what constitutes a mansion? It's a word you don't hear much anymore, almost an anachronism—an old-school descriptor that conjures images of Beverly Hills movie-star homes or places where Hugh Hefner frolics with his Bunnies. Steven said the word applied only to truly gigantic homes that lie on multiacre gated estates. "I don't think our house is a mansion," he says, pointing to their one-acre lot as key evidence. Tammy agrees with him, but she points out a description in *People* magazine of a celebrity who lives in a 4,000-square-foot mansion. "How is a 4,000-square-foot house a 'mansion'?" she says.

She raises a good point. As our notions of size have changed, how does one define what constitutes a truly high-end home? And how crucial is size to the definition?

The definition has blurred in large part because so many of the amenities once found only in humongous homes owned by rich people have trickled down into moderately priced houses. That's one reason people who'll never live in the kinds of houses featured in *Architectural Digest*—or even in a Potomac View home—are keenly interested in what's inside them. Features like Jacuzzis, bars, and exercise rooms all used to be exclusively the province of high-end houses, but nowadays it's easy to find those features in smaller, middle-class homes.

Lately no feature has trickled down farther than the home theater. For decades showing a movie at home required a full-blown projector, so "screening rooms" remained limited to people connected to the Industry. But in the 1980s, VCRs and primitive big-screen TVs allowed regular consumers to enjoy more cinematic experiences at home. Then came surround sound and giant plasma TVs that hang on the wall. So many homeowners have been putting in home theaters that it may soon be seen as an essential feature of a modern home.

And you can find superb examples of these spaces even in tiny dwellings. Since 1979 Glenn Mosby has lived in an 850-square-foot postwar bungalow a few miles south of Detroit. But when he walks guests downstairs to his basement, they stare in stunned silence. Inside this very modest house sits a $37,000, state-of-the-art home theater. It took Mosby twenty-six months to build and it's won a design award from a home theater magazine. With a 1,000-watt subwoofer, cinema-style seating, stage lighting, and a remote control that automatically dims the lights—dramatically, taking thirty seconds—watching a movie with Mosby can rival anything you'd experience at the multiplex. "People don't know what to say when they see it, because they see this little house, and they don't expect it," he says.

But all around his neighborhood he sees more of his small-house neighbors copying the things they see in bigger, more expensive homes. They're adding multigabled rooflines and exterior columns. Instead of simple foundation plantings, they're installing exotic landscape beds in the middle of the yard, and built-by-hand stone walls. Mosby attributes some of this to the growth of Home Depot, which doesn't ask, "How big is your house?" before selling you high-end appliances, fixtures, or shrubbery. It's also a function of the growth of HGTV and home magazines, which have made more middle-class homeowners aware of what's inside upscale homes. "You're starting to see it infiltrate the middle-class ranks," Mosby says.

A few days after I talked to Mosby, the *New York Times* ran a piece on the item that's emerging as the next have-to-have: the mudroom. The first mudroom was in a mansion built in the 1920s by automotive heir Edsel Ford not far from Mosby's home, but the story cites many examples of middle-class homeowners who covet the clutter-busting storage benches, shelving, and book-bag hangers. Just how mainstream could the mudroom go? In fact, I have architectural drawings (and a variance from our town planning department) to add one to my home. And mudroom by mudroom, the line between mansions and everyday homes will become a bit blurrier.

Back in Potomac View, Steven and Tammy Goldberg and their three children are living on land with a storied past. At the south edge of their subdivision, just above the namesake river, lies a stately home called Marwood, to which all this surrounding land once belonged. Built in 1930, the thirty-three room residence once served as the capital residence of Joseph P. Kennedy, father of the future president and ambassador to Great Britain before World War II. During those years the Kennedys entertained Franklin Roosevelt so often that the family installed an elevator to accommodate the disabled president. After dinner—often lobsters shipped down from New England—the family and FDR would retire to the 200-seat movie theater.

During the postwar years, as developers transformed Potomac from a farming-and-foxhunting region into a sought-after suburb, the acreage behind the Marwood estate remained vacant. Some builders used it to dump the dirt they dug out of backyard swimming pools. By the 1990s the parcel had changed hands among developers, but no one could figure out an economical way to build homes on it, since this would require removing decades of debris and compressing what was left to make stable ground.

It would become a job for Toll Brothers. The company, founded outside Philadelphia by brothers Robert and Bruce in the 1960s, started out selling basic $17,990 homes to families flocking to the suburbs. But over time Toll Brothers began focusing on luxury residences. During the 1990s economic boom, more people chose to upsize into Toll's brand of trophy homes, and the company thrived. By 2002, in the midst of the real estate boom, Toll controlled 40,000 lots in twenty-two states.

On the forty-six lots at Potomac View, where crews began pouring foundations in 2003, Toll set out to build some of its largest models. Its customers have been desiring larger and larger homes the last few years, and the company has worked hard to keep ahead of demand. To illustrate the point, one page in Toll Brothers' 2005 annual report shows two homes. One is called the Columbia, offering 3,200 square feet. In 2000 it was the company's best seller. Above it sits a photo of the Hampton, the best seller in 2005. With 4,800 square feet, it's exactly 50 percent larger.

When the company started selling houses here, executives figured an average selling price of around $2 million. But thanks to the soaring housing market, by 2006 (with only seven lots left unsold) the average Potomac View home was selling for nearly $3 million—and the sales team hoped the house on the best remaining river-view lot might top $4 million. The average Potomac View buyer earns around $400,000 a year, puts down $1 million in cash, and ends up with a monthly mortgage payment of perhaps $12,000 to $14,000. Initially the sales team figured most buyers would be doctors, lawyers, or entrepreneurs, but the reality illustrates how our House Lust has reconfigured socioeconomic status: Instead, the community is dominated by mortgage brokers who grew rich during wave after wave of refinancing.

As big as these homes are, many buyers wish they were even bigger. So the Potomac View construction team has responded. They've figured a way to bump out the family room wall by eight feet, an option they've named the "Super-Expanded Family Room." Adding six feet to the width of the conservatory creates a "Grand Conservatory." Project manager Pat Kirby and his construction team say nearly every buyer here obsesses over the square footage of his home, and when buyers talk about their home's size, they round up. In third-grade math class, students learn that if you round 8,175 to the nearest thousand, you get 8,000. But here if you ask the buyer of an 8,175-square-foot home how big it is, he'll probably tell you 9,000.

For some buyers, space isn't the prime draw. Tammy Goldberg says she didn't even want such a large home, but ended up with one by default. The Goldbergs have three children, an eight-year-old and twin four-year-olds. They relocated here from New Jersey in 2006 to advance Steven's career as an investment banker. This home is the fourth the family has built, and over the years their homes have increased in size from 2,000 square feet to 3,200 to 4,500 to 9,000. "It wasn't like we said we need a house double the size of our last one," Tammy says. "It's just if you look at all these houses in a specific price range"—theirs was around $3 million—"you're going to get all large houses. That's just what they are." While few Americans live in 9,000-square-foot, $3 million homes, the other elements of their story are familiar. Today's professional jobs often require more relocation than in the past, and each time a family relocates and buys another home they opt for something a bit nicer. Nowadays nicer usually implies bigger.

Showing me around her home, Tammy admits that when they first moved in everything seemed really large. But they've gotten used to it. Today every kitchen cabinet is filled. So are the closets. "We use every room," she says.

The exception, of course, is the living room—a space that remains nicely decorated but never used in many suburban homes. "We don't really sit in there, but I'll sit in there to talk on the phone by myself," Tammy says. When they entertain, they try to encourage people to move away from the kitchen island and into the living room, but it rarely happens. Instead, it's mostly become a pass-through area that one must cross to get from the foyer to the kitchen. As Tammy admits, "The living room is a really pretty room we really don't use."

Big-house critics point to unused spaces—especially living rooms—as smoking-gun evidence that these homes are dysfunctional. But, in fact, there's nothing new about the phenomenon. In colonial

America, the earliest homes were one-room spaces, but as homes expanded to two or three rooms and beyond, residents quickly began demarcating "public" versus "private" spaces, and the more formal public space, which became known as "best rooms" or "parlors," were often used only when company visited. "By 1820, parlor had come to mean a formal and often rarely-used room for entertaining," writes home historian Jack Larkin. As homes have enlarged, the "best room" concept lives on; it's become a deeply held custom to make one room in the house a formal space, but most of us prefer living informally, so we gravitate instead to the family room and kitchen to hang out. One of my friends calls her living room "the Museum," since it always has that pristine, never-lived-in look; she once threw a small party with the intent of forcing guests to sit in it. (We acquiesced for predinner cocktails, but after dinner everyone moved into the kitchen, as usual.)

In the Goldbergs' expansive kitchen, Tammy's favorite feature is the twin dishwashers. Instead of piling dirty stuff on the counter while a single dishwasher runs, she always has a spare machine ready to load. "I could go back to a small house, but I could never go back to not having two dishwashers," she says. Across the family room from the kitchen is a men's hangout room, with poker and pool tables. Downstairs, in the finished basement, is a sprawling play area, along with two bedrooms and one and a half baths. The previous week, during Passover, the Goldbergs had ten relatives stay overnight for most of the week. The house has so much space, it caused no inconvenience at all. At Halloween the family hosted fifty neighbors for a party. Steven says their need for a large home is partly because they live far from their extended family and want lots of room for everyone to visit often.

It's easy to mock these sentiments—*I simply can't live without my two dishwashers*. But this ratcheting-up of our expectations is a familiar phenomenon, and I have my own slightly ridiculous example of it. In college and my first twenty-something apartment, I hauled my dirty clothes down the block to a Laundromat. When my wife and I shared our first apartment, we felt spoiled to have a communal, coin-operated washer and dryer just down the hall. And when we bought our home, having our own washer and dryer in the basement felt like a luxury. But while it freed us from finding correct change, the basement setup required hauling laundry baskets up and down two flights of stairs (a trip that once landed my wife in the ER after a slip-and-fall). So when we renovated we added an upstairs laundry, but we still kept the old one in the basement, giving our modest, middle-class house . . . two laundries. The basement laundry is useful for washing bulky comforters, or for when we want to do a lot of laundry quickly by running two loads at a time. What some might see as excessive, we call convenient.

Likewise, Steve's desire to have a home large enough to accommodate lots of overnight visitors or dozens of party guests is an example of what some market researchers call the "maximum-use imperative." It's a phenomenon that helps explain why people like owning sport-utility vehicles. Most SUV owners probably tow a boat, carry eight passengers, or use four-wheel drive to get their car unstuck only a couple of times a year (if ever), but even if we use these capabilities infrequently, we still feel better knowing we *can*. Our houses are the same way: We'd prefer not to send relatives to Motel 6 when they visit, or rent the Knights of Columbus hall for a family get-together. Ideally, we'd like our homes to be large enough to accommodate our "maximum-use imperative," even if much of the space sits empty the 360 nights a year we're not throwing parties. Some big-house owners flick at this when they explain, a little apologetically, that they need such a big house for business-related entertaining.

Multiple appliances and "maximum-use" space are both examples of how, over time, Americans' concept of wants and needs have changed dramatically, due mostly to our society's growing affluence. It's a progression recounted in *The Good Life and Its Discontents,* by my *Newsweek* colleague Robert J. Samuelson. "Neither individuals nor nations are ever satisfied, because people always want more," Samuelson writes. "Yesterday's luxuries become today's necessities. They are what middle-class Americans think they 'have to have' to qualify as being middle class." Writing in the early 1990s, Samuelson cited the VCR as a then-current example of this phenomenon, but what's striking is how many new necessities have emerged since then. Today most middle-class homes have broadband Internet service; its owners almost certainly carry cell phones; its teenaged residents probably have iPods. Together these products and services can add thousands a year to the household budget, but they're considered basic have-to-haves, not luxuries. Likewise, a generation ago people were thrilled to own their own home, but today they "need" something far bigger.

Still, this ever-changing mix of wants and needs can leave people who live in nice homes feeling a little uncomfortable with their abundance. Tammy recalls her kids visiting a friend's home and commenting on how small it seemed—even though it was probably larger than 90 percent of the homes in America. Living in a space as large as theirs—Tammy calls it "a little bit over-the-top"—leaves her worrying whether her children's worldview may be a little bit skewed. "My kids have no concept," she says.

While it's hard to find anything lacking in her home, Tammy did make one trade-off in its design. Its floor plan called for two first-floor half baths (or "powder rooms"). Instead, Tammy opted to replace one powder room with a mudroom, with custom-built cubbies to hold the family's coats, boots, and book bags. She adores the mudroom, but whenever she tells the kids to go to the bathroom before getting in the car, she misses the two first-floor baths she had in her last house, which allowed multiple kids to use the bathroom simultaneously.

Steven has small regrets, too. The costs are one of them. When you buy such a large home, every bill—from the property taxes to the money you'll spend to have it painted—becomes supersized, too. He sounds like he's only half kidding when he says he regrets the size of the home every time he checks his bank balance. He's also less than enthusiastic about the two-story family room. Though Tammy adores it, Steven says the noise from that room travels throughout the house, and he'd prefer a space that's more intimate. "It's completely non-functional to have a two-story family room," he says. Instead of four bedrooms upstairs and two in the basement, he wishes one of those basement bedrooms were on the first floor. Finally, he wishes they had a bigger backyard. There's a lesson here: Even someone who spends $3 million on a home isn't going to be completely satisfied.

The Goldbergs furnished their home themselves, but for many affluent families, figuring out how to outfit houses this big can require professional assistance. "It's absolutely ridiculous the kind of space that has to be filled—houses where there are ten rooms on the first floor, two different sunrooms plus two-story family rooms, windows like you wouldn't believe," says Katie Goldfarb, a Potomac-based interior designer. Lots of novices rely on oversize furniture to fill floor space, but that often interferes with traffic flow. Instead, in the soaring family rooms Goldfarb uses rich, warm paint colors, and sometimes has painters stop the wall color several feet shy of the ceilings to try to make the ceilings seem lower. She uses table lamps to try to create intimacy, which can be difficult to achieve with recessed lights in high ceilings. And she's always looking for large-scale, three-dimensional artwork to try to fill the giant walls. "You have to do things which bring the space down to a human size," she says.

Upstairs the job can be even more difficult, thanks to gigantic master suites. "They're so large you have to furnish them almost as if you're furnishing a small studio apartment," she says. Goldfarb usually starts with a huge bed. She wishes she could use more dressers to fill space, but these homes already have so much closet space that there's really no need for furniture to store clothing. So she often opts for an arrangement of traditional-size sofas and armchairs. By the time she's finished, there's sometimes enough seating to throw a small cocktail party in the master bedroom.

In the finished basements Goldfarb has helped outfit her share of exercise rooms, nanny suites, pool table rooms, and bars. When those rooms aren't enough, she's seen homeowners opt for gift-wrapping rooms or plant-potting rooms that would make Martha Stewart proud. "After a certain point you run out of rooms to put down there," Goldfarb says. "Unless these houses have families that are very large, most of these large spaces go unused."

The people who live in these giant homes often point to their investment potential, and during the real estate boom that seemed like a valid justification. But the need to furnish, heat, and cool all this space represents very real costs that take away from whatever appreciation a trophy home might enjoy. Back when home prices were rising rapidly, an unused living room might have been a great investment, but the couches and end tables the owner buys to fill it up will only depreciate—as will the junk that tends to fill up basements of large homes. Living in tight spaces can force people to be choosier about what they'll buy; in contrast, people who live in big houses have the freedom of knowing they'll always have space for whatever they'll buy—and some may have the credit card statements to prove it.

At Toll Brothers' headquarters outside Philadelphia, executives don't pretend that anyone really needs this much space. Despite a net worth that's measured in the hundreds of millions of dollars, company founder Robert Toll lives in a 1750 farmhouse with bedrooms that are smaller than the master bathrooms of the homes his company builds. He jokes about his yuppie customers' long-running fascination with Jacuzzi tubs. He suspects many hope their new "love tubs" will provide a boost to their sex lives, but he's skeptical. "People have an image of producing children in a tub, but I don't think it really works—that's only for fish," he says.

Toll and his colleagues acknowledge that people buy these homes mostly to show off. They argue: So what? "'Judge not, lest ye be judged,'" Toll says, quoting the New Testament. "None of us needs the square footage that we use, but none of us needs the jewelry we wear, either," he says. "If we lived only by common sense and logic with respect to our needs, there'd be no Tiffany and no Toll Brothers." The company's president, Zvi Barzilay, puts it differently: "We're not selling shelter. We're selling extreme-ego, look-at-me types of homes."

When critics of big homes pick on Toll Brothers' designs, the company's chief architect, Jed Gibson, reminds them that beauty is in the eye of the customer. He tells a story—a favorite around Toll headquarters—of CEO Robert Toll looking over the plans for a particularly unfortunate design. "Oh, my God—that's the ugliest house I've ever seen," Toll said, grimacing in disgust. Then a vice president spoke up, telling Toll that in his region, the model was selling fast at $700,000 apiece. Toll didn't miss a beat: "This is the most beautiful house I've ever seen." It's an anecdote that speaks to the uneasy tension between giving buyers what they want and creating a home that's architecturally refined. For Toll Brothers, that choice is easy. "Did I like that house? No, I agreed with Bob," Gibson says. "It was one of the ugliest things I'd ever seen, and I hated the fact that it was coming out of my shop. But it was selling. It was what the customer wanted."

There is, of course, a word used to describe America's new breed of megahomes. The *Oxford English Dictionary* defines "McMansion" as "an ostentatiously large house, hastily constructed, with minimal attention to building quality and architectural detail." *Webster's* isn't much kinder, defining it as "an excessively large home built on relatively small acreage."

As these homes proliferated, a whole industry has risen up to draw attention to their alleged shortcomings. At the head of this movement stands Sarah Susanka. "More rooms, bigger spaces and vaulted ceilings do not necessarily give us what we need in a home," Susanka wrote in her 1998 manifesto, *The Not So Big House*. "It's time for a different kind of house. A house that is more than square footage . . . A house with a floor plan inspired by our informal lifestyle instead of the way our grandparents lived."

In the book, replete with photos of the cozy, exquisitely detailed homes Susanka designs, she lays out her philosophy. The traditional configuration of a home's public rooms—living room, dining room, family room—is really obsolete, she argues, since families rarely use their formal living room or dining room anymore. Better to replace them with a single open, multipurpose space. Likewise, soaring ceilings may look impressive, but they inhibit intimacy and cause acoustical problems. Better to vary ceiling heights, with some tall and some short. Instead of large spaces she favors lots of wood trim, built-in bookcases, window seats, and stonework. To create a refuge from the open living area, she advocates an "away room"—a TV-free spot where adults can shut the door to talk or read without noise. While Susanka has designed homes as large as 7,000 square feet, most of her projects tend to measure around 2,400 square feet. Few families need more than that, she believes.

The Not So Big House was so successful it spawned a stream of sequels and a full-fledged architectural movement. As a result, today Susanka spends most of her time writing books and giving speeches. She rarely designs homes anymore, and she hardly ever steps foot in the homes she and her followers love to hate. So one afternoon I aimed to remedy that. Together Susanka and I would go shopping for our own starter castle.

I pick her up at a hotel in downtown Boston and we drive west to a Toll Brothers development about fifteen miles away. I've been to attractive Toll subdivisions, but this isn't one of them. Containing just twelve homes, it's located on a small island of land, crammed between two relatively busy streets and a cemetery, without so much as a cul-de-sac to provide the illusion of space.

We drive around the project. Susanka immediately notices that while the houses have brick facades, the three remaining walls are vinyl-sided. In stark contrast to the elegant front windows, the side and back windows are untrimmed. "That's really tacky," she says. "Just the front gets any attention, and the sides are leftover." She says the builder is responding to the fact that homebuyers typically focus on two things: the way the house looks from the street (what architects call the "front elevation") and the two-dimensional floor plan showing the layout of the rooms. If buyers don't notice the rear window trim, builders figure, why spend money there?

Susanka and I walk into the four-bedroom, three-and-a-half-bath model home, called a Chelsea Georgian. Jane, the sales agent, greets us. "We're just driving by," I tell her, introducing Susanka as "my friend." The agent asks a few questions to get a sense if we're serious. I tell her that my in-laws live nearby and that my wife has talked about moving to this town (both true statements). She asks me where I live now. When I answer, her expression changes: Based on where I live, she's concluded I can't really afford a home like this model, priced at $1,487,975. (She's right.) She tells us to look around at our leisure, and sits back at her desk.

This model has a strange layout. The living room, to the right of the front hallway, dead-ends at its back and feels disconnected from the rest of the house. The kitchen, usually at the center of Toll Brothers homes (and almost always adjoining the family room), is instead sequestered at the rear left of the house, behind the garage. Susanka walks around, wrinkling her nose and occasionally frowning. Upstairs in the master suite, located behind double doors, she has a hard time figuring out where the bed would go. Inside the master bath, with a cathedral ceiling and a corner Jacuzzi overlooking the cemetery, she shrugs, unimpressed.

As we go down the stairs, Jane greets us again. Several homes will be ready for us to move in within two months, she tells us. I mention that the basement seems quite large. "You can get a lot of square footage down there" if we were to finish it off, Jane says helpfully. Even without the basement, this home is 3,800 square feet. "Price per square foot, we're competitive with everybody, if not lower," Jane says. And unlike other builders, who calculate a home's square footage by simply measuring the first floor and multiplying it by two, she boasts that Toll Brothers measures the true square footage by subtracting the upstairs floor space lost by the two-story foyers and family rooms. Susanka and I thank her for her time and head for the car.

Outside, I ask the architect what she thinks. "It's very basic," she says. "What they promote are the tall ceilings and the granite—everything else is pretty darn simple." The appliances are all standard-issue. The sidewalks are concrete, not stone. Many of the door openings are untrimmed. "What they're selling is a full, front-on facial, and space, and that's about it. In terms of detail, there's very little. . . . There's nothing that's sophisticated or has any quality to it, but most people don't know to look for that. They walk in and feel it's airy and has lots of space, and that's about as far as they go."

The floor plan—with its disconnected kitchen and family room—seems hopelessly flawed. "The kitchen and eating area would be by far the most-used space in that house, which, when you look at it, is a pretty small area," she says. She also disliked the master bedroom setup. "I would never want to have double French doors opening into a bedroom—that's the most uncomfortable place to sleep you can imagine."

Homes like this are all about square footage, she says, which is one reason the sales agent brought up the low price per square foot. Susanka doesn't blame the builder alone for making houses like this—she describes a complex set of forces that lead developers to behave this way. Land here is really expensive, and developers feel they have to build $1 million houses to justify the land cost and turn a profit. And since every twenty-first-century buyer is going to crunch the numbers to calculate the cost per square foot, the builder who delivers the biggest spaces at the lowest prices (by skimping on things like window trim) will be seen as the best value.

"Dollars per square foot are a very poor measure of anything that matters," she says. "A house that fits you may feel a lot bigger than it is, and it may have a higher dollar-per-square-foot cost. But if you've been told you're getting a bad deal if you spend more than $250 per square foot, you're not going to get the kind of house you want. . . . It's this measure that's misleading you from the get-go."

She asks me what I thought of the house. I really disliked this particular floor plan, I say. But on the other hand, I have friends who live in Toll Brothers houses, or homes that share the same basic size and design, and while I don't covet their spaces, they certainly don't offend my sense of aesthetics. When I visit, it's usually for a dinner party or a cookout, and I've always thought these homes work extremely well for entertaining large groups. The kids disappear to the finished basements; the adults have plenty of space to hang out—even if, as Susanka points out, everyone congregates in the kitchen, leaving the living and dining rooms empty. Sure, maybe this is a misleading way to assess a home's functionality, since I'm seeing these houses used on these "maximum-usage imperative" occasions—for parties—when all the extra space really pays off. But who says it's a bad thing if a living or dining room doesn't get used all that often, particularly as homes have come to be seen more as investments? When was the last time anyone *used* a share of IBM stock?

With all this talk about square footage, I begin to wonder: Exactly how big was the center-hall colonial in which I grew up? I lived there for twenty years, but despite my intimacy with this structure, I don't know the square footage. Hoping to find the answer, I go online to look up its size, but it turns out my hometown's tax collector isn't wired yet. So I ask my parents, separately, if they remember how big the house was. Neither knows offhand, and each e-mails me back calculations of the size based on their guesstimates of its length and width. Dad figures 2,000 square feet; Mom says 1,730.

Today a homeowner who doesn't know the square footage of his house is becoming as rare as a high school senior who doesn't know his SAT score. But Mom says that's a generational phenomenon. When people her age were buying and building their homes, they didn't focus on square footage. "I don't know the square footage of the house your stepfather and I own now," she says. "And the only reason I know the square footage of our last house is because the Realtor made an issue of it when we sold it."

It turns out she's got a point—apparently people didn't always obsess about square footage the way we do now. But in the same way that "body mass index" is supplanting weight as a measure of our bodies, or that our ratio of LDL to HDL is becoming more relevant than our raw cholesterol score, square footage has emerged as the prime measure of housing. In an episode from season three of the NBC comedy *The Office*, Dwight is invited to a cocktail party at the home of his company's chief financial officer. Looking around the man's house, Dwight drills down: "What's the square footage?" When the CFO answers ("About 5,000"), Dwight still wants to know more. "Does that include the garage?" he says skeptically. Dwight's fascination with the house is intentionally over-the-top—in the next scene he's shown tapping the walls and yanking the banister to test its sturdiness. But like the best of this show's studies-in-awkwardness moments, it begins with a perfectly reasonable premise: In particularly house-obsessed regions of the country, when you see someone's house, inquiring about the size has become perfectly reasonable behavior.

As Manhattan's best-known residential appraiser, Jonathan Miller has witnessed this evolution. When he started this work, in the late 1980s, many real estate listings didn't provide the apartment's square footage—instead, they'd list the number of rooms. "In co-ops, no one looked at square footage," Miller says. "It was, 'It's a seven-room apartment.' But a seven-room apartment could be 1,500 square feet or 2,800 square feet."

The standard real estate metric began to change in New York, Miller recalls, because of a boom in condominium building during the 1980s. By law, condominium listings had to disclose the square footage, and that measurement began catching on with the public. Real estate agents were initially reluctant to list the square footage of resales, because if the measurement they gave wasn't correct, the misinformation could result in lawsuits. But over time they acquiesced. Now square footage is the sine qua non of a home's characteristics, second only to its address.

Of course, that doesn't necessarily mean the numbers sellers tout are accurate. Few of us ever pull out tape measures to double-check the number, and Miller says most brokers unintentionally inflate the size by 10 percent. "If it says 2,000 square feet in the listing, I can almost guarantee it's really 1,800 or 1,825 square feet," he says.

Once the public became used to talking about apartment sizes in square footage, it was only a matter of time before more savvy buyers began crunching those numbers the same way appraisers do. The simplest way to do that—whether you're building from scratch or buying an existing home—is to divide the price of a property by its size, giving you the price per square foot. In 2006 in Manhattan, the average apartment was valued at $1,002 per square foot—meaning a decent closet on the Upper East Side is worth more than a new Toyota Camry.

But the fascination with square footage isn't only a city phenomenon. In Scottsdale, Arizona, custom homebuilder Dennis Dixon gets a steady stream of buyers whose first question is some variation of: "How much per square foot will it cost to build me a house?" His answer is: "It depends."

Dixon bemoans the industry's reliance on cost-per-square-foot as the primary metric. At a seminar for contractors, he clicks through PowerPoint slides showing why. Consider a 4,500-square-foot house. It could be one story or two stories. The one-story home will require a much bigger foundation and roof—both big-ticket items—so despite the identical square footage, it will cost much more. Next consider the shape. The exterior walls of a home—a sandwich built of siding, plywood, insulation, two-by-fours, and drywall—are a big expense. That's why, instead of looking at square footage, he looks at the length of the walls as a key variable when figuring cost. He shows one slide with two shapes. The first is a ten-by-ten square, which has forty feet of exterior walls. The second is a skinny rectangle, two feet by fifty feet, which requires 104 linear feet of walls. Both are 100 square feet, but the cost to build the walls for the skinny rectangle would be more than two and a half times the cost of building the square. This slide explains why colonial-style homes are so popular: Their square shape and two-story structure give buyers the maximum square footage with the least possible roofing and exterior walls.

Beyond the shape of a house, all square footage isn't created equal. Garages are cheap, as is bumping out a wall by a couple of feet in a family room, as Potomac View's builders routinely do. High ceilings can drive up costs without changing the square footage at all. (To account for this, Dixon suggests builders calculate the price per cubic foot for homes with lots of cathedral ceilings.) Appliances and fixtures matter, too: Dixon recalls one client who built a 4,000-square-foot house that included a $60,000 stove, and the stove alone added $15 to the cost per square foot.

Pricing houses by the square foot, Dixon tells builders, makes about as much sense as if car dealers sold automobiles by the pound, or if booksellers priced books based on the number of words. But builders have to learn to deal with it, because it's the language the public speaks nowadays.

America's hunger for more space puts it in stark contrast with other countries, whose inhabitants are forced to learn to construct full lives in what are, by U.S. standards, far smaller spaces.

An ideal illustration of this contrast lies in Americus, Georgia, a few blocks from the headquarters of the nonprofit group Habitat for Humanity. There, the charity operates a Global Village and Discovery Center, where visitors can walk through a model of the slumlike conditions in which one billion people live around the world. Next to it are models of the simple homes the charity builds for the needy. Many of the shelters it's building overseas are Spartan, three-room, cabinlike structures, some without plumbing or glass windows. Many models are made of earthen blocks, measure a couple of hundred square feet, and can cost as little as $2,280 in the Philippines or $3,120 in Guatemala. In the United States, the typical Habitat for Humanity home is wood-framed, measures 1,200 square feet or less, and costs about $60,000 (including land).

But lately the dimensions of its U.S. homes have been growing. Today even the working-class people who are depending on charity for a home desire bigger kitchens and laundry rooms, and Habitat for Humanity has felt compelled to upsize its designs, albeit slightly.

You can't walk through this tour—looking inside rudimentary

homes that are smaller than some suburban garden sheds—without asking a fundamental question: Americans have grown to *want* more space, but how much do we really *need*?

Different cultures answer the question in different ways. In Japan the average home measures about 1,033 square feet (though in Tokyo the average is just 694 square feet). On a list of twenty developed countries, only the United States and Australia are building new homes that average more than 2,000 square feet. In Sweden, Ireland, Italy, Portugal, and the United Kingdom, the average new house is less than 1,000 square feet.

For Americans the smallest living accommodations many of us experience are in cramped college dormitories. According to the Association of College and University Housing Officers International, the median-size new residence at U.S. colleges in 2005 contained 338 square feet per student.

That may seem like a lot of space to residents of Manhattan. In hot urban markets, every square inch is so expensive that, like people living on wartime rations, nearly every resident is forced to calculate exactly how much space he truly needs—and often find creative ways to do with less. To really appreciate the excessive spaces being built in places like Potomac View, it's necessary to stop in the Big Apple, a place where square footages are experienced so differently.

If you've never lived in New York City, it's hard to have sufficient appreciation for just how small the average resident's living space really is. In *Through the Children's Gate*, writer Adam Gopnik describes hunting for a family-size Manhattan apartment. It's only when he began looking at multimillion-dollar residences that he found "the old American representations of normalcy and domestic comfort . . . kitchens that look like kitchens, living rooms like living rooms, bedrooms like bedrooms," he writes. Gopnik says most non–New Yorkers imagine the typical city resident living in something that looks like Meg Ryan's character's apartment in a Nora Ephron movie, or one of the charming spaces depicted in a Woody Allen film. In truth, only hedge-fund managers live in places like that.

At the other extreme is the apartment—if you use the word

loosely—inhabited by Seth Herzog, an actor and comedian. He is thirty-five years old, and since 1994 he has lived in an apartment on Broadway between Twenty-eighth and Twenty-ninth streets. It's a vaguely trapezoidish-shaped room, with clothes and junk everywhere. Manhattan is an island of small spaces, but Herzog claims his home is one of the city's smallest. It measures 175 square feet.

"I tell people who are coming over, 'Whatever you're thinking of when I say, "I live in a small apartment," cut it in half. Then cut it in half again. Now you're getting close,'" he says.

When I go to visit, I'm wearing a backpack. The space is so tiny—and cluttered—that I can't get through the door with it on, because the piles inside prevent the door from opening very wide. So I take the backpack off, walk inside, then drag the backpack in behind me. A few feet to my left, past clothes hanging from a pipe by the ceiling, I spy the sink. To my right is a wall lined with shelves filled with a hodgepodge of belongings: old mail, an Uncle Sam hat, action figures. Herzog sits on an old plaid couch under a loft bed. In the corner is a window. There's no place for me to sit down, so I take him out to lunch at a coffee shop.

Technically speaking, his space isn't really an "apartment." There is no bathroom (it's down the hall) and no kitchen, so legally it's a "single-room occupancy" dwelling. Herzog rents it, paying $393 a month. If he moved to anything even slightly larger, he figures, he'd spend at least $1,000 a month. The way Herzog sees it, he's making a sacrifice in comfort to invest in himself and his career. "That's a huge part of living in New York City," he says. "People who live in a small space in New York, they're sacrificing for the potential of their dreams and hopes. It's a whole part of the bargain of being here."

There are obvious downsides to living in cramped quarters. Though he has a small refrigerator and a microwave, Herzog eats most meals out. His bachelor pad is far from an ideal place to bring a date—though over lunch, he regales me with a story about once sharing his loft bed with two women simultaneously. (Due to the cramped space, he suggests you imagine a coupling better suited for Comedy Central than for the Playboy Channel.) The apartment would be tiny no matter how organized it was, but the clutter—much of it props that Herzog uses in his comedy routines—makes the space a complete nightmare. Among his friends, Herzog's packrat tendencies are so notorious that two of his buddies, William Doble and Toby Miller, made an independent short film called *Zog's Place*, focusing on his dysfunctional living arrangement. Herzog says he's recently agreed to let a different friend who's a designer help him conduct a makeover, though when I call her later, she's not sure she'll make much headway. The space is just too small, she says, and Herzog is too unwilling to part with his treasures.

By one estimate, New York City contains 5,000 so-called "microapartments" of less than 300 square feet, most of them on the Lower East Side. Unlike Herzog's place, these are full-fledged apartments, with kitchens and baths. Jonathan Miller, the appraiser, has visited an apartment measuring 160 square feet, and a colleague saw one with just 130 square feet. The *New York Times* runs a steady stream of stories in its House & Home section describing how design pros configure and make over these tiny apartments. Most of the solutions involve loft or Murphy beds, tons of built-in cabinetry, white paint, mirrors, and the careful culling of possessions. "In my mind the apartment is much bigger," says Giuseppe Pica, one of these House & Home celebrants, whose design scheme for his 305 square feet utilizes transparent Lucite furniture.

Devotees of this way of life can be a passionate crowd. They've always reminded me of people who live on sailboats, where space is so tight that dining tables must convert into beds, and where one's possessions are chosen and edited with a care and precision few landlubbers can replicate. Among the most evangelical is small-apartment dweller Maxwell Gillingham-Ryan, a thirty-nine-year-old former Waldorf teacher. In 2001 he quit teaching to become an interior designer and start a Web site called apartmenttherapy.com. Maxwell and his wife share a 250-square-foot apartment in Greenwich Village. His tricks for making their space work include ruthless purging (of CDs, shoes, and books, in particular), eschewing sofas, and replacing doors with soft curtains. "That's the struggle of a small space—you just don't have all the rooms to do all that you want to do," he told me. "You have to take that space and figure out how to give it that multi-function feel in one footprint without making it feel like a train wreck, so that one wall becomes an office and another wall becomes a living room." In the Gillingham-Ryans' microapartment, the bedroom doubles as the living room, with the other room working as a dining room/kitchen.

The disconnect between the lifestyles of these microhomeowners and their supersize suburban counterparts continues to grow. In the city, where tight spaces make accumulating possessions a zero-sum game, parents go through an annual ritual of throwing away selected children's toys each December in order to make room for new Christmas presents. In the suburbs, meanwhile, large-home residents struggle to find Christmas trees that won't look too small in a humongous two-story family room. In cities residents (and their designers) commission complicated built-ins and storage systems to try to fit more stuff into a small space. In the suburbs the contrasting problem is how to find a TV wide enough to fill up the walls in those ever-larger spaces. In cities studio dwellers love their fold-up Murphy beds, but in the suburbs bigger master bedrooms have led to the advent of the "extreme ultra king" bed, the new top end of the mattress world. It measures 12 feet wide and 10 feet long, or roughly 184 percent larger than the "California king" mattresses that once reigned supreme.

As big-home denizens lie on this expanse, shouting to their spouses on the other side of the bed, they can take a special comfort in knowing that their mattress is about two-thirds as big as Seth Herzog's entire apartment.

When I tell people who live in ordinary-size houses that I've been visiting 9,000- (and even 29,000-) square-foot homes, I hear two common reactions. The first involves the cost of these homes: People marvel at how anyone could (or would want to) foot the seven- (or eight-) figure price tags homes like this carry. But the second reaction is more common, and it has less to do with finances and everything to do with family dynamics. People worry that if they lived in such a large space, they'd become disconnected or isolated from other family members, as everyone hangs out solo in sunrooms, grand conservatories, or luxurious bedrooms. In Potomac View, where nearly every child's bedroom features an en suite sitting area and bath (and very often their own TV and video-game system), it seems like a valid concern. Indeed, so many kids today are being raised in homes that feature a bathroom for every bedroom, some experts say today's teenagers have grown unusually squeamish about undressing in school locker rooms or sharing gang-style dormitory showers.

These are issues that researchers haven't studied very much, largely because megahome living is a recent phenomenon. When sociologists have examined house size and family life, they've usually focused on the other extreme: the extent to which living in cramped or overcrowded circumstances leads to problems. In fact, research suggests that it does. New York University sociologist Dalton Conley cites studies showing that people who live in homes where the number of rooms is fewer than the number of inhabitants suffer from increased irritability, withdrawal, weariness, and poor physical and mental health. Conley's own research goes even further, suggesting that children who grow up in an overcrowded home tend to suffer in educational attainment, perhaps because they don't have sufficient space to study or because the crowded conditions affect their sleep.

But as more Americans supersize their homes, researchers are becoming interested in what's going on inside. Anthony Graesch is an ethno-archaeologist at UCLA's Center for the Study of Everyday Lives of Families. "I'm very interested in people's relationships with their houses—how intensively they use spaces, the range of activities that occur in these spaces, and how they change their houses over time," he says. For his Ph.D. dissertation, he worked on a project that involved videotaping daily life inside the homes of thirty-two dual-income, married-with-kids families in Los Angeles. Most of these families are middle-class, and the homes average around 2,000 square feet. But several live in houses of more than 3,000 square feet, and one family, with household earnings above $500,000, lives in a house that measures 4,000 square feet. In each home Graesch's team spent four days videotaping family members as they went about their daily activities. They also tracked, at ten-minute intervals, which rooms were occupied by which family members. Then Graesch compared how the traffic patterns varied based on the size of the different houses.

No matter what the home size, Graesch says, people tended to spend most of their time near the kitchen—generally congregating around the nearest flat surface, whether it was a kitchen island or an adjacent dining room table. "That ends up being the primary locus of activity," he says. "These become multipurpose rooms, whether for paying bills, reading the paper, eating, talking, or playing games." Contrary to speculation, Graesch found that even kids living in large homes didn't seem to spend inordinate time in their bedrooms or away from their parents. Those results might be colored by the recruiting criteria: For this study, each family had to have at least one child between eight and ten years old, and by the time these children are teenagers some may spend more time alone in their bedrooms, as big-house critics fear.

Beyond the home's floor plans, Graesch's research also suggests that technology plays a big role in how families use their homes. His team's data show that regardless of a home's size or layout, people tend to spend a ton of time wherever there's a TV or a computer. Indeed, as both adults and children spend more time online, how families actually utilize space may depend less on the work of the architect, and more on the work of the electrician who installed outlets offering broadband Internet access.

Graesch isn't the only one who suspects technology may ultimately trump square footage when it comes to family interactions. Kathryn Anthony is an architecture professor at the University of Illinois at Champagne–Urbana. Anthony believes that while people may worry about a family in a 9,000-square-foot home losing touch with one another, it may be just as easy to lose touch in a 1,500-square-foot home in which each family member plugs into his own iPod while tapping on a wireless-equipped laptop. "These kind of electronic devices allow people to get into their own worlds and really divorce themselves, at least temporarily, from what's going on," Anthony says. It's no wonder that pediatricians advise parents to keep TVs and computers out of children's bedrooms.

And whatever the size of a family's home, Anthony says there's usually one key factor that supercedes all other indicators of how connected the family is: Do they sit down to eat together on a regular basis? Back in Potomac View, nobody seems to be using their formal dining rooms very much. But no matter how big the family, there's plenty of room to sit around the oversize kitchen islands.

As the real estate boom faded, sales of trophy homes—in places like Potomac View and elsewhere—cooled substantially. By 2006 it was clear that the days when gigantic houses appreciated like dot-com stocks did in 1998 had definitely come to an end.

As the real estate bust continues, there will certainly be people who question whether buying supersize houses remains a wise investment. *Wall Street Journal* columnist Jonathan Clements, one of the housing boom's leading skeptics, has crunched the numbers and concluded that most people who trade up to a large house end up with less wealth than if they'd stayed in a moderate-size home and poured the money they saved (by keeping a smaller mortgage payment) into their retirement accounts. "Buying a bigger house isn't an investment," Clements writes. "It's a lifestyle choice—and it comes with a brutally large price tag."

There are early indicators that more Americans may be realizing that. As the market cooled off, "all the evidence we have is that the average home size will stabilize at around 2,400 square feet," says Gopal Ahluwalia, chief researcher for the National Association of

Homebuilders. Part of that change, some forecasters say, will come as more baby boomers enter their empty-nest years and begin downsizing to smaller homes. But the trend isn't just a function of age: Ahluwalia cites consumer surveys suggesting that people's preference for square footage is waning. Lately, he says, they're showing more interest in quality features, like hardwood floors or fireplaces, than in sheer size.

Still, even if the square footage of homes plateaus, Ahluwalia sees people trying to create the illusion of size in different ways. In many new homes the ceilings, once a standard eight feet, are moving toward nine, ten, or even twelve feet. (Basketball, anyone?) He's seeing more homes—even in the suburbs—embrace the wall-less feel of modernist loftlike spaces. Even if the outside walls of the home stop their outward movement, inside the home people still want the feel of limitless space.

It remains to be seen whether people who already own these XXL homes will have a difficult time selling them if, as Ahluwalia and others say, our preference for really big homes is starting to fade. If the majority of consumers really do start to long for the kind of architectural detail—fancy moldings and window trim, bookcases and fine stone fireplaces—that critics like Susanka prescribe, some of these elements can be added into homes later, during renovations, so that's not a big concern. But it's also possible that some of these gigantic spaces may come to be seen as albratrosses.

Near the end of my reporting for this book, I visited a subdivision a mile from my home where a builder had started work on three large homes, two of which measured more than 5,000 square feet. Two of the homes were nearly complete, with plaster on the walls; the third stood as just a shell. You could tell that work had stopped abruptly—one family room had just half its flooring installed—because the builder, unable to find buyers, had run out of money. A few days after my visit the bank would auction off the properties. Among the curiosity seekers who'd come out for this Sunday walkthrough, the big question was whether anyone would submit bids, since the next street over featured two similar finished houses that had been languishing on the market for months. Once finished, these would be impressive homes—but with home values no longer escalating, homes this big and this expensive were no longer as attractive to buyers as they'd been a year or two earlier.

It's no surprise, perhaps, that even in the face of predictions that the heyday for trophy homes has passed, people like Bob Toll remain bullish on the business of building gigantic houses. His company's sales dropped steeply as the boom turned to bust, but he argues that once supply and demand return to balance, people will still continue to dream about buying houses in places like Potomac View—and when they do, the square footage will still matter. Toll scoffs at critics who predict Americans might turn en masse to European-sized (or Susanka-styled) housing. Even if Americans come to view real estate as less of a sure-fire route to riches than it was during the first half of the '00s, Toll believes a certain segment of the population will always desire a home that makes a simple statement: I've arrived. "If you can afford a large home and believe in the investment, why not?" Toll says. "You live in your dream, and you've made a smart investment, which is the extra kick necessary to convince yourself to buy a home that's bigger than anything you'd really need just for living."

As for the Goldbergs, after more than a year in their megahome, they have no regrets. Their family is just as close as ever. "When we go upstairs at 7:00 p.m., it's family time, and we're really close," says Steven, who notes that despite all their square footage, the family's bedroom doors are all within 10 feet of one another. Says Tammy: "The kids don't get lost."

And if they ever do, there's a good chance they're simply hiding in one of the bathrooms.

CHAPTER TWO

THAT NEW-HOUSE SMELL: LAS VEGAS, NEVADA

When Only New Will Do

In a simpler time, Mark and Tina Giles probably wouldn't have been looking to move. The couple—he's fifty, she's forty-seven—had lived in the same Las Vegas home for twenty years. They'd raised their children there, and settled happily into the empty-nest phase of life. They'd paid off most of their mortgage—and if they stayed put, they could look ahead toward a retirement free of house payments.

But the Gileses' longtime home was built thirty years ago, and to them it felt well past its prime. They were restless. They looked briefly at existing homes for sale, but they were unimpressed. So rather than settle for the things they didn't like in an older home, they decided to avoid compromising by having a house made to order and built just for them. By doing so, they got to choose every doorknob and cabinet pull. They got to watch their new home rise from the desert one stick of lumber at a time. But their biggest thrill was knowing they were the first residents of an immaculate, unblemished space. It's a feeling Tina describes succinctly.

"You're not moving into somebody else's 'ick,'" she says. "That's a strange way to put it, but we wanted to start fresh."

It's becoming a common sentiment. In the auto industry, car

buyers have long been captivated by that "new-car smell"—the plastic-scented perfume that pervades the interior for the first few weeks after you drive an automobile away from the showroom. Now a growing number of families like the Gileses want the same experience when it comes to their homes. They want to be the ones to rip the cellophane wrap off of shiny new appliances. They want to apply the first coat of paint, instead of painting over a half dozen previous owners' color choices. They want the latest in technologies, from heating and cooling to "smart-house" electronics. In places like Las Vegas, some people refer to an existing home as a "used house"—and who wants to settle for used when you can buy new?

It's an ideal that can carry a big cost in both time and money. Even if the process goes perfectly, buying a new home where the Gileses did, in a new subdivision called Huntington being built on the southwestern edge of Las Vegas, takes at least nine months. The Gileses remained patient. They visited the job site on weekends when workers weren't around. They wrote their names on the un-painted drywall as a sort of time capsule. They added their own small touches to its construction, like stuffing extra insulation around their whirlpool tub before the tile was installed, in hopes that it would help keep their hot baths a little warmer. Mostly, though, they mar-veled at the structure's rise. "The most exciting thing was just watch-ing the house go up piece by piece," Tina says.

For this privilege they paid around $380,000, not including the in-ground pool, hot tub, and deck they installed after moving in. That's not as much as it costs to buy a new house in more expensive places, but it's still left them with what feels like an uncomfortably large mortgage. The Gileses, however, have no regrets. They moved into the home in early 2006, and they love it. To them it couldn't be more perfect.

If you grew up on the East Coast, as I did, you may be a bit unfamiliar with this fascination for living in a new home. I grew up in a house built in the 1920s, and very few of my childhood friends lived in a home less than ten years old. Today, within a mile of my house in Massachusetts, there are dozens of homes that date back to the 1700s. My own home was built in the 1970s, and I some-times wish that it were older, so that it might have a little more char-acter. In Manhattan, likewise, there's cachet to "prewar" apartments, which usually feature thicker walls, higher ceilings, and more charm.

Throughout most of the country, existing homes remain the norm. According to census data, the median U.S. home is thirty-two years old, and nationally 80 percent of the homes that are bought and sold each year have been previously occupied.

But in the land-rich, fast-growing cities in the West—and espe-cially in places like Las Vegas and Phoenix—many buyers have grown to covet new homes. And even in the exurbs surrounding older East Coast cities, there is plenty of new construction going on. Despite all the century-old (and older) homes in my suburb, many of the neigh-borhoods around mine were built in the last decade—and there are still new homes being built within a mile or two of mine.

As I toured model homes and watched families choose options for their new residences, I struggled to understand what's fueling this desire. Finally one afternoon, standing in a basement, a salesperson lowered her voice and explained it to me in simple terms. Many Americans, she told me, are absolutely horrified at the idea of bathing in a bathtub a stranger has used. And the metaphor extends beyond the bathroom. No matter how well we scrub a preowned house, we know somebody else's invisible grime still surrounds us. The only way to truly eliminate it is to build from scratch. In the same way that some religious and conservative cultures are obsessed with vir-ginity, a group of homebuyers has developed a fetish of their own: They want a virgin home.

In truth, calling this a fetish may be a poor choice of words, if only because the new-home aspiration has become so prevalent in the last few years. In 1993, when the National Association of Home-builders conducted its annual survey, 48 percent of Americans said they hoped their next home would be newly built. But in the 2004 survey, an astonishing 74 percent of would-be buyers said they hoped to purchase a home unsullied by a previous owner. In less than a decade, the proportion of us dreaming of new homes has grown by half.

Most of those dreams won't materialize. It costs more to build a new home than it does to buy a preexisting house similar in size, look, features, and location. Furthermore, many towns lack the land for significant homebuilding; together those are two of the key reasons most buyers end up buying an existing home. Still, between 2000 and 2005, 6.3 million Americans experienced the thrill of moving into a built-from-scratch house, spending more than $1 trillion for all those shiny sets of house keys.

There are perfectly rational reasons for making this choice.

First, new homes feature the latest and greatest in technology and accoutrements. In a culture that's obsessed with staying up-to-date, many of us want to satisfy the same impulse when it comes to our houses.

Second, purchasing a new home will allow buyers to enjoy the layouts and floor plans that have evolved into the twenty-first-century ideal.

Third, homebuilders have become especially sophisticated at marketing their wares, utilizing perfectly designed model homes and specially trained salespeople to sell their version of the American Dream.

Fourth, in the last decade some big homebuilders have moved away from building one-size-fits-all houses and found ways to offer buyers thousands of choices. The result is that people can feel like they're customizing their house, the same way they love crafting their own skinny, no-foam, half-caf mocha lattes at Starbucks.

But beyond these logical explanations, there may also be a deeper psychological explanation driving many buyers—and it's driven by an impulse that's as old as our country.

To better understand it I called Dr. G. Clotaire Rapaille, a French-born market researcher with a specialty in psychiatry and anthropology. Rapaille has consulted for companies like Chrysler, General

Electric, and IBM, and he's developed his theories into a framework he calls the "culture code."

According to Rapaille, many of our purchases are driven by urges hidden deep in our national subconscious. For instance, our fascination with luxurious bathrooms is a result of the importance American culture places on toilet training, Rapaille says. Once we learn to wipe ourselves our parents leave us alone in the bathroom, so we subconsciously associate this space with freedom and independence. Or consider advertisements for diamond jewelry. The reason the diamond industry makes subtle flicks at the investment value of gems, Rapaille says, is because anyone buying (or receiving) an engagement ring is subconsciously thinking of America's high divorce rate. Love may die, but at least the signifier you're wearing on your finger should increase in value—and remembering that helps steel a buyer's confidence as he plunks down two months' salary for the bauble.

And when it comes to Americans' growing fondness for new homes, Rapaille sees a deep connection with our history of expanding across the frontier.

"The whole issue here is we're going West—we are the New World," Rapaille says. He compares families who watch their new split-levels being banged together by immigrant labor in modern-day Las Vegas to the nineteenth-century settlers who once gathered for community barn raisings. "In America, it has to be new," he says. "We cannot move into somebody else's bedroom, bathroom, or living room. That doesn't fit the American mind. We are pioneers. We like to create, to go where nobody has gone before. That's the American ideal and the American Dream."

I tell Rapaille about the new-home saleswoman and her bathtub theory of what's driving new-home buyers. Rapaille agrees with her analysis, and goes further. Even if we buy a house with a brand-new bathtub, a lot of Americans will be a little uneasy about soaking in it. Rapaille says many of us are aware that when you take a bath, you're not so much washing off the grime as steeping in it. "Americans want to be clean and ready for action," he says, which is why we're a culture that vastly prefers showers. Those pulsating showerheads are simply better at washing away the dirt and giving us a new beginning.

Building a new house is a lot like showering—it's the best way to get a fresh start. And for a generation afflicted with House Lust, nothing can compare with the spotless, neat-and-clean experience of designing your own new home.

There's a prerequisite to fulfilling this desire, however. Before buyers like the Giles family can snap keepsake photos of their half-built home, an industry had to become adept at building new homes cheaply, quickly, and in large numbers. How they've come to do it is an important part of this story.

Over the last several years, few places have seen a bigger boom in new houses than Las Vegas. A few miles off the iconic Strip, the desert is rife with new subdivisions. At intersections miles from town, immigrant workers stand on street corners waving huge directional signs to try to steer drivers toward model homes. During the early twenty-first century, fifteen hundred people a week were relocating to Sin City. The result is a city that feels somewhat lacking in history, a place where a person who moved here in 1990 is practically a native son.

Housing all these arriving families has been no small task: By some accounts, during the building boom the number of construction jobs here nearly rivaled employment in the casinos. Homes have been going up so quickly in Vegas that the landscape seems to change each month. As Susan Denton and Roger Morris describe it in their history of the city: "Tracts of pale, tile-roofed houses flow over the valley and up the sloping foothills of the bare, jagged mountains at its edge."

Kent Butler's job is to keep those new homes flowing. Butler, a muscular man with a goatee, is director of construction for KB

Home's Huntington community, a neighborhood rising from the foothills a few miles west of the Strip, which the Gileses now call home. Sitting in a trailer, Butler looks at the construction schedules displayed on his Dell laptop, a tool he utilizes far more often than a hammer. Nowadays big builders employ managers, not carpenters. The actual work of homebuilding—hanging the drywall and laying the tile—is outsourced to subcontractors, who use mostly immigrant labor to get the work done cheap and fast. Gone are the days when your home was built by a small-time entrepreneur who managed his affairs from the back of a pickup truck. Today a growing number of homes—at least one in four, by most estimates—are built by multibillion-dollar companies like KB, whose executives clock time in a Los Angeles high-rise and whose shares trade on the New York Stock Exchange.

Butler and his team are modern-day heirs to Levitt and Sons, the family-owned construction company that did for postwar homebuilding what Henry Ford did for the auto industry. In the wake of World War II and the dawn of the baby boom, the nation was desperately short of housing. "Six million families were doubling up with relatives or friends by 1947, and another 500,000 were occupying Quonset huts or temporary quarters," historian Kenneth T. Jackson writes in *Crabgrass Frontier*, his history of America's suburbs. But the G.I. Bill gave these vets easy access to mortgages, and builders responded by buying up huge swaths of farmland on which to build homes.

On 4,000 acres of Long Island, the Levitt family commenced the largest private housing project in history, which became known as Levittown. Like Ford, the Levitts' big breakthrough was their assembly-line approach to building. Their construction process was broken into twenty-seven routinized steps, from pouring the foundation to sweeping out the dust before the moving van arrived. Teams of workers swept through nascent neighborhoods, performing their assigned task in home after home. By the time they finished they'd built 17,400 houses in Levittown. The structures were modest affairs: standardized four-room Cape Cods or ranches measuring 750 square feet and starting at $6,990. Buyers waited in line for up to four days to place their order, and on a single day in March 1949, 1,400 families signed contracts.

KB's Huntington community is tiny by comparison. When complete—by 2009, the company hopes—it will contain just over 1,400 homes. But the smaller size doesn't mean it's any easier to build, because twenty-first-century buyers aren't interested in basic one-size-fits-all housing. In contrast to the standard models of Levittown, KB's Huntington community contains five different product lines, each with multiple floor plans and hundreds of options. If a buyer chooses Huntington's most modest Liberty town house and avoids pricey add-ons, he can buy here for just $240,000. But if he chooses the top-of-the-line Villa home on a premium lot and loads it up with extras, he could spend as much as $750,000.

This improvement on the assembly-line approach might sound familiar, as other industries have been doing it for years. Back in the 1920s General Motors famously trumped Ford's hyperefficient production scheme by utilizing marketing prowess. While Ford offered "Any Color as Long as It's Black," General Motors countered with a laddered product line of entry-level Chevrolets, midpriced Buicks, and aspirational Cadillacs, a system it dubbed "A Car for Every Purse and Purpose." Today builders like KB attempt to meld the production efficiencies of Ford while offering the marketing choices championed by GM.

Butler hops in his truck and drives up to New Quay Court. "We're running out of street names here," he jokes. On each side of this new street sit eleven building lots, with twenty-two homes in various stages of construction. Unlike custom builders, who work with clients and their architects to construct one-of-a-kind residences, KB is a so-called production builder (or, more derisively, a "tract builder"). Beyond the local building codes (and the laws of physics), there are no constraints on a custom builder—anything a buyer and his architect dream of, they can create, assuming the client has the money to pay for it. Custom building can routinely take two years, and often costs twice as much as a production home. That's why it remains for the most part an option that only the affluent can enjoy.

In contrast, production builders like KB build giant neighborhoods of middle-class homes. Builders offer buyers some choices, but they carefully constrain the options to keep the homes easy to build. "As far as the main structure of the house, we don't let them customize anything," Butler says. "No moving the walls, unless it's an offered option." For instance, in the downstairs of its Huntington homes, buyers can choose to turn the half bath into a full bath in order to turn the downstairs study into a guest room. Upstairs they can expand the master bath into a "super-master bath" (which allows for a separate tub and shower). Outdoors, the builder offers a small menu of back decks and patios. But if it's not on the menu, KB won't build it.

Critics of these mammoth builders fear that such neighborhoods will end up looking monolithic. With so many identical side-by-side houses, you'd almost expect people to drive into the wrong garage. In truth, today's builders do a better job of differentiating houses than they used to. Not only are there more models of homes to choose from, but builders like KB work to prevent buyers from putting too-similar homes too close to one another. The builder forces buyers to vary the colors of adjacent homes, and use different landscape schemes to create more differentiation. If you move into a place like Huntington, you will almost certainly meet a neighbor with the same floor plan as yours, but chances are your home won't look that similar to the one on the left and right.

Out on New Quay Court, a forklift beeps as it backs up, loading drywall into a home. Slowly the houses continue to rise, becoming a tad closer to completion each day. And for each one, a family is waiting patiently.

Inside those houses, Butler's subcontractors are installing technology that didn't exist when my 1970s home was built. In the attics they're putting in radiant barriers to prevent the sun's rays from driving up air-conditioning bills. In the walls water runs through plastic tubing that's easier to install and less likely to leak than traditional copper pipes. In the ceilings built-in audio speakers distribute music throughout the house. When Butler outfitted his own KB house, he opted for a high-tech security system that allows him to see who's at the front door or in his swimming pool by clicking on his TV remote while he lies in bed.

These technical innovations remain a key reason why so many people want a newly built home. In a society where plenty of folks long for the latest iPod or cell phone, it's only natural to want an up-to-date house. And nowadays building companies are rolling out so many cutting-edge products so frequently, you can't help feeling that a home built just a couple of years ago seems technologically behind.

The potential for buyers' remorse—even for homes that are just a few years old—is huge. Houses are the ultimate big-ticket item, and retrofitting them can be extremely tricky, since much of the technology that drives a home lies inside its walls, under its floors, or above its ceilings. Upgrading from Windows 98 to Windows Vista requires an hour of slipping CDs in and out of your computer, but installing central air-conditioning or smart house technology could involve ripping apart large sections of an older house. Often these projects don't make economic sense, even if you could tolerate the noise and dust. If you want these technologies, it usually makes more sense to build new.

To get an idea of just how out-of-date your not-so-new house really is, there's no better place to visit than the International Builders' Show—the place where home-products companies converge each winter to show off their latest wares.

Out on the vast convention-center floor, I stop at the Owens Corning booth. The company is best-known for the pink fiberglass insulation used to maintain a home's temperature. But today Owens Corning is touting a different product line: acoustical insulation. It's a new kind of material they sell to builders to stuff between interior walls. The aim is to make the house quieter.

I don a headset and watch a promotional video. "Today's housing," says a grave-sounding narrator, followed by a montage of crying babies, loud video games, and a child who's an aspiring rock drummer. "It's noisy and getting noisier." The video flashes to a group of women sitting around a table, focus-group style. "I never knew my house is loud," says a woman who appears so ashamed you'd think she's admitting she has a sexually transmitted disease. "I never knew that standing downstairs and hearing the bathtub upstairs affected me. If I didn't have to hear that, I might have less wrinkles." Another woman talks about how the noise contributes to "the stress, the blood pressure, the anxiety." The total effect is something like those teasers the local TV news stations run during sweeps weeks: "Your noisy house—could it be quietly killing you? News at 11:00."

Adding insulation to the interior walls of a new house will increase the cost by about $1,000. But after hearing the Owens Corning pitch, not only am I sold on the product, but I momentarily ponder how I'd go about ripping down walls to retrofit my own noisy, wrinkle-inducing, blood-pressure-raising home.

I keep walking. Executives from lumber giant Georgia-Pacific whiz by on Segway scooters, looking self-important and slightly ridiculous. At the Stanley tools exhibit, carpenters compete to see who can hammer nails the fastest. At nearly every exhibit there's a product you probably never thought your home might need—but if you stop to listen to the sales pitch, you start to rationalize why it'd make perfect sense for your home and your life.

At the Gerber booth, a rep shows off their lineup of toilets, from the Viper to the Avalanche to the Ultra-Flusher, which he says is able to flush an entire loaf of bread. (It should come with a disclaimer: "If you really need a toilet this powerful, please consult a gastroenterologist.") But Gerber's more innovative product isn't about power—it's about size.

Behold the Pee Wee. It's a toilet that's ten inches high (compared to the regular fourteen-inch toilet) and looks like a Shetland pony grazing amid Thoroughbreds. The Pee Wee, which retails for $395, is made for kids' bathrooms. Gone are the days when a child required a step stool to perch anxiously atop an adult-size toilet. Now that so many new homes include a bathroom for every bedroom, toddlers can have their own junior-size commode. It's certainly cute, but the company argues that the Pee Wee is about function, not form. One of the big reasons American kids delay potty training is because they're scared of falling into an adult-size toilet. With the Pee Wee that anxiety goes away, the Gerber rep claims, and kids will be more likely to use the bathroom by themselves at younger ages. (Yes, Dr. Rapaille would have a field day analyzing the appeal of this product.) Given the costs and unpleasantness of changing diapers, can you really afford *not* to have the Pee Wee in your house?

The toilet makers are hardly the only ones who employ these rationalizations. I stroll by a German company that's showing off an ultra-high-tech coffee-and-cappuccino maker that's installed directly into a kitchen wall, with built-in plumbing and electric supply lines. The unit runs about $2,000, not including installation. Sound ridiculous? Not really, a kitchen designer explains. Consider a husband and wife who each drink just one $3 Starbucks concoction a day. If their fancy in-wall unit lets them kick their pricey Starbucks habit, it will pay for itself after just a year.

I keep walking. Soon I'm talking to a sales rep for an elevator company. Once upon a time elevators were mainly for office buildings, hotels, and hospitals, but lately they've begun appearing in upscale homes. Prices start in the $30,000 range, with the key variable being how many floors are in your house. It's possible to retrofit one into an existing house, but far more cost-effective to build it into new construction.

A home elevator sounds like an over-the-top luxury (at least for able-bodied people who aren't in wheelchairs), but as with tiny toilets and $2,000 coffeemakers, there's an economic rationalization. The baby boom generation is aging, and someday many of them will be reluctant to deal with stairs. If your house has an elevator, this argument goes, it could increase the number of potential buyers. That extra demand could bring a higher price for your house, meaning that the elevator very well could—*say it along with me*—pay for itself in the long run.

These economic justifications are pretty sketchy, of course. Anyone who tries to drink enough coffee to justify a $2,000 coffeemaker risks behaving like Robin Williams. But beyond the dubious financial arguments, the marketing that surrounds many of these products smacks slightly of businesses trying to scare consumers into identifying new problems where none previously existed. Perhaps the best contemporary example is teeth whitening. Until a decade or two ago we wouldn't worry about someone judging us by the hue of our dental enamel. Today some Americans worry as much about their off-white teeth as they do bad breath or body odor, and sales of teeth whiteners are a $300 million business. Spend time on this convention floor and you may start to suffer from subtle anxieties that your house is too noisy, has too many stairs, or is plagued by substandard toilets. It's an insidious way of selling products—but if my reaction to these pitches is any indication, it's also pretty darn effective.

To be fair, some of the gizmos being shown off aren't just about luxury longings or early-adopter snobbishness. Environmentalism is a driving force, too. Many of the products I see are aimed at making homes more energy efficient. There are multipane, superinsulated windows, some with special coatings to decrease the effect of sunlight on the internal temperature. There are fancy tankless water heaters, and solar panels that generate do-it-yourself electricity. Some home-building pros speculate that rising concern about global warming has started to transform homebuyers the same way the 1970s gasoline shortages affected drivers. Nowadays nobody buys a car without checking its gas mileage, and likewise tomorrow's homebuyers won't consider buying a new home that's not overflowing with insulation and stocked with superefficient Energy Star appliances.

Even for people who aren't considering trading up to a new home, seeing the newest home accoutrements available at the Builders' Show can have a corrosive effect. I think about this when I meet a female executive for a homebuilding company who's in the process of relocating from the Rocky Mountains to Los Angeles. She mentions that she can hardly stand going to the gym anymore, since everyone in Southern California seems to be so thin, tan, and beautiful. In the Midwest she saw herself as perfectly fit, but in Los Angeles she feels like she's fallen down a few notches on the fitness curve.

As I walk around the Builders' Show, I notice the same thing is happening with my self-image of my house. I live in a perfectly nice home. But spend enough time around the people who make and market the latest upscale home gadgets, and no matter how nice your house is, you'll end up loving it just a little less. In the same way the ultrathin models in fashion magazines can affect women's body images, the growth of shelter magazines, Home Depot, and HGTV have exposed more Americans to the latest-and-greatest gear that's becoming essential to an idealized home. If you spend time wandering among these home-products extravaganzas, the appeal of buying a new home becomes clearer and clearer. It's contagious.

In late 2006, investment manager Hilary Wiek was moving from Cleveland, Ohio, to Columbia, South Carolina. Before buying a house, she toured more than a dozen properties, ranging from homes built in the 1920s and 1930s to brand-new homes in move-in condition.

Initially Wiek wasn't dead set on buying new, but she did have some reservations about buying an older home. As a single woman with no interest in playing handyperson, she liked the fact that new homes typically come with a warranty. If something broke in the first year or two, she'd be able to call the builder to come and fix it, the same way a renter can call her landlord. As she toured older homes, she'd eye the old refrigerators and water heaters with suspicion, worrying that soon after she closed on the home, the appliance would kick the bucket, costing her time, money, and inconvenience to get it replaced.

But as she toured homes old and new, her big reaction was to a different element: the floor plans.

Wiek was raised on the West Coast, where she and most of her friends lived in houses built in the 1970s. The ceilings were high. The living spaces were mostly open. You could see over countertops from the kitchen into the dining room and living spaces. Instead of the traditional living room, her parents' house had a single "great room" that served as an all-purpose hangout space. It's an informal setup she prefers.

The layout of the older homes she looked at, in contrast, seemed hopelessly out-of-date. "The further you move east with these older homes, the more you get these tiny little rooms that feel claustrophobic," she says. The ceilings are low. There are too many walls and too many doors. The bathrooms are cramped, without enough storage or electrical outlets. And the kitchens—yikes. "The kitchens are teenytiny in these older homes—I don't know how people deal with that, and I don't even cook," she says. In some of these 1920s kitchens, she couldn't even figure out where she'd find room to put a microwave.

Instead, Wiek chose a newly built home that was all ready for her to move in. Its floor plan is more in keeping with her modern sensibilities. The kitchen opens into a great room, dining room, and sunroom. The master bedroom has plenty of space for a seating area. There's a two-car garage, of course. The house isn't extraordinarily large, but its 1,900 square feet are better allocated to the way Wiek wants to live. She's seen plenty of homes with unused living and dining rooms, and she finds her open layout far more functional. "I don't understand the point of having space that's not being used," she says.

These updated floor plans are another big attraction of buying a brand-new home. If you tour model homes in new developments— I've visited dozens of them in at least eight states—you'll observe a lot of regional differences. In the West homes have stucco exteriors and often feature one-floor living. In Florida homes have exceptionally high ceilings and expansive screened-in lanais. In New England homes are more likely to feature clapboards outside and the traditional center-hall foyer inside, with adjacent living room and dining room.

But despite these differences, there are elements of these new homes' floor plans that are nearly universal, whatever their location.

The kitchens tend to be large and open, with islands, acres of counter space, and even room for a desk and a television. It's a reflection of how we live today. Modern kitchens are engineered to serve as the hub of the house.

In new homes family rooms are almost always adjacent to the kitchen, and similarly open. Master bedrooms are often twice the size of secondary bedrooms, usually with two walk-in closets; even in relatively modest homes most master bedrooms now feature a private bathroom. The garages are enormous; measured by square footage, they're often the largest single space in a modern home.

When it comes to American homes, these features are all relatively new.

Until a few decades ago kitchens were usually hidden away in the rear of the home, a design remnant from the time when these spaces were mostly the domain of domestic servants. (As recently as 1870, one in eight American families had full-time domestic help.) Even during the first half of the 1900s, as millions of servantless middle-class families attained homeownership, many architects believed the best kind of kitchen was a small one—it was easier to keep clean, and required less walking to migrate between appliances.

Likewise, the twentieth-century living room—which had supplanted the parlors and "best rooms" of nineteenth-century homes—were meant to serve as multifunction spaces. The desire to be able to use this room for both formal entertaining and everyday family life reflected the twentieth-century desire to live less formally than in the Victorian era, and to have less of a division between a home's public and private spaces. Living rooms were where you entertained company, where children played, and where the family listened to the radio.

During the postwar homebuilding binge, however, these ideals changed. In a nod toward even more informal living, open floor plans, which first became popular in California ranch-style homes, migrated east. Kitchens opened up so mothers could cook while keeping an eye on their children's play. And as they became a more visible part of the home, kitchens evolved into modern-day hearths, drawing people toward them the way fireplaces had in earlier times. And as kitchens morphed into gathering places, they've grown larger and larger.

At the same time two trends led families to want a living space beyond the living room. As Dr. Spock's more permissive style of parenting gained popularity, so did the desire for a separate play area where kids could keep toys and play more freely than they could in a fancy living room. And as television took hold, homeowners who could afford a larger home desired a separate space apart from the living room where they could watch TV together. Architectural writer Winifred Gallagher calls this migration from living rooms to family rooms to all-purpose great rooms "a hundred-year-long experiment in which American culture has gradually shed traditional manners and mores to become more informal and open, while the home dropped walls and doors to the same end."

To see how quickly the idealized floor plan can change, consider two television homes. On *Leave It to Beaver*, which hit the airwaves in 1957, the Cleaver home features small, discrete rooms, and the on-screen family spends most of its time in the traditional living room. By 1969 Carol and Mike Brady and their blended California family enjoy a home with a large and open kitchen, an adjacent family room, and a nearly wall-free first floor; from the front door you can see through the living room and kitchen and over a countertop into the family room beyond.

Those sorts of changes have continued, driven by shifts in the way we live. The average American today owns far more clothing than a person in the 1970s, which created the need for far larger closets (and pricey closet organization systems to go inside them). The sport-utility vehicle craze has made traditional-size garages feel horribly cramped, leading to a profusion of oversize garages (which nowadays often have three bays—two for cars and one for possessions). Even the pantry has been supersized the last few years. Why? Blame Costco. Until the 1990s families didn't feel the need to buy gallon vats of mayonnaise or olive oil. Now we do, and the modern home has been reconfigured.

The more familiar you become with the advantages of these up-to-date floor plans, the more you'll regret not having them. When my home was built in the early 1970s, it featured a living room and a dining room as primary public spaces, and a 10-by-12-foot kitchen (then standard-size). A few years later the owner added a large family room onto the side of the house farthest from the kitchen.

My family loves our home, but the more time we've spent in newer homes, the more aware we've become of just how less-than-ideal our floor plan is. In more modern homes the kitchens are often twice as large as ours, so guests can hang out with the cook. In my kitchen it's hard to do any serious cooking with more than two people in the room without tripping all over one another.

Furthermore, our family room is 30 feet down a hallway from the kitchen. When we throw a party we have two choices: One person stays in the kitchen and misses most of the fun, or else we cook everything ahead and keep it warm in order to spend time with guests.

As hardships go, we're hardly suffering. But as I shuttle back and forth from our kitchen to our family room, I'm keenly aware of our outmoded floor plan. And as the ideal home layout changes in the years ahead, this dissatisfaction may grow. If I wander through a newly built home in 2018, there will probably be new twists to the size and positioning of rooms we can't dream of today—which will make me even more aware of the shortcomings of my not-so-new house.

When Melissa Schmidtberger was growing up in California, her parents had a strange hobby. On weekends they'd drive into the desert to tour model homes at new developments. "We never bought them—it was just my parents' pastime," Schmidtberger says. "They've always been lookie-loos."

It's a habit that influenced Schmidtberger's career choice. We're sitting in the sales office at KB Home's Huntington development. Schmidtberger, a thirty-four-year-old blonde in a KB Home blazer, is one of the community's top salespeople. Her job is simple: getting you to dream about living in a new home, just like her parents did. To do it she uses her well-honed sales skills, along with a tool that's carefully calibrated to spark House Lust: the model home.

Schmidtberger spent a few years as a traditional real estate agent before migrating into new-home sales. The jobs are like night and day, she says. When she'd take a buyer to see an existing home listed for sale, she often knew hardly anything about it. Sometimes she'd never been inside the house before, and she could only guess what surprises the existing homeowner might leave for her, from dirty dishes to horrendous decor. "It makes it harder to sell a house when you see it with somebody's clutter," Schmidtberger says. "You can't really experience it on your own with somebody's stuff lingering around the corner."

In new-home sales, by contrast, the whole process is highly choreographed. In the sales office Schmidtberger greets customers near a topographical display, a three-dimensional model covered with Monopoly-size houses that shows the streets and land features of the community. While Schmidtberger might know next to nothing about an existing home she used to try to sell, today she knows virtually everything about KB's offerings, from the warranty on the stain-proof carpeting to the precise commuting time to various office parks.

Schmidtberger describes her job as a residential matchmaker. As she asks questions ("What do you like about your current home?"), she's trying to understand your inner desires and match them to a KB model. The biggest variable is your family structure: Once she knows how many people will live in the house, she can figure how many bedrooms you'll want. Then she'll try to gauge whether a gourmet kitchen, a formal dining room, or a more open floor plan is a bigger priority. She'll help you look over floor plan diagrams, but before long she'll escort you across the street to view the model homes.

The whole point of a model home is to get you to imagine what it's like to live inside. But the industry's research shows that the average shopper spends about eight minutes touring a model. That's an extremely quick walk-around for a huge purchase. To gain a fuller appreciation for the new-home lifestyle, I asked the builder if I could spend the night in a model home, the way some affluent car buyers are allowed to take a new car home for the weekend for an "extended test drive."

It wasn't an easy sell. If I spent the night in a model home the sales staff would need to deactivate the home's security system, so they assigned a security guard to patrol the perimeter. Builders usually disconnect the toilets in model homes so visitors don't use them, but since I'll need to use the facilities during my stay, they send a plumber in to hook one up. And late one Sunday afternoon one of the builder's employees hands me a key and shows me inside. As a parting gift she hands me a knapsack filled with toilet paper, a granola bar, and a water bottle. "Have a good night," she says.

My home for the evening is the Burnham, a 3,308-square-foot, top-of-the line model. When you walk in the front door you enter a tiled foyer, with a living room to the right and the dining room straight ahead. Behind the curving staircase is a wide kitchen with a broad Corian island. "Just $243 a month!" reads the brochure touting the kitchen upgrades.

Upon arrival I sit out on the patio, watching the last few minutes of sunshine. The backyard is a tiny patch of synthetic grass, about a fifth of what you'd need for a decent Wiffle ball game. But the covered patio (a $12,000 option) is nice, with a built-in stainless-steel grill and a couple of lounge chairs. I'm momentarily bummed to see that the model next door has its own swimming pool. I'd love to be staying there, but the builder probably would have insisted on hiring a lifeguard.

If you spend enough time going through model homes, you begin to notice small details about the decor. There's the randomness of the books, which are usually bought by the pound without respect to the titles. (The Burnham's pretend owner seems to own memoirs by every attorney in the O. J. Simpson trial.) On the walls are dozens of "family" photos, featuring people of every imaginable ethnic hue.

Some walls feature diplomas and civic awards—meant to help you imagine that this neighborhood will soon be filled with accomplished people *just like you*. Some of the models I visited featured nonstop Muzak and security cameras, to prevent visitors from doing anything untoward. Thankfully the Burnham is Muzak and Webcam free.

This home's most personalized decorating touch is a chalkboard in the laundry room, where the home's faux Mom has scrawled out her to-do list for the week: "Bake 200 cupcakes for Sean's baseball fund-raiser on Monday. Attend Julia's swim meet Tuesday. Take a Cantonese cooking class on Wednesday. Host Uncle Bob's retirement party on Thursday. Buy a gift for Tina's baby shower on Friday." Whew. Someone needs to talk to Mom about the hazards of over-scheduling herself.

A lot of thought goes into these touches. Like most big home-builders, KB hires outside design pros to "merchandise" its models. They're paid by the size of the house; in Las Vegas, prices range from $21 to $28 per square foot, meaning this model probably cost more than $90,000 to decorate.

The interior of the Burnham is the handiwork of Cathy Hurst. The daughter of a homebuilder, she grew up in California and attended design school in Los Angeles before moving to Las Vegas in the 1980s. Her work is a bit different than traditional interior design, which gears everything toward a client. In contrast, a model home has to work for the masses. "Your colors can't be quite as saturated," Hurst says. "Your furniture placement is different. If you're space-planning for a family, you're going to fit their needs—how they watch TV, how they really live, how they entertain, the ages of their children." In a model she aims for stylishness *and* universal appeal.

To guide their work the designers usually imagine exactly who's living in the home. "Sometimes we even role-play," Hurst says. "We'll say, 'I'm the Mom, I have two kids, I work at home. . . .'" The goal is to go beyond bland and sterile. The same way Method actors try to understand the backstory and motivations of a character, a good model-home merchandiser creates a backstory—and a faux family—for each model home.

Some builders take things a bit further. In California, one Centex development has employed actors to play the pretend family in one high-end model. The fake husband, a barefoot, affable man in his thirties (who once played a lifeguard on *Baywatch*) would greet visitors and offer them juice, while his wife—"slim, blonde and agreeable," reported the *New York Times*, in a story on this marketing gimmick—offered cookies. Two kids showed visitors to "their" rooms. The marketers who dreamed up the idea said the practice would make the home tour more memorable. Outside experts said the tactic risked coming off as a little bit creepy.

As evening turns to night, I wander these empty rooms, trying to imagine my family living in the Burnham. It's a bit of a stretch. I'm accustomed to my East Coast home, with its smaller rooms and lower ceilings; here I feel a bit dwarfed by all the space. But I'd probably get used to it in time.

My biggest concern, however, stems from the realization that if I really lived here, my house wouldn't look nearly this good. While I admire the decorating scheme, my family isn't likely to have $90,000 to spend on interior design, so we'd probably have the same furniture that's in our existing house. So in a way the model seems aimed at selling me a dream I couldn't possibly make true.

As I wander, I find myself gravitating back to the features I covet the most: the spacious kitchen, the adjoining family room, and the gigantic closets. But even if I were buying at KB, I'm not sure the Burnham would be right for me.

The next day I'm back in the sales office with Schmidtberger. If I'd liked the Burnham, she would carefully shift the conversation to my finances. "Has anyone taken the time to show you what your purchasing power is?" she'd ask, implying that she's doing me a *favor* by asking questions about my earnings, peeking at my credit score, and gauging my ability to afford what she's selling. It's all part of her training: Nearly everything she says has been carefully scripted and coached, via frequent training classes. Each quarter her employer sends a "mystery shopper" out to evaluate her by pretending to be a buyer and grading her sales pitch.

Her ability to connect with buyers is the key to driving transactions. Artur Nazaryan, a mechanic at a Mercedes dealership a few miles from Huntington, put a deposit on a 2,500-square-foot home here in 2005, but he was torn. While his new house was being built, he found an existing home a few miles away. It had a pool and a bigger backyard. "I could get a better deal on the used house," he said, and he told Schmidtberger about his second thoughts on his Huntington purchase.

She empathized. She cajoled. And she wheeled-and-dealed, convincing her bosses to cut Nazaryan a $20,000 price break and to pay for all his closing costs. He agreed to the offer. When it came time to sign the reams of closing papers, Schmidtberger explained every page in as much detail as he wanted.

Today he lives a few blocks from the Burnham model where I very briefly resided myself. He has no regrets.

"It's a beautiful feeling to get a new house that nobody has ever lived in," Nazaryan says. "You're the first one, and it smells like a new house. Everybody should have that excitement at least once."

If salespeople like Melissa Schmidtberger have their way, many more of us will.

If the builder's sales pitch works, you'll choose a floor plan and leave a deposit. Within days a construction crew will begin pouring its foundation.

Meanwhile, you've got some big decisions to make.

Catalino and Guadelia Ferrer are in the middle of this process one Sunday afternoon. When I meet them at the KB Home Design Studio, located in a strip mall a few miles from downtown Las Vegas, they're focused on a single choice: How many cable outlets would they like in their new home?

At $225 apiece (including wiring and installation), the cable wall plates are among the cheapest items the couple will consider today.

Just before arriving in the electrical department they'd decided on the carpets, tile, and hardwood flooring they'll put in the Spanish-style, two-story home. The flooring alone cost $13,507. But as Bridget, their design consultant, stands patiently waiting, the couple debates the cable outlets. Do they really need one in each of their three children's bedrooms—and if so, on which walls? They sketch out where the beds will go, then mull the choice.

The minutes tick by. The time they spend in the electrical department—where, after more than four minutes of discussion, they decide to splurge on a cable outlet in every bedroom—gives a window into just how complicated their choices will be. Exactly where outside the house do they plan to store their garbage cans, and would they like a floodlight above the spot? Have they given thought to whether they'll put Christmas lights on the house—and how many? They'd better decide now, because this is their chance to order special exterior electrical outlets for that purpose. Act now or their light-up Frosty the Snowman will require an extremely long and unsightly extension cord come December.

Next up: What kind of toilet-paper holders would they prefer?

"This is the first time we're buying a new house, where we have to make choices," says Guadelia, a fifty-ish Filipino immigrant wearing shorts, a bright yellow blouse, and lots of jewelry. For many of the options Catalino, dressed in a blue-striped golf shirt, is inclined to go with the standard, no-extra-cost features the builder offers. But even though he resists fancy granite countertops and cherry cabinets, he and his wife still get to make dozens of choices, from the Mojave Desert #1 Landscaping package to the forty-gallon water heater. As the afternoon drags on, Guadelia's cell phone—its ring tone set to the "Electric Slide"—goes off repeatedly. Their kids want to know what's taking so long.

Burger King has spent years marketing itself as the fast-food outlet where you can "Hold the pickles, hold the lettuce . . ." in order to "Have It Your Way" at lunchtime. While baby boomers made do with one-size-fits-all stuffed animals, today's kids can customize their plush toys at Build-A-Bear Workshops. You can build your computer at

Dell.com, custom-design your sneakers at Nike.com, or choose your own color combinations for a Ralph Lauren shirt at Polo.com. These behaviors are all evidence that we're in the era of "mass customization"—and lately it's a phenomenon that applies even to tract homes.

This degree of customer choice is a relatively new development. Until the early 1990s most homebuilders constructed "spec houses"—generic-looking homes built without a particular buyer in mind. But when the housing market slowed in the early 1990s, builders lost billions on the carrying costs of all these unsold finished homes. In reaction to that, many big builders changed their methods. Now many builders will begin construction only once a confirmed buyer has made a deposit. One side effect of this shift is that buyers get to make more choices, and builders like KB use this as a potent marketing tool.

Huntington customers make their selections inside a design studio the size of a small grocery store. The showroom is filled with bathroom fixtures, window treatments, and built-in backyard grills. It's a place where buyers can load up their house the way Dagwood loads up his sandwiches—and roll the entire cost into their mortgage payment.

A lot of buyers become fixated on the process. "We've seen a real shift in how people perceive their homes," says Miquel Hutton, who runs KB's Vegas design outpost. "What we're seeing is a shift toward people trying to deck the house out. They want to put [in] all the amenities they want, and they're much more focused on the aesthetics." That's hardly surprising: In an era of HGTV and *Martha Stewart Living*, people aren't just looking for their home to be a comfortable setting for their lives, but a showpiece of which they can be proud. That's leading them to spend more money. In 2005 the average KB buyer in Las Vegas spent $25,000 on upgrades. A year later the average option cost was $32,000.

To keep that number rising, Hutton's staff shows buyers the upsides of ordering many of the things they'll need for their new home directly from KB, instead of buying it somewhere else after they move in. That way buyers can roll the costs right into the purchase price—and doing that, they argue, is just one more benefit of buying a built-from-scratch house.

Hutton walks to the kitchen displays and launches into a demonstration of new-home math, the power of which comes from the mortgage financing. "Keep in mind that for every $1,000 you spend here, that's about $7 per month on your monthly mortgage payment," Hutton explains. He points to a stainless-steel refrigerator, which costs $2,000. Rolled into the mortgage, that fridge costs just $14 per month, or $168 per year. Assume you stay in your house five years' before moving, he says—about typical for someone buying a starter home. At $168 per year, you'll pay roughly $840 for five years usage of that refrigerator. "If you buy it at retail, you'll pay $2,000, plus installation, plus delivery, plus sales tax, plus the extended warranty," Hutton says, explaining that the builder doesn't charge for any of those things. And if you roll the cost into your mortgage, the interest is tax deductible. "So which makes more sense?"

No matter how a buyer chooses to finance these choices, not everyone finds all this decision-making pleasurable. Swarthmore College economist Barry Schwartz, author of *The Paradox of Choice*, sees the new-home-buying process as an example of how too many options can leave customers worse off. "The lure of being able to customize everything is irresistible," Schwartz says, "[but] there are some people who can't make a decision and will regret whatever decision they make." Schwartz has spent years studying how this overabundant choice can decrease customer satisfaction—research he began after becoming paralyzed by indecision when shopping for jeans.

While some buyers love all the choices, Schwartz speculates that homebuilding may be one industry—like the automobile industry—where a company can find a competitive advantage in simplifying things. "Think of what happened with cars," he says. When Toyota and Honda entered the U.S. market, instead of offering customers a long list of options (like American carmakers did), the Japanese manufacturers offered groups of options and didn't allow customers to cherry-pick. If you want power windows and a DVD player in a Honda minivan, chances are you have to take heated seats and power mirrors as part of the package.

In fact, some homebuilders are embracing this limited-choice model. "We asked a ton of people, 'What do you think of the process of buying a home? Do you enjoy [choosing] upgrade after upgrade after upgrade?'" says Erik Pekarski, national vice president for strategic initiatives at Pulte, a giant Michigan-based homebuilder. "The consistent response was, 'We thought that was something we wanted, but it became so difficult sometimes to try to figure out how far we should upgrade, and how much more money we should spend.' Everybody said they got excited about that process, but in the end there was remorse." Pekarski's team likes to compare the typical new-home upgrade process to dining at the Cheesecake Factory, a restaurant chain whose menus run to fifteen pages—leading a lot of diners to agonize over what to choose. "I can't even eat there," he says.

Pulte's solution is to radically cut the number of options and upgrades it offers consumers. They still offer a wide selection of countertops, flooring, and cabinets—high-visibility items customers really do care about. But they've reduced the number of toilets from twenty to just one. Pulte's research suggests that, at a minimum, this won't hurt customer satisfaction, because homebuyers care most about a home's location and floor plan. But the company's hope is that customers will like this system better—and just as important, Pulte will save millions in supply costs, inventory management, and paperwork.

Still, as I wander around the KB Home Studio, I can see the appeal of having so many choices—and not having to live with decisions made by the previous homeowner. The night my wife and I closed on our home, I spent long hours scraping and repainting the dark kitchen cabinets to try to lighten up the hideous kitchen. Over time we've done something substantial to nearly every room in the house. Being able to avoid so many lost weekends by making our own choices all at once in a design center like this one seems pretty compelling.

The Ferrers seem to enjoy it, too. By the time the couple walks into the afternoon sun, they've chosen oak cabinets, Corian counters, insulated garage doors, and a half-horsepower garbage disposal. Total cost: $34,365, which comes on top of the $300,000 they'll spend for their new home. But when they cross the threshold seven months from now, their made-to-order home will fit them perfectly.

When Charles and Carolyn Kingdon moved from England to Rhode Island in 2003, they never considered moving to a new subdivision. Their former home in Britain was built in 1723, and even in the New World, they preferred to live in a historic residence.

They found it in downtown Providence—a home built in 1780 that boasts eight working fireplaces. The walls are out of square and the floors aren't completely level, but their house has a character they adore. "You know other people have been here," Charles says—and he wouldn't have it any other way.

While the vast majority of Americans hope to move into a new home, a minority feel precisely the opposite way. They find older homes to be more distinctive. They're suspicious of newer construction methods. Like fans of Civil War reenactment, they see living in an older home as a way of connecting with the past—and a desirable alternative to the new-home developments they deride as sterile commodities.

It's a lifestyle that requires a degree of commitment. A lot of people romanticize old homes, but many of them are drafty, uninsulated, and extremely costly to heat; unless they've been updated, they probably have finicky plumbing and wheezing electrical systems. While conservationists may think it's less wasteful to save an old house, the owners had better be prepared to use a lot of energy to keep it warm enough, cool enough, and functioning properly. That's not the only sacrifice. Unless they've been renovated, few will offer oversize Jacuzzis or gourmet kitchens. And forget about adding a rec room to the dungeonlike basements. Compared to life in the Burnham model home where I (briefly) lived while in Las Vegas, living in a 200-year-old home can feel like roughing it.

That's why some people who covet the land beneath these houses are inclined to knock them down and build from scratch. Indeed, while most new homebuilding takes place on empty acreage far from cities, in many older towns the only way to get a new home is to do a teardown of an older one. It's a trend that infuriates a lot of residents of these places, but even as the real estate boom ended, teardowns have continued in some suburbs near my home. In Manhattan, meanwhile, builders are now gutting dozens of existing commercial buildings to turn them into condominiums—meaning that you no longer need to move to the exurbs to find the virginal spaces today's buyers covet.

Traditionalists hate to see older homes torn down, and they're doing what they can to fight it. Len Baum is a Rhode Island architect who specializes in saving these structures. He maintains a network of like-minded enthusiasts. When they hear a historic property is slated for demolition, Baum tries to find a client who will pay for him to meticulously map, measure, and dismantle each piece of the home. Then he'll relocate it to a faraway building lot and rebuild and restore it, bit by bit—often at a cost of millions of dollars. "A lot of clients have either a family connection with the American Revolution, or they just see themselves as being philosophically connected with the beginning of America," Baum says. "They just love the rich, handmade fabric of these homes."

Baum lives in a home built in 1913, but he'd prefer to be in something older—something more like his office, an 1880 shingle-style home that he's totally restored. He's so devoted to working on old homes that he usually declines to accept jobs on any home built after 1930.

When Baum visits new-home developments, he's appalled by much of what he sees. He's not reacting to just the mishmash of architectural styles, but to the quality of the construction. He believes modern builders try to maximize profits in ways that would seem foreign to a nineteenth-century builder. Baum regards some of the corner-cutting allowed by twenty-first-century building codes—such as framing that places studs twenty-four inches apart, instead of the traditional sixteen inches—as woefully substandard. Over time he expects the walls in some of today's newest homes to warp and bend.

He's not alone in worrying whether production houses are as well built as the homes of yesteryear. In a 2001 investigation by the *Boston Globe*'s Spotlight Team (which later won the Pulitzer Prize for uncovering widespread sex abuse by Catholic priests), reporters zeroed in on one builder's use of Thermo-ply, a thin recycled board, instead of traditional plywood for the external "sheathing" of homes. At least 700 homes in Massachusetts have been built of Thermo-ply. To illustrate how flimsy they are, *Globe* reporters were able to slice through a Thermo-ply wall (to simulate breaking into a home) using nothing but a razor blade in just six minutes.

Nita Leger Casey shares Baum's disregard for newer homes. She lives in a house built in 1885, and when she visits new homes, "they're just cold to me—they're all the same," she says. "They're plasticky, phony." It's a common view, one popularized by the 1968 Malvina Reynolds song "Little Boxes," with the lyrics: "Little boxes on the hillside, little boxes all the same . . . And they're all made out of ticky tacky and they all look just the same."

When Casey moved into her vintage Victorian twenty-two years ago, she wanted to do something nice for the sellers. So she used her art training to do a pen-and-ink sketch of the home's exterior, which she presented to the previous owners at the closing. They loved it. Today Casey specializes in painting house portraits. She's done more than 300 in all. The only time she's painted a newer house is when a builder or real estate agent has hired her for it. Usually if someone loves his house enough to want a professional portrait, it's at least a century old.

"I'm kind of hooked on houses—I always have been," Casey says. "I love old colonials and old Victorians." Sometimes she visits the ocean in Maine with a fellow artist. While her friend gazes east and paints seascapes, Casey turns toward the land and paints the old beachfront homes.

Fans like Casey are driven by sentimentality and aesthetics, but there are more cold-eyed reasons to prefer an older home, even in a place as obsessed with the new as Las Vegas. Jimmy Dague is the co-founder of Century 21 Aadvantage Gold, the biggest real estate brokerage in the city. He trains his agents to explain to buyers all the advantages of existing homes. They usually have far larger backyards, since they were built before land prices escalated so sharply. With an older home you know what the neighborhood looks like. You can tell if the neighbors keep an RV parked in the driveway or blast Black Sabbath on their backyard deck. "With new homes you're taking a little bit of a gamble as to what it's going to look like when the neighborhood is totally built out," Dague says. Older homes also tend to be closer to the city, cutting commutes.

Back in Providence, Charles Kingdon believes socioeconomics goes a long way toward explaining why some people prefer new houses and some adore old ones. "In Britain, the higher your social status, the older your property, invariably," Charles says. He associates the desire for a new residence with a working-class, blue-collar mentality. "People aspiring to be middle-class want everything new, and it displays a lack of confidence," he says, expressing a particularly uncharitable sense of British class-consciousness.

His attitude may stem, in part, from the fact that those historical European estates are likely to be handed down from one generation to the next, providing a visible reminder of a family's wealth and heritage. In America it's much less common to find adults owning a home once owned by their forebears, and there's no shortage of upper-class families who want to build anew. But just as people like Tina Giles and Artur Nazaryan are convinced a new home provides a better way to live, Kingdon remains resolute in his sensibilities.

"Anybody can build a new home, but nobody can replicate this house," he says. He'd no sooner move to a new subdivision, he says, than the Queen of England would sell Buckingham Palace and move to a condominium.

On his 1982 acoustic album *Nebraska*, Bruce Springsteen sang "Used Cars," a song that offered insight into the longings of a class of people who've grown accustomed to hand-me-downs. Narrated by a child, the song describes the thrill of a family buying a "brand-new used car." But beneath the excitement the child is all too aware that the preowned automobile is a sign of his family's second-class status. The chorus repeats: "Now, mister, the day the lottery I win, I ain't ever gonna ride in no used car again."

During the go-go years of the early 2000s, this attitude extended to homes, too.

After months of touring model homes and design centers, of studying floor plans and the latest high-tech home gizmos, I've come to better understand the appeal. My wife and I have a sentimental attachment to our 1970s home, and we hope to stay put for quite some time. If we were to move, we've always talked about the possibilities of living in a century-old home. Still, one day at work I see an e-mail from my wife that piques my curiosity. "This is that house I love on Adams Street," it says, followed by a link to a real estate Web site. The link shows a sprawling, newly built Cape Cod home on three acres. The ad says the inside is only partially complete, so there's still time for the buyer to decide on the floor plan and choose fixtures and amenities. Best of all, it's only a few blocks from our current home, so we'd remain in walking distance of our current neighbors, and our kids wouldn't have to switch schools. But even if we did want to move, this listing is far too expensive, so I quickly scroll through the photos, then get back to work.

As the real estate boom has faded, more people are holding off on turning their new-home dreams into reality. During 2006 and 2007, new-home sales plummeted. Many of the people who'd agreed to buy houses in developments like Huntington canceled their deals and walked away from their deposits—leaving builders struggling to find buyers for vast neighborhoods of half-built homes.

The people who went ahead with their purchases—including Mark and Tina Giles—did so knowing that financially they might have been better off pulling out of the deal. In fact, shortly after the Giles family closed on their house in early 2006, the builder announced it was cutting prices. As the new-house smell faded from the Gileses' home, they were left knowing that if they'd waited a few months they could have bought the same house for $40,000 less. "We were really, really, really not happy about that," Tina says.

Still, even if their new home has proven to be a negative investment in the short term, the Gileses play down any regrets. "I'm in love with this house—it couldn't be more perfect," Tina says. "We thought, Should we choose money, or what will make us happy? We picked what will make us happy."

This built-from-scratch dream may cost a lot of money, require months of patience, and at times present buyers with far too many choices. But as we sit on the ultrapowerful, previously unsat-upon toilets in our sprawling new master bathrooms, it's worth reflecting on the bright side of this lifestyle. Here we can glance down at the brushed-nickel toilet-paper holder—the one we chose from more than a dozen options—and contemplate it with genuine satisfaction and pride. Like Frank Sinatra, we did it our way.

CHAPTER THREE

FIX-UP FEVER:
NEWTON, MASSACHUSETTS

Imagining the House It Could Become

On a November day in 1996, Paula Giannetto was driving around Newton, Massachusetts, with a real estate agent when the agent used a tried-and-true technique to prod her to spend more than she'd planned. Giannetto had been clear about her price range: $300,000 to $325,000. But after they'd looked at a half dozen less-than-inspiring homes, the agent detoured to Dwhinda Road, slowed down, and pointed to the Dutch colonial on the corner. "You're going to love that house, but it's too much money." After the agent announced its price—$399,000—Giannetto reluctantly suggested they drive away and look at cheaper houses. But it wasn't long before Giannetto told the agent to drive back to Dwhinda, price be damned.

Giannetto, a medical equipment saleswoman, was relocating to Boston from Hoboken, New Jersey. For her house-hunting odyssey she'd brought along Mark Ito, a high-tech marketing manager from Boston whom she'd been dating for a year. Together with the agent they walked into the home on Dwhinda. Built in 1931, the three-bedroom, two-bath house measured 2,000 square feet. The foyer and stairway had the roomy, solid feel of prewar construction. The living room was spacious, with built-in bookcases. Ito loved the butler's pantry between the kitchen and the dining room. Giannetto fell for the hardwood floors.

But they also saw problems. The kitchen was cramped and out-dated—even the town's tax assessment records listed it (along with the baths) as "below average." Upstairs, under the gambrel roof, one bedroom had an awkward layout and a tiny closet. Downstairs a sitting room off the foyer didn't seem particularly useful, nor did the full bath off the kitchen. Out the dining room window you could see Route 128, the region's major highway. With the windows open you could hear it, too.

As they walked through the property with the agent, they talked about whether these problems might be fixable. It's a phenomenon that's common when house hunters tour older homes: From their first walk around the place, potential buyers aren't just looking at the house as it currently exists, but envisioning the home it might become.

"You could knock all that out and make an updated kitchen," the agent told them, referring to the awkward front room and the over-size downstairs bath. Giannetto knew it'd be some time before she'd attack a project that big. But looking around, she felt confident that the house's strong points outweighed its shortcomings. "This house has charm," she said.

Even though they were looking at property together, this would be Giannetto's house, not Ito's. Their romance was progressing nicely, but they weren't serious enough to be buying property together. But with Ito's moral support, Giannetto offered $360,000. The buyer accepted. She closed on the house on Valentine's Day 1997. For the next couple of years Ito kept his own apartment in downtown Boston, but he usually spent a few nights a week on Dwhinda Road. In 1999 they married.

During those early years the Itos painted most of the rooms and replaced the kitchen's linoleum floor. They talked about doing a full-scale renovation, and even hired an architect to draw up plans. But as the dot-com bubble burst, Mark's foothold in the high-tech industry began to feel a little shaky, and he decided to go back to grad school to become an English teacher. With his studies consuming his time, and with Paula temporarily serving as the family's sole breadwinner, they postponed their remodeling plans.

But by 2005, with two small children, they'd had enough. Paula, who works at home when she's not on the road, had commandeered one of the upstairs bedrooms as her office. That meant their two children—Luke, age four, and Nora, age one—had to share a bedroom. "Nobody was getting any sleep," says Mark, who rises soon after dawn to get to work at a nearby middle school. They needed to make a change.

They never really considered looking at other homes. The Itos love living in Newton, a suburb of 84,000 people just west of Boston that's known for its superb schools. It's an idyllic place to live, which is partly why home prices jumped 40 percent between 2000 and 2005, when the median-priced Newton home hit $736,400. Those stratospheric prices mean the Itos would have to leave Newton to afford a much nicer home, and during their time on Dwhinda they'd grown attached to their neighborhood, which is filled with children the same ages as theirs. So instead of moving they decided to act on the plan the real estate agent had suggested during their first walk-through: They would rebuild their Dutch colonial to make it better accommodate twenty-first-century family life.

One of Paula's coworkers explained how to do a cash-out refinance to pay for the job. The Itos put aside the initial plans they'd had drawn up a few years before, and instead hired a different architect, who quickly conceived plans to add a family room, mudroom, laundry, master suite, and to radically expand the kitchen. They went before the local historical commission to get their project approved. They interviewed contractors, ultimately picking one who was friendly with their architect and could start the job in just a few weeks.

And on a blustery February morning, a tall orange excavator labored over a growing hole in their backyard. A few days later a concrete foundation lined the hole, and a team of framers began pounding together the skeleton of their addition. By the time the project is finished—seven months later, the Itos hope—their home will have increased in size by more than half, to 3,385 square feet. And if they stick to their budget, they will spend about $360,000 on the renovation—as much as Paula originally spent to buy the home. They believe it's a smart investment. Before they began the job an appraiser told them their house was worth around $800,000. By the time they finish its value should top $1.1 million.

It's a breathtaking number, and whether consciously or not, the Itos drop their voices a few decibels when they talk about it, as if they're a little embarrassed that they'll soon be living in a home whose value runs to seven figures. "I grew up in a ranch with one bathroom, and Mark grew up in a house with two baths, but it wasn't huge," says Paula, who was thirty-nine when the remodeling project began. "Now all of a sudden we're building this dream house."

But all around them their neighbors are doing—or have already done—the same thing. As the Itos' job gets under way, a big renovation across the street is just finishing up. New windows sit outside another home, awaiting installation. Their architect has designed additions for three other houses within sight of the Itos'. All around them a young generation that grew up in cramped postwar houses is adding luxurious master suites, oversize mudrooms, marble bars, and gourmet kitchens. As Mark, also thirty-nine, stood outside one evening on the exposed plywood floor of what would become his master bedroom, neighbors walking by yelled up to him, offering congratulations and encouragement.

The Itos realize that no matter how smoothly the job goes, the months ahead will be stressful. They'll be without a kitchen, eating off paper plates. They'll have no room to entertain friends. They'll be writing five-figure checks, using borrowed money, at an alarming rate. In short, they'll be entering the life stage that's become known as "renovation hell." It's a place where couples are prone to bicker (and sometimes even divorce), where homeowners can feel torn between the desires of their architects, their builders, and themselves, and where there's so much potential for anxiety and conflict that some family counselors have begun to focus on a hot new specialty: treating renovation-addled clients.

But no matter how difficult the next few months become, the Itos will have lots of sympathy, because everyone they know seems to be renovating, too. "There's this sort of sense of camaraderie, because we're all going through it," Mark says. "Our kids and our home renovations are the two biggest topics we talk about when we're with other families." He looks down at the architectural drawings spread over their dining room table. "I remember being single and talking to people in their thirties, and thinking how boring it was that they talked about renovations and Home Depot. But now we bring these drawings out at parties and people are like, 'Let us see.'"

On dining room tables across America, the architectural plans have been multiplying. In 2006 Americans spent roughly $180 billion on home remodeling, according to Harvard's Joint Center for Housing Studies. Although renovation fever has receded a bit as the real estate boom has ended, at the height of the boom, home improvement expenditures were growing by more than 20 percent a year. Part of this is a function of age. We're now fifty years beyond the post–World War II homebuilding binge, and that's more time than homeowners should expect to get out of basic systems like roofing or furnaces. A house, David Owen wrote in his memoir of home repair, "is essentially a huge box filled with complicated things that want to break—a box that sits outside, day and night, in the rain and snow, surrounded by creatures that would like to eat it."

More than half of Americans' home improvement spending, however, isn't aimed at replacing things that have worn out. Rather, it's going toward "discretionary" remodels that let older homes boast some of the features—like family rooms and master bathrooms—that either didn't exist when they were built, or were considered proper amenities for only upper-class housing. According to those Harvard researchers, between 1985 and 1999 nearly one in five owner-occupied U.S. homes gained an additional bathroom, nearly one in seven gained a bedroom, and one in four added some other type of room.

Most of these remodels are driven by basic changes in family size or economics. A family has a third child and needs a new bedroom. A baby boomer inherits money and decides to redo the kitchen. But beyond those basic drivers, there's a complicated psychology that fuels these pursuits, and there's a small contingent of academics who try to better understand why we covet closet-organizing systems, wine cellars, and home theaters. Their theories fill dissertations, but to simplify them a bit, the experts see three main drivers that account for the contractors' pickup trucks that fill so many suburban driveways.

Some of these experts continue to cite the long-standing theory that home remodeling is mostly about keeping up with the Joneses. "The relentless status-seeking of the Boomer generation has created something of a permanent state of fix-up fever," writes June Fletcher, who covers real estate for the *Wall Street Journal* and has witnessed remodels that featured hand-embroidered wall-to-wall carpeting, car wash–equipped garages, life-size Broadway-style stages for kids' play-rooms, underwater stereo systems for swimming pools, and gold-plated gun safes. There's no doubt many of us have our friends at least partly in mind when we start tearing out walls. Life doesn't often resemble a television show, but for a generation that's become accustomed to watching the climactic "reveals" on shows like *Trading Spaces* or *Extreme Makeover: Home Edition*, people who undergo a renovation can't help but imagine how friends will ooh and aah at their own postmakeover space.

And in this Jones-beating-Jones competition, housing has become the weapon of choice. Boston College economist Juliet Schor points to homes (along with clothing and automobiles) as a key element in "the visible triad," that trio of possessions that are most evident to the people we meet and factor most heavily into how we assess people's status. The idea that we spend money partly in an attempt to affect how others view us has been around at least since Thorstein Veblen coined the phrase "conspicuous consumption" in the waning days of the nineteenth century. But in the twenty-first century, when outlet stores and credit cards give nearly everyone access to designer clothing, and cheap lease deals can put middle-class people into luxury cars, our homes have emerged as the primary arena for this one-upmanship.

There is a subtle, modern twist on these theories, however. It's a view best articulated by Cornell economist Robert Frank, author of *Luxury Fever*, and it's a theory I've come to think of as the "I've earned it" hypothesis. Frank believes people spend big money on visible goods like watches, cars, or kitchen remodels not only to impress and compete with friends, but also to treat and comfort themselves. He points to an acquaintance who bought a Lexus not because he wanted to impress anyone, but because he was wowed by the quiet, smooth ride and mechanical perfection. This man doesn't care what friends or valets say—he just wants to enjoy his daily commute. That's not to say these choices aren't driven partly by envy or competition—only that it's not simply about impressing anyone. After seeing a friend's recent acquisition, we can't help but tell ourselves, "I'm just as accomplished and just as deserving." Frank believes that even people who eschew materialism and don't give a damn about the Joneses can't help thinking, "He has something nicer than me, and I feel bad about it." So when we get out our home equity checkbook and start calling contractors, we're not just aiming to impress people. We're doing it to treat ourselves right.

Perhaps the best illustration of "I've earned it"–driven spending is the rising demand for spa services like facials and massages. But for modern-day renovators, the best examples of the phenomenon are master bathroom remodels. Veteran homebuilders say that until the 1980s, someone who just bought a new home (or did a renovation to an old one) wouldn't think to show someone else their upstairs bathroom. Nowadays some people include a master bath on their house tour, but it's still mainly a private space. Yet these spaces have become a key focus of renovators and builders, and homeowners are spending fortunes on them: Today a top-of-the-line master bath might include a multiple-head steam shower, a $5,000 remote-controlled toilet, and a jetted tub with nearly as much horsepower as a riding lawn mower. Few people in our lives will ever catch a glimpse of these improvements, but we still covet them. Why? Because we've earned it.

We're also doing renovations—theoretically, at least—for the people who'll buy our homes someday. Resale value—the third big driver of renovation projects—has always been a factor in the urge to upgrade our habitat. Most of the things we buy (including that Lexus) depreciate and wind up in a dump, but the fact that our houses appreciate and are someday resold adds a fair bit of complexity to every decision we make about them. For decades homeowners have passed along conventional wisdom like, "Don't build the biggest house on the block." But in the last two decades, as renovating has become an all-out national sport, its economics have been studied with increasing rigor. The most relied-upon source is *Remodeling* magazine, which since 1988 has commissioned surveys of appraisers, real estate agents, and remodeling contractors to determine the expected payback of various projects. In its 2005 study, for instance, the magazine declared that the most lucrative improvements were replacing siding or doing a moderate bathroom remodel. Each of those projects is estimated to cost a little more than $10,000, and would result in a price increase of slightly more than that cost if the home were sold immediately. At the bottom of the list are home office and sunroom additions. For every dollar you spend on these jobs, be prepared to recoup less than 75 cents.

Deciding to plunge into a big renovation is a complicated exercise. Some buyers, like the Itos, begin the mental process of imagining how they'll reconfigure spaces from the first moment they walk into the house they wind up buying. It's a behavior Harvard economist Kermit Baker, who studies the remodeling market, sees more frequently today. "A lot of households buy a home, and within a month or two have sort of a twenty-year time horizon in place—'We'd like to do this and do that,'" he says. The fact that these wish lists usually go far beyond whatever money or energy the homeowners have to spend is why so many houses today seem to be in a near-constant state of renovation. As soon as one project ends, it's just a matter of paying off the Home Depot credit card before the next one begins.

For families that go through these renovations, the projects can become all-consuming—the same way a couple experiencing their first pregnancy talk endlessly about the impending birth. For an example of how much time and energy can go into a renovation, consider Rodney Paige, President Bush's former secretary of education. When Paige resigned from his post in 2004, he told the president he needed to leave his job in order to complete a "personal project." The project, it turned out, was remodeling his Houston home.

Some of America's penchant for adding on and fixing up is timeless. Read Laura Ingalls Wilder's Little House books and you'll lose count of the number of times Pa beckons Mr. Edwards over to help put on a roof or bump out the kitchen to accommodate Ma's new stove. The biggest change between those rudimentary frontier renovations and today's remodels is that nowadays far fewer of us know enough about carpentry or plumbing to do even a simple remodeling job ourselves.

There's an irony here. In the same way that Americans watch more cooking shows but spend less time cooking, fewer of us know how to replace a faucet or build a bookcase despite endless hours spent watching HGTV. Baker, the Harvard economist, estimates that between 1985 and 2001 the percent of home improvement projects that were hired out to a professional increased from 50 percent to 60 percent.

That's true despite the phenomenal rise in Home Depot, which has grown from a single Atlanta location in 1978 to have 1,984 stores and $81.5 billion in sales in 2005. The chain's motto is, "You Can Do It. We Can Help," but the sad truth is that no matter how much tutoring we get from the Depot's orange-aproned staff, many of us just aren't interested. Even as battery-powered drills have come to rival ties as America's favorite Father's Day present, many of these tools will gather dust. It's an unfortunate side effect of the Information Age that many of us are now living in a post-handy world.

So many men are clueless about home repair that lately Home Depot has begun helping women pick up the slack. One evening I stop by a Home Depot location a few miles from the Ito home. The store is holding a "Do-It-Herself" workshop, teaching women how to install laminate flooring. For more than an hour instructor Fred Strelke shows four women how easily the modular flooring snaps together. Shoppers pause to watch, as if he were performing a magic trick. On a wall nearby hangs a list of other classes, including lessons on installing ceramic tile and closet organizers.

After class I ask the women why their husbands aren't here. A round of male bashing ensues. Their husbands, mostly in their thirties and forties, talk a good game about being handy, the women explain, but they rarely pick up a tool. None of these women wants to be the household handywoman. (One even admits that power tools scare her.) But if they want a job done at all, they say, they'd better do it themselves. They're not alone. In a survey commissioned by Home Depot, 45 percent of women said they'd purchased hand tools in the last twelve months, and 26 percent said they did all or most of their household's routine maintenance themselves.

One of the women at the workshop is Judy Brasher, a full-time fund-raiser. Her husband Brad, a biochemist, is plenty handy: He builds intricately detailed model rockets. "I'd like him to redirect his energies toward more useful projects," she says, citing her desire to add chair rails, crown moldings, and built-in bookcases to their home. "I try to stress how much fun it's going to be, how we'll feel so much satisfaction when we're finished, and really try to sell him on it," she says. At the Home Depot workshop, she discloses her strategy for getting a new laminate floor. She'll start installing one herself, knowing her husband will likely jump in to finish. "I can be a little bit sloppy," she says, praising Brad's meticulousness. "If he saw me start a project like this, he'd at least take it over or let me be his assistant."

In other families, the husbands explain away their diminishing interest in do-it-yourself-ism as a function of basic economics. Too many of us spend all day sitting at computers; all our hands are good for is typing thoughtful e-mails, clicking through PowerPoint presentations, or writing checks to people who actually know how to fix cars or rewire outlets. We're clumsy enough with a hammer that we'd probably do more harm than good, and even if we could do a decent remodeling job, it would take us so much longer than a pro that it's more efficient to hire the job out.

Clumsiness and lack of experience aren't the only things deterring men from remodeling. Heather Peck, another woman at the laminate-floor class, says her husband Chris, an investment banker, is so busy at work he usually wants to hire professionals to make home improvements. She'd like to see him in a tool belt a little more often. "He's really big and strong—it's convincing him that this is something we can do that's the challenge," she says. Heather admits she once took a sledgehammer to their kitchen while he was on a fishing trip to motivate him to start a remodeling job.

That episode is an example of how tensions over home renovations aren't limited to couples who are in the middle of a remodel. Even before that first hammer hits the first nail, figuring out what piece of a home is most in need of fixing up can be a strain. Tales of renovation-fueled marital strife have become a fixture in newspapers' home section pages. "Irreconcilable Interiors: When Mates Don't Match" reads a typical example in the *New York Times*, which chronicled how couples who are perfectly able to agree on issues like vacations or child rearing can reach an impasse when deciding between adding a painting studio for the wife or a den for the husband. And hiring the work out to a professional builder may only add to their angst. Contractors, the *Times* reported, have become objects of lust that rival the vaunted UPS man. ("I can't tell you how many times I hear somebody give a recommendation for a contractor that ends with the four words, 'And he's really cute,'" says one observer.) With so many shirtless, muscled carpenters around our houses, it seems inevitable that some of them end up getting horizontal with the woman of the house to test whether the floorboards in the new bedroom squeak.

Shirtless or not, contractors are especially prevalent in the driveways of Newton. Its residents are affluent enough—median household income in 2005 stood at $86,000—that there's plenty of disposable income for home improvement. In this, Newton is a prime example of the kind of "inner-ring" suburb that cultural critic David Brooks had in mind when he described places where dinner-party conversations routinely devolve into debates over granite countertops versus Corian. "People here talk about their relationships with architects the way they used to talk about priests, rabbis, and ministers," Brooks writes of America's rehab-crazed suburbanites. "Bathroom tile is their cocaine."

And like any addicts, rehabbers don't let bad weather deter them. In January the average temperature in Newton is 28 degrees—not exactly the ideal time to start a construction project. But in January of 2006, homeowners and contractors obtained building permits to start 156 projects in this city, with a combined value of $16.24 million. Among the permits issued that month was one for Mark and Paula Ito's home on Dwhinda Road.

For a frontline look at how these renovation jobs play out, step into the Inspectional Services office inside Newton's Town Hall. For the residents of Newton's northeast quadrant, the ultimate say over any remodeling job lies with Charles "Buddy" Lamplough, one of the city's four building inspectors.

Walking outside Town Hall, Lamplough gets into his '95 Mercury Sable, emblazoned with the city's seal. He fires up a Palm Tungsten to consult today's list of inspections. Lamplough is forty years old, with short reddish hair, a goatee, and a gold hoop earring in his left ear.

He looks a bit like Danny Bonaduce, the troubled former *Partridge Family* child actor. Clad in brown corduroys and an earth-toned checked shirt, Lamplough has a 30-foot Stanley tape measure and a small black flashlight attached to his belt. Before becoming an inspector four years ago, he worked in construction. "For fifteen years I worked outside, freezing my ass off all winter long, spending summers on the roof, in the sun, dealing with bees," he says, pulling the car onto Commonwealth Avenue. "Now I'm in a nice environment, in an office or in the car. And I still get to see the work I love."

His first stop is a brick-front colonial on Franklin Street. During the last inspection he noticed some wet insulation, so he's checking back to see that the contractor has replaced it before installing the wallboard. In the backyard a carpenter cuts trim on a portable workbench as a radio blares. Inside a new room at the back of the house two workers are hanging drywall. Lamplough pokes at the new insulation to make sure it's dry. It is. Outside he banters with the carpenter about the great weather. "Tell Steve it's all set. I'll see you at the final."

The addition to this home is pretty typical: an expanded family room, with a master bedroom upstairs. In Newton a job like this generally starts at $250,000. "These little additions on the backs of these houses cost more than I spent to buy my house," says Lamplough, who lives with his wife and three children in a 1,200-square-foot ranch in Stoughton, a much less affluent town. Of course, the price of anything can vary based on how much the clients know about construction and how much money they have to spend. In Newton, inhabited mostly by upscale professionals who work with words and ideas instead of nails or two-by-fours, contractors assume homeowners have little construction knowledge and lots to spend. Some charge accordingly.

That's evident as Lamplough drives away from Franklin Street and locates his second stop, another brick-front colonial on a busier street. There's a SOLD sign in the front lawn—apparently the house is under contract, and the sellers have been forced to make some last-minute repairs to seal the deal. A contractor pulled a building permit for this job just a few hours ago, and he's already finished. In the basement the homeowner explains that the buyer required them to replace a section of the sill, the wood that connects a house to its foundation. He points to a small piece of pressure-treated wood that's clearly new. Lamplough says it's fine. Walking to the car, he looks at the permit, which shows the contractor charged $1,500 for the job, which might have taken two hours. "Given that we're in Newton, that's probably ballpark," Lamplough says. "In my town that'd probably cost $500."

Lamplough's next stop is on Morton Road. A contractor's sign is planted in the front lawn, and the front porch is covered in blue tarps. Pulling them aside we find a two-burner Coleman camp stove, three propane tanks, a cooler, and a garbage can. Despite the brutal Boston winter, this is the family's temporary kitchen. Inside, most of the first floor of the house is reduced to studs and plywood. Lamplough says that in his experience, most people aren't prepared for how much discomfort a renovation causes. "As a contractor, you don't tell people, 'You're going to go through hell on this,'" Lamplough says. "It's always, 'The dust won't be bad and it won't be too noisy.'"

By the time this Morton Road project ended, the family had lived for eight months without a kitchen, but they were unusually good sports about it. Homeowner John Huth, a Harvard physicist and an assistant Boy Scout troop leader, embraced the challenge of outdoor cooking. "My proudest moment was when I was able to roast two whole chickens and make home fries and broccoli," he says. (His least proud moment: starting a grease fire by spilling chicken fat on his camp stove.) His wife, Karen Agnew, got used to cooking breakfast—still in her pajamas—under the front-porch tarp in below-freezing temperatures. In her view, the biggest drawback of their temporary accommodation was having to use a tiny upstairs bathroom sink for all cooking and dishwashing. The family lost weight going up and down the stairs so often, she says, and most of their dishes and glassware broke in the cramped sink or while in transit up and down. But both parents say the harsh living conditions brought them closer to their three teenagers during the project. "We just sort of rallied together as a family," says Huth, who now whips up meals on an eight-burner Thermador cooktop in his dream kitchen. "I'm not saying it wasn't a hardship, but it forced us to live in a smaller space and do more things together, and I actually liked that."

In Newton, as everywhere, the biggest home renovation problems involve finances, rather than physical discomfort. "A lot of people are not terribly realistic about what they can get for the money," says John Lojek, Newton's building commissioner (and Lamplough's boss). The average homeowners embarking on a big renovation in Newton may have paid $250,000 or $300,000 for their home ten or fifteen years ago. Now they're preparing to spend an equivalent amount to remodel it. It sounds like a lot of money, but as a construction budget, it disappears quickly. "Some of them think they're going to get a whole new house for that money, but that's just not how it happens," Lojek says.

There are issues besides money that drive renovation jobs off the rails. Some clients do everything too fast. In their desperation to start the job they don't spend enough time plotting things out. Some try to save money by hiring part-time tradesmen to do jobs at night and on weekends, often with poor results. Other homeowners try to oversee a job themselves by serving as the general contractor. "That's not unlike me walking into a hospital and saying, 'How difficult can it be to do an appendectomy? Give me the scalpel,'" Lojek says. Lamplough says one of his least favorite parts of the job comes when he watches an unsuspecting homeowner sign on to do business with a bad contractor. "There are contractors who are absolutely horrible, and we know it," Lamplough says. "When somebody's about to pull a permit, I want to just tell them to run. He's going to take a deposit and that's the last they'll ever see of him. But we can't say a word."

You don't have to search hard to find stories like that. Dan Bradford is a securities lawyer who lives in Sudbury, a short drive from Newton. When his family decided to add a master bedroom, mudroom, and study to their house, he found a superb contractor. But when the contractor's preferred excavator bid more than $40,000 for the site work, Bradford tried to save $10,000 by hiring his own sub-contractor. At first the subcontractor seemed great: He even let Bradford's five-year-old drive his backhoe on his birthday. But with the job half-finished, the guy disappeared. Bradford called him every day for a month, to no avail. Bradford's wife called the excavator's wife, begging for him to return. Finally he came back and did a little more work. "He told me, 'I'm practically done,' and I wasn't experienced enough to know he still had a fair amount of work to do," says Bradford, who paid him nearly all the money he was owed.

Bradford learned the hard way how much work remained. While he was on a business trip to London, his wife called in a panic. Because the backyard hadn't yet been graded (in which dirt is sloped to send rainwater away from the foundation), their basement was completely flooded. A few weeks later it rained again, and Bradford found himself in the backyard with a shop vacuum, trying to keep water from flowing into the house. By the time the job ended, the family had spent thousands on bringing in cleaning crews and hiring another excavator to actually finish the job. Bradford is able to look on the bright side. "At the end of the day the guy's work will all be covered up with dirt, so it's not something where I'm worried about the soundness of my house, the way it's built, or we're going to have to tear something apart to fix it," he says. Still, as the job neared completion, the Bradford family remained beyond irritated—and was seriously considering a lawsuit.

For Lamplough, those types of stories are all too familiar, but they're not unique to Newton. To his mind, what makes his job particularly interesting is that the city's affluence lets him witness families who are transforming their homes into unimaginably luxurious residences. Driving back to the office near the end of his workday, Lamplough recalls a recent inspection. The house had a swimming pool enclosed by a mechanical retractable roof, a fancy home theater with three levels of elevated seating, and a giant horseshoe bar. Behind the bar were two Sub-Zero refrigerators: one filled with soda, the other with half pints of ice cream in assorted flavors. The family living there has two children, ages five and six. "I hope these kids grow up with respect for what they have," Lamplough says. "I'd like to put them in my home for a month, then send them back to live in their house. They'd be like, 'We've got it so good.'"

A few days before Easter, architect Peter Sachs pulls up in front of the Ito home and knocks on the door. Paula apologizes for the house being a mess. Mark, just home from school, meets them in what used to be the dining room. It now has a stove, refrigerator, and sink installed along one wall. The entire south side of the downstairs—the old kitchen, sitting room, bathroom, and butler's pantry—is walled off by plywood. "We're kid-free for the next hour," Paula says as they sit down at the dining room table.

The job is going well. The addition is weather-tight, with siding on and windows in place. Inside, the interior walls are mostly framed. Mark's chief concern is that they haven't yet made some big decisions, like how to configure the kitchen cabinets. If they don't make these decisions soon, he worries it could delay the job.

The architect and his clients step outside to look at the south wall of the house. The builder has already put the new windows into the addition, but now the Itos and Sachs need to decide how to reposition the windows on the old part of the house so that they'll flank the new stove in the kitchen. Sachs has drawn the elevation with three downstairs windows, which have already been purchased. Privately, the Itos think he's adding too many windows to their house. In the master bedroom they worry they'll have no place to put dressers; in the family room Paula thinks they won't find spots for bookshelves. Likewise, the Itos think three kitchen windows will limit their cabinet space. Sachs asks if they're going to replace the old windows on the other sides of the house. "We're still trying to decide," Paula says. The additional work will cost $10,000, and they're not sure it's in their budget.

They move inside the addition. It smells of sawdust. Their old kitchen sink sits on the floor of the new family room; tomorrow it will go in the Dumpster. Toward the east side of the spacious, L-shaped space that will eventually constitute their kitchen and family room is the existing house, its walls now opened and its framing exposed. The old lumber, more than three-quarters of a century old, is darker, somewhere between copper and cappuccino, compared to the pale, fresh lumber that comprises the addition. In the existing house, built before plywood was even invented, the exterior walls are sheathed with long, wide boards. In the addition, everything is sealed tightly with plywood and Tyvek.

At the front end of the kitchen the trio talks about whether the coat closet will really be deep enough to fit coats, and whether the pantry will be large enough. Sachs tries to explain how the finished space will look. Paula has her finger on her chin, and Mark has a faraway look. Each seems to have entered that place in their brains where they try to merge the half-built space with the two-dimensional blueprint sitting on their dining room table. It's a visualization exercise that architects are adept at, but for untrained homeowners, it can be all but impossible to imagine the finished space. The architect tells them to think about how the new windows will look at 5:00 on a winter's night, when the sun is low in the west. They mention glass-front cabinets, and he discourages them. "It looks nice if it's done right, but you have to be a complete neat freak," he says.

The exchange is part of the delicate interplay between an architect and his clients. Although it's a discipline that involves math and computers, architecture is, at root, an art. And as with any art, a lot of it is subjective. Taste matters. On some issues—like the glass cabinets—the Itos defer to their architect's expertise and experience. But when his design calls for something they don't like—like too many windows—they can be hesitant to speak up, for fear of offending him or questioning his judgment. On certain issues it can be less confrontational to simply tell the contractor to deviate from the drawing without involving the architect in the refiguring. Sachs is generally easygoing and amiable—late in the job, when he makes a mistake ordering their doorknobs, he dips into his fee to send them $800 to buy replacements. Still, as they debate changes to the architectural plans, everyone tends to speak carefully, so as not to offend anyone else's taste. As the clients, the Itos know that when Sachs leaves, they can tell the contractor to do whatever they want.

Other clients wind up at the other end of the spectrum: Instead of covertly overriding the architect's choices, they become so dependent on his (or her) calls that they come to lack any trust in their own taste. Several years ago I met a couple who'd built a smart-looking family room and master suite onto a Victorian home in a college town. By the end of the job, they'd spent so much time deferring to their architect and interior designer that they joked that they lacked the confidence to choose which movie they were going to watch on Friday night without calling each one for a professional consultation.

The Itos and Sachs move from the kitchen to the family room. After a brief discussion they decide to put a four-foot French door between the dining room and the family room, and to ask the builder to shorten a railing he's already built to accommodate the larger opening. "Okay, we've made a decision," Paula says. Mark moves to the opposite wall. "If we had a plasma TV here, would it sit too low?" he asks the architect.

Outside, a car door slams. The nanny walks up the front yard with Luke and Nora, who run into the backyard to play. Nora runs around the portable outhouse set up for the builder near the driveway.

The Porta Potti, the Dumpsters, and the constant stream of trucks clogging the street can test the neighbors' patience. In the 2006 film *Friends with Money*, a married couple adds a new floor to the top of their house, giving them a picture-perfect view of the ocean—and completely blocking their neighbors'. A streetwide war erupts, and the renovating couple's marriage crumbles. When it comes to their neighbors, however, the Itos are fortunate: Most of them have already done renovations, so they're sympathetic. Their support is also bolstered by the more enlightened attitude that came to take hold during the real estate boom. Instead of focusing on the noise and inconvenience, today most people look positively on neighbors' home improvements, hoping the spiffed-up home will increase the value of their own adjacent property.

Complaining neighbors are just one of the expected stresses of renovating. For the Itos, the most unexpected one comes from being buffeted by a constant stream of decisions that need to be made quickly. No matter how complete the architectural drawings are, lots of things get figured out on the fly. By midproject, Paula has learned that if she needs to leave on a sales call, she'll probably spend fifteen minutes kibitzing on the front lawn with the builder, talking about, say, where to put the handrail on the new porch.

"The number of decisions you need to make to keep the contractors and subcontractors going is very hectic," Mark says. "And each decision seems to affect some other decision in the house, and every decision seems to be more urgent than the one prior to it." At one point, when Mark is on a trip to California and the contractor needs a decision made right now, Paula resorts to frantically e-mailing Mark digital pictures of some cabinetry to try to get his input without holding up the job.

Mark's other big concern is security. While they're comfortable with their builder and his workers, they've now entered the phase of the job when a larger group of subcontractors they've never met is on site. Mark recalls that the Boston Strangler was a handyman whose work routinely had him visiting suburban homes just like this one. "I'll be happy when it's all over so we don't have this flow of people," he says. One architect recalls a female client with children who compared the lack of privacy she felt during her renovation to the hours she spent in the hospital delivery room. During labor, it seemed like dozens of random hospital staffers came in to do pelvic exams. For this woman, watching a constant flow of unknown workers enter the home each morning—many without knocking—felt nearly as invasive.

The biggest stress, of course, is money. If the Itos' home hadn't doubled in value since they bought it, they never would have attempted a job like this. The fact that the mortgage industry has made it so easy to liquidate that equity is one reason millions of families like theirs are renovating, too. At the height of the refinancing boom in 2006, Americans liquidated $352 billion in home equity by utilizing "cash-out" refinancing, with most people using the newfound dough to pay down credit card debt or make home improvements.

Still, even though they have money to cover the job, keeping track of it all—and deciding how to spend it—can seem like a full-time job. Sitting at the dining room table, Paula, a pretty, chatty brunette, and Mark, a more reserved, thoughtful Asian-American, pull out the his-and-hers spreadsheets they're using to manage the job. Paula's is more of a basic accounting document that tracks the money they've already committed to spend. One page shows the payment schedule they've agreed to with their builder, from the $84,500 they paid him upon signing the contract, to the $5,000 check they owe when the windows are delivered, to the $15,300 they'll pay when he's completely finished. In all, they'll pay the builder $260,000.

Mark's spreadsheet is more forward-looking, and covers all the money beyond what they'll pay the contractor. Their custom-built kitchen cabinets will cost $31,000, and their new BlueStar stove, installed with a hood, will be $6,000. Mark's spreadsheet is color-coded, reflecting whether the money is a guesstimate, a solid quote, or has already been spent. Along one side the expenses are broken down into percentages, telling him that 30 percent of their budget will be spent in the kitchen, which they intend to be the focal point of the whole house.

But despite the meticulousness, there's a lot more uncertainty than they expected. "Every time we turn the corner there's something additional we should be doing," Paula says. Do they replace all the old windows and the entire roof, or just what's necessary to get the addition done? If they don't replace the whole roof now, will contractors even return their calls for a smaller job a year from now? Some homeowners get addicted to the "while-you're-here" syndrome, and are constantly asking their contractor to add bookcases, built-ins, or other features that weren't on their original wish list. Needless to say, these extras can add up quickly.

In contrast, most of the Itos' unbudgeted expenditures feel necessary. Their add-ons have been things like $4,500 to fix the siding, $2,000 to redo the chimney, and $3,500 to add air-conditioning to the upstairs. At the same time they've tried to make sensible cuts where possible. Their architect designed their laundry room to use a new stackable washer-dryer, instead of the existing side-by-side units they already own. They've nixed that plan, telling the builder to ignore the architect and build the laundry to accommodate their existing appliances. Still, they worry they're going to run out of money. "In the beginning you feel like it's this unlimited budget, so the decisions are easier," Mark says. "I don't want to get to the last room in the house, which may be the most important one to us, and realize we can't do what we want to because we changed the windows." Their top priority remains the kitchen, even if they have to finish other rooms (like the master bedroom) later on.

For most big decisions they're on the same page. The major disagreement concerns that wall on the north side of the family room, just opposite where the couch will go. They agree that it makes sense to have an electrician install the wiring to someday accommodate a flat-screen TV. But in the early weeks of the project, Mark and his father visited a local electronics store to look at models, and now Mark wants to include the TV (and surround-sound audio) as part of the renovation. Aside from wanting to spend the money on other things, Paula objects to using money from their cash-out refinancing to purchase a consumer appliance that doesn't enhance the value of their home. "Why would we pay for a plasma TV over thirty years?" she says. Mark agrees with her logic, but thinks that they'll save money and aggravation by having the electrician and carpenters install it now. "That's been the biggest argument we've had," Mark says. They first tell me about this disagreement when the job has just begun. Nearly three months later, it's still unresolved.

When it comes to making decisions, Mark tends to move on quickly, without looking back. Paula, in contrast, tends to revisit the things they've already decided—like agreeing to put so many windows in the family room—and worry whether she'll regret them. "I feel like any project is never going to be 100 percent perfect, so you live with 90 percent," Mark says. Until they've lived in the space for a while, they won't know exactly how perfect it is. And no matter how many spreadsheets they've concocted, they have no idea how much they'll end up spending until the day, many months from now, when the builder drives away for the last time.

The Itos, fortunately, don't get to the point where they need counseling to resolve their renovation-fueled conflicts. But if they should, there's a small group of pros who stand ready to serve them. And on a Saturday afternoon at a booth at the Civic Arena in Manchester, New Hampshire, one of them is plying her trade.

"Have you ever heard of Renovation Psychology?" a woman in white painter's pants and a purple shirt asks, smiling at a passerby. The target of her sales pitch, a man in a black T-shirt, stops, looking a little confused. The woman continues. "It's everything on the human side of the hammer. I'm Dr. Debi, and I invented Renovation Psychology."

Debi Warner has long grayish black hair, green eyes, an energetic smile—and a degree in clinical psychology. For more than a decade she used that training on patients in northern New Hampshire. Over time she recognized a trend: Many of her patients' stress seemed to be caused—or at least exacerbated—by home remodeling jobs. "They'd come in and say, 'We're doing our kitchen and fighting all the time over the design. He wants this and I want that.' They're depressed, aggravated, and things are going poorly," she says. To help them Warner applied the basic techniques of couples therapy, teaching communication skills and conflict resolution. But the more she thought about it, the more she wanted to do something to help people anticipate the stress and bickering, which is as inevitable as the noise from power saws. Why not attack this problem upstream, she wondered, by teaching people doing renovations how to spot early warning signs of stress and solve these problems before they turned into crises? Many churches routinely send engaged couples for counseling before their wedding. Likewise, Dr. Debi hopes to equip couples to ward off construction-related interpersonal conflicts. Instead of renovations from hell, she aims for couples to experience renovation ecstasy.

So in 2005 Warner quit her job, trademarked the phrase "Renovation Psychology," built a Web site, and self-published a 273-page book, *Renovation Psychology: Putting the Home Team to Work*. Illustrated with black-and-white photos of Warner and her husband in wedding attire and goofing with power tools, the book advises couples how to turn renovation projects into opportunities for self-actualization and discovery. "Renovation is a spiritual experience by nature, so you should take some time to view the job ahead through your own spiritual framework," she writes. "If you have faith, pray about it. If you have a seeking, look toward your higher consciousness to give you a pinnacle to aspire to." What God has joined, let no master-bedroom addition rend asunder.

On this weekend Warner has spent $750 for a booth at the Manchester Home Show. From 9:00 a.m. to 8:00 p.m. on Saturday and Sunday, she stands on a foam pad (to ease leg strain), trying to talk showgoers into paying $28 for her book. To her left is a company selling granite mailbox posts. To her right sit sales reps for a lumber company. "At least we're under a skylight," she says, pointing up at the sunlight streaming through the ceiling. By late afternoon the crowd is thinning, but Dr. Debi is still smiling, despite having sold just six copies of her book.

The book, however, is only the first step in her effort to spread her message. On a TV screen at the back of her booth there's a video showing her walking around a construction project with a family. The "family," it turns out, are actors; her son and his girlfriend play starring roles. The show is a pilot for what Warner hopes will be a Renovation Psychology television show, which she bills as a cross between *Oprah* and *This Old House*. On a table in her booth sits a clip-board where people can sign up to be in the studio audience at the first show. Today she's brought a freelance videographer to tape inter-views with home show attendees talking about the stress of their own renovation jobs. "This is a good test today—are people comfortable having this kind of conversation on camera?" she says. Over nearly eight hours, her team has taped four would-be guests.

Among the tradesmen who invade America's homes to execute our *Architectural Digest*–inspired dream, there's no question she's onto something. If you spend your days talking couples through the end-less list of decisions required to complete a remodel—and giving them near-daily bad news that everything will cost more than they expect—you wind up with unique insights into the strain it can cause on a marriage.

For some pros it can be too much. Danielle Fraser spent four years as an upscale kitchen designer in Crested Butte, Colorado, be-fore switching careers—largely because she was tired of watching couples fight. "Initially people were so excited about their remodel," she says. But Fraser often wound up with a ringside seat as couples viciously fought over the job. "The most common situation was the wife wanted to make upgrades in their choices, and the husband would say, 'No, I'm sorry, that's too expensive.' She would say, 'You said I could do this.' He'd say, 'I know what I said, but I'm changing my mind.' That unfolds right there in front of you, and it's very un-comfortable," Fraser says. "The whole project starts creating resent-ment. . . . They're not happy with each other, and you can feel the air get really thick." During the four years Fraser worked as a designer, as many as one-third of her clients ended up divorcing during the course of a job or soon afterward. "To see their marriages break up was extremely disappointing," says Fraser.

It's a risk that's well known to several of the couples who've lived in the old Georgian colonial on Charles Street in Fredericksburg, Vir-ginia. When Pamela and Jeff Graham bought the house, built in 1785, a few years ago, the owner warned them that previous couples who'd tried to fix it up had a tendency to fight a lot. In fact, the couple who sold it to the Grahams, Tim and Martha Garrett, had gotten divorced, and Tim counts the stress of the renovations as a key contributor to the demise of their marriage. He says his wife had an unrealistic expectation of how quickly the renovation would get done. "You might finish up an area, and it looks great, but there's another area waiting," Tim says. "That's the old joke about old houses—you never actually finish renovating them." Today Tim lives in a house built in 1851 that he's renovating, while Martha lives in a newly built town house. "There's virtually zero maintenance," Tim says—just the way his ex-wife likes it. Before the Garretts owned it, the house had been rented out by Harrison and Peggy Jett. As renters, they didn't try to renovate the Charles Street house, but their time there inspired them to buy and rehab another old local home. "By the end we were hardly even speaking—it became such a negative influence in our lives," recalls Harrison. "The week after the house was completely done, she asked for a divorce. She said: 'I'm done, it's over.'"

The Grahams keep those couples' troubles in mind as they rebuild their home room by room. "When we feel ourselves getting irritated at each other, if it's a tiny situation we take a walk," Pamela says. "If it's big, we go away for an overnight." When the stress gets insurmountable, Pamela likes to go into a room they've finished refurbishing, which now looks absolutely perfect. She pours a glass of wine, puts on her iPod, and looks around at how beautiful their last project came out. She waits until she calms down. Then they plunge ahead, hoping their next project comes out just as nice.

In California, a licensed family and marriage counselor named Rachel Cox has also found a specialty in treating renovation anxiety and distress. Cox, who's married to a contractor, saw firsthand how her husband's clients would come unhinged during renovations. So she placed an advertisement in a publication called *California Marriage and Family Therapist* suggesting that counselors refer their renovation-addled clients to her. Calls started trickling in. To boost business Cox began tracking building permits and mailing letters to local families embarking on big renovations. Nowadays she might see fourteen couples a week, charging $90 a session. Don't bother asking about health insurance coverage: Renovationitis is not yet a recognized psychological disorder, so patients pay the bills themselves.

In Cox's practice, the course of treatment typically lasts between four and six sessions. Beyond the financial stresses caused by renovations, Cox sees common problems that result from one spouse getting saddled with more of the work, whether it's dealing with the contractor or running to plumbing supply stores to choose fixtures. "The remodeling doesn't cause [marital stress] so much as magnify it—the marriages that are not always superstrong get fractured even more during the course of a project," she says.

Cox sees larger problems that sometimes continue even once the certificate of occupancy is issued. Even the best renovations, she says, can't live up to the homeowners' idealization of what they might accomplish. If you renovate a kitchen, you can't help dreaming about the sophisticated dinner parties you'll throw in the new space. But no matter how nice the countertops look, many people are still mainly microwaving hot dogs for the kids, not making witty banter over pinot noir with friends while whipping up a soufflé. "It's a lot like buyer's remorse," Cox says. "It's like, 'All that money for this and I still have to live here with myself and my kids and my mess.'" For other buyers, the end of a job brings an emotional letdown, since renovations can be fun and exhilarating, despite the stress. "It's almost like becoming an artist for eight months and producing this beautiful sculpture—that's the rush people miss," Cox says, recalling one client who required Zoloft to fight a postrenovation depression. Cox even sees a few clients become addicted to the process, serially renovating spaces again and again.

Back at the Manchester Home Show, Dr. Debi hopes that if she can find a soapbox to communicate her teachings loudly enough, more of the families who go through remodeling will see it as a life-affirming, relationship-enhancing process, rather than as a painful, short-term experience that's worthwhile only as a means to an end. She's on a mission that, at present, isn't very lucrative, but so be it.

"I'm at a stage of my life where I have to make my dreams happen," she says, before returning to the front of her booth. A couple walks by, and Dr. Debi steps forward, smiling.

"Have you ever heard of Renovation Psychology?"

As the Ito job hits the six-month mark, the work is going quite smoothly. All the rough plumbing and electrical work are complete, the drywall is up, and carpenters are installing trim. The couple gives much of the credit for the lack of surprises to their architect, Peter Sachs.

Sachs works from an office he built out of the garage behind his house a few miles from the Itos' home. There are two large drafting tables, a grandfather clock in one corner, and a guitar sitting on a stand. On a chair next to him sits an orange cat.

Many people go into architecture because they have a lifelong aesthetic fascination with buildings, but Sachs took a different route. "I did a lot of construction work on houses as a kid—I started working on framing crews when I was fourteen. My interest in architecture evolved out of making a living in construction and realizing that the top guy in the pyramid is the architect," he says. He attended the University of Pennsylvania in the mid-1970s and studied under well-known architects Louis Kahn and Robert Venturi. Unlike Saab-driving architects who've never held a hammer, Sachs believes his construction background sets him apart. "Builders know that I could put on a tool belt and work a day on their project and be a valuable framer," he says. "A lot of people I build with respect that and know that I'm not posing." Today he works almost exclusively designing renovations for homes in Newton, doing about fifteen projects a year.

Most people have a basic grasp of why renovations are harder than new construction, but Sachs believes they underestimate the level of difficulty. "Renovating an older house is triage," Sachs says. "You're starting with a product that has problems already." Before you open up the walls, you never really know what you're going to find: rotten beams, an immovable support member exactly where you'd planned to run the plumbing lines, carpenter ants. In addition to the surprises, renovation starts with demolition, an extra step that adds to the cost and disruption. It's no wonder so many people just decide to demolish an old house and build from scratch.

The Itos are unusual for having hired an architect to design their addition. Most home renovations are designed by the homeowner or the builder, without professional guidance. Sachs says only 4 percent of home renovations involve an architect, and, like everyone in his profession, he sees that as regrettable. Homeowners who do hire an architect usually end up with a renovation that is more in keeping with how the client really lives. When Sachs renovated his own kitchen, for instance, he began by focusing on the size of his dining room table, and bumped the wall out just enough to accommodate it and a window seat. For a mudroom, the architect will likely ask questions about what sports your children play (hockey players require far more storage for equipment than baseball players or ballerinas). Some of the questions can get intensely personal. Are you comfortable having your spouse in the same room while you use the toilet? If not, the architect will create a separate "toilet room" in a master bathroom. When discussing master bedrooms, architects and clients often have euphemistic discussions about "privacy" and "acoustics"—often a discreet way of acknowledging that the client wants the bedroom placed and constructed in such a way that their kids won't hear Mom and Dad having sex.

As happy as the Itos have been with his work, Sachs has been similarly impressed by their ability to quickly make choices and decide on compromises. "When both people are working, their time is limited, their time is valuable, and they are accustomed to making decisions," he says. That's not to say the Itos and Sachs have agreed about everything. When the Itos first saw the design for their remodel, they were shocked at how big it was. They also wondered if he'd made the right decision about how to use the space over the family room. Sachs called for a door in the second-floor master bedroom that would lead out to a roof deck. With two small children, the Itos never really cared for the roof deck, and sometimes they've wondered if they shouldn't have asked him to bag the flat roof in order to create a cathedral ceiling in the family room instead.

These tensions—between the architect's creative vision, the builder's pragmatic desire for a design that's easy to build, and the homeowner's desire for something affordable that fits his life—are a factor in every job. In the early 1980s writer Tracy Kidder hung around the building lot where Jonathan and Judith Souweine worked with a Boston architect and a local building crew to construct a custom house in Amherst, Massachusetts. The result was *House*, his narrative of custom home construction. It's largely a story of conflict: Every few pages, the architect and the builder disagree over which would be responsible for some problem, or the Souweines are trying to renegotiate the expenses with the builder in an attempt to cut costs.

Every job has its trouble spots, and likewise every architect has client-from-hell stories. Sachs says that as in poker, there are tells that let architects predict which clients are going to cause headaches. At the top of the list is a client who's already worked with another architect but has been unhappy. Problem number two is driven by economics: People without enough resources are often frustrated to learn how little they'll get for their limited budget. At the other extreme, families with unlimited resources tend to dither endlessly, paying little attention to how much time the planning process is taking. Says Sachs: "My most successful clients and my most successful projects are ones that are well defined by constraints, financial and maybe even aesthetic."

Coincidentally, Sachs is dealing with a problem client the morning I visit. He's been on vacation, and returned home to a letter from a client who is unhappy it's taking him so long to complete a design for her renovation. "She's already spent $20,000 on another architect. She's made changes over and over again," he says. His fee for the job will be $30,000, and he's holding a large check from her that he hasn't yet deposited. After reading the letter, he's wondering if it's worth the aggravation. He's about to call her to discuss the job. "I'm going to say, 'We can't do this project because you can't make any compromises.'"

He picks up the phone and dials her number. I can hear only his end of the conversation. They chat about his vacation and make small talk. Then he launches into the architectural version of the "It's not you; it's me" speech.

"My biggest priority here is my relationship with you," he tells the client, whom I've agreed not to name. "To the extent that if you've been unhappy in any way with the work I've done so far, I'd give that check back to you. I haven't put it in the bank yet."

The dispute isn't only about the time the project is taking—it's also about money. Of the $30,000 fee, about $7,000 is designated for up-front design work, in which Sachs will explore various design options before making final construction blueprints. Sachs says things are progressing just as he'd planned, but the client is frustrated that the summer building season is approaching, and she doesn't have construction drawings yet. "I'm not being defensive about it," he tells her. "I think we've come a long way in three months. . . . Maybe I'm guilty of not performing speedily enough, but I can't diminish the complexity of you as a client. I mean that in a good sense," he says.

The client talks for a long while. Sachs winks at me. Although most architects say they like dealing with clients, in truth some of them are happiest at their drafting table, pencils in hand and the clients nowhere in sight. But there's no escaping this part of the job. Decisions about one's home are especially difficult because they're expensive and you'll live with them for a very long time. So architects have little choice but to engage in handholding—and sometimes a little amateur psychology—as clients dawdle and kvetch over tough choices or budgetary woes. During today's conversation, Sachs's client tries to steer the discussion toward whether to add a bulkhead under an office window. Sachs moves their chat back from the specifics of their design to their relationship. The client takes the wheel again. Sachs rolls his eyes. Then he resumes control and, while remaining polite, his voice starts to rise.

"I'm sensitive to your feeling that things aren't happening quickly enough. But I'm more sensitive to the bigger picture, which is to prevent a finished project that is lousy with a capital L. I'd rather have you discharge me as your architect than to have you spend $300,000 to build something and then say, 'You idiot!'"

On the phone, the situation stays unresolved. But a few mornings later they meet for coffee. Sachs is carrying her uncashed check in his pocket, ready to hand it back to her. He opens the meeting by asking: "Am I getting fired or not?" He's not. After another long conversation, he tells me a few days later, his client has come to realize the benefits of his proceeding cautiously before they commit to a final design. He will continue as her architect—and he deposits her check in the bank.

The Itos' renovation was supposed to be finished in August. But a few days after Labor Day work continues. There's tile awaiting installation in the upstairs master bathroom. The family room lacks carpeting. The walls require touch-up painting. By October, the family hopes, the builder should disappear from their lives.

The kitchen is finished, however, and it's stunning. The dark wood of the custom cabinetry looks hand-polished, and the drawers open and close with soft precision. True, the bill for these cabinets was more than the average worker earns annually in much of the United States, but the result is a kitchen far nicer than anything you'd find at Home Depot. Under-cabinet lighting casts a warm glow onto the Giallo Ornamental granite, imported from Brazil; the light highlights the way the granite complements both the cabinets and the earth tones in the tile floor. The new stainless-steel appliances are sparkling and smudgeless. Mark moves to the BlueStar range and flicks on one of the 22,000-Btu burners. The blue flames dance.

Usually an addition feels really big when the two-by-four walls go up, but then everything seems dramatically smaller once the drywall is hung, separating the rooms from one another. But the Itos' space still feels remarkably large. In fact, the kitchen is so big that they may add a small island to fill up the space. But first they want to live with it for a spell. Overall, this job has turned out so nicely that their architect has asked to take photos to use in advertisements.

It's come at a big price tag. Originally the Itos planned to spend $360,000. As the job nears completion, they're $80,000 over budget. Their finances became so stretched that in late July they liquidated a retirement account to keep the job going. As soon as the renovation is complete, they plan to refinance the house again and replenish the account before they get hit with tax penalties. After their next refinancing, they'll be left with a mortgage of roughly $750,000.

They rattle off a long list of items—including the windows and a huge painting bill—that led them to overspend. But on the north side of the family room lies another reason. A big mass of wires dangles from a hole in the wall, which also has speaker cutouts and an electrical outlet mounted at eye level. Mark smiles, describing the forty-two-inch high-definition LCD television that will be mounted here next week. It will attach to a sound system that features speakers located in ceilings throughout the first floor. The audiovisual equipment has added about $12,000 to the job. The couple debated this expense long after most big decisions had been made. On July 4, while driving home from a vacation in Maine, Mark and Paula got in a loud argument over the flat-screen TV. From the backseat Luke, now five, told them: "Guys, you have to calm down." Ultimately, Paula decided that she got so much of what she wanted out of the renovation that Mark deserved to get his way with the television.

Sitting in the new breakfast area behind the kitchen, Paula reflects on the project. "I've learned things about my relationship with Mark through this," Paula says. One of these lessons has been positive and affirming. The renovation has reinforced their sense that they make aesthetic decisions well together, and that they generally have the same priorities and sense of style. Paula recalls visiting a tile store where the sales rep complimented them on their ability to reach agreements easily, unlike couples who often bicker over choices.

"Part of the reason you're with someone is because you enjoy the same things and you have the same tastes, and this project has brought out what we really do well together," Paula says.

On the other hand, for all their meticulous spreadsheets, the project has also illustrated a weakness of their union. "We are really bad at budgeting—we have a bad tendency to say, 'Oh, the hell with it, we'll deal with it later,'" she says. While she's very pleased with how the project turned out, she can't help thinking that if they'd sold their unrenovated house, taken the proceeds, and added in the $440,000 they spent on their renovation, they could have bought a $1.1 million home without suffering through dust and disruption.

It's a common sentiment. No matter how many spreadsheets you construct, every renovation project is destined to go over budget. And as those *Remodeling* magazine surveys show, very few remodel jobs pay back $1 in value for every $1 that's spent, at least in the short term. So after a renovation, homeowners are left to ponder a depressing equation: "My house was worth X, I spent Y, but now I have a house worth less than X + Y." Still, even though we understand that math in advance, millions of us plunge ahead anyway. Particularly during the real estate boom, when money spent on home improvements seemed all but guaranteed to outperform your 401(k), deciding to splurge could feel irresistible. Besides, no matter how magnificent your 401(k) balance, you can't invite friends over to have dinner in it.

Despite going over budget, Mark has no regrets. "This way you get what you want—you're not buying something and then living with it," he says. Yes, they spent more than they planned, but he's convinced it was a smart investment. The big mortgage doesn't worry him. With Luke now in kindergarten, their child-care expenses have already dropped; when Nora goes off to school in a few years, their disposable income will grow even more. If a financial crisis hit, they could probably find more lucrative jobs, ask their parents for help, or even sell the house and move to something cheaper.

As the job winds down, the Itos already sense that a small part of them will miss the excitement of seeing their home transformed a little bit each day. They'll miss the decision making, as stressful as it was at times. "What are we going to talk about now that this is done?" Paula wonders.

Mark compares their renovation to the stress and excitement of getting married. He looks over at Paula and smiles. "We've now planned a wedding and survived a renovation, so we're probably going to be together for a long time," he says.

And if the end of this project leaves them feeling too let down, all they have to do is look out the back window of their new family room. All the construction has wreaked havoc on their backyard. There's a big tree that really should be removed. The yard would look a lot better if they added some new stone walls, a few fresh shrubs, and a walkway from the garage. Newton suffers no shortage of top-notch landscape designers. After all, the Itos have earned it.

CHAPTER FOUR

WHY WE LIKE TO WATCH: NEW YORK CITY

Shelter and Gossip

Just after 7:15 on a Wednesday evening, Braden Keil sits in a cluttered cubicle in the newsroom of the *New York Post*, the city's feisty tabloid. A few yards away sits Richard Johnson, editor of the paper's white-hot Page Six gossip column, reading a story about Paris Hilton on a gossip blog. It's just after deadline in the newsroom—Keil filed his "Gimme Shelter" column for Thursday's paper a few minutes ago—and he's on the telephone with an unhappy source.

"Hi, Don," he says. The caller is Donald Trump Junior, twenty-nine, an executive in his famous father's real estate empire. Earlier in the day Keil had received a tip that the rapper Jay-Z would be moving out of his $40,000-a-month rental in the Time Warner Center into a $65,000-a-month, fourteen-room penthouse near the top of the ninety-story Trump World Tower. Early in the afternoon Keil had called Trump's people to confirm the story. Hours later Trump Junior has finally returned the call, after deadline, and is trying to convince Keil not to run the item.

Keil tells him the column is finished, and the Jay-Z item is staying in it. He politely chides Trump for not returning his call earlier, and promises that readers won't be left thinking that Trump's people have planted the item, which seems to be Trump's primary concern. After a couple of minutes, Keil hangs up the phone. The next morning the Jay-Z item—headlined "King of the World"—leads his column.

In a world in which Americans have developed a voracious appetite for the latest gossip on celebrity hookups and hairstyles, drunken escapades and intramural rivalries, it's not very surprising that people are hungry for stories about celebrity real estate moves, too. And to stay apprised of these developments, many of them turn to Braden Keil.

Keil is fifty years old, but could pass for a decade younger. He's been writing about real estate since only the late 1990s, but he's always been extraordinarily interested in houses. He recalls sitting in elementary school as a child, doodling big castles with tennis courts and ponds, and thinking: "I could live in something like that." The reality is less grandiose: Despite his deep knowledge of Manhattan real estate, Keil spent the early 2000s convinced that apartment prices were set to drop, so he's still living in an Upper West Side rental.

At work he keeps a Rolodex filled with names and numbers of real estate agents. But many of his best items come from a core group of fifteen brokers he speaks with each week. Keil has three criteria for what constitutes a great real estate gossip item: a transaction involving an A-list celebrity, a record-breaking price paid for a property, or a deal involving a home with an interesting history, such as an apartment once owned by a U.S. president or the scene of a spectacular murder. In this worldview, the perfect "Gimme Shelter" item might carry the headline "Britney Spears Drops $200 Mil on Kennedy Compound."

Keil also keeps a close eye on celebrities who've shown an unusual adeptness at turning big profits when buying and selling homes, a group that includes fashion designer Calvin Klein, music executive Tommy Mottola, and especially the actress Uma Thurman. "Uma is very savvy—she's made money on all her transactions," he says.

Some stars and brokers welcome his coverage. Keil has been inside homes owned by Ricky Martin, Sting, and Lorraine Bracco. When Keil heard that onetime *Frasier* star Kelsey Grammer was buying a Hamptons estate, he left him a voice mail. Grammer called back promptly, happy to dish about his spectacular new home. Other celebrities, seeking privacy, try to talk him out of running items. They rarely prevail, though Keil does respect their need for security by hewing to his own ethical code: He prints celebrity addresses only if they live in a doorman-guarded building in Manhattan. For stars in stand-alone town houses or suburban manses, Keil declines to give readers precise coordinates.

Like all reporters, Keil is happiest when he's breaking exclusives. One of his greatest hits involved Christie Brinkley. In 2003 Brinkley and her architect husband, Peter Cook, bought a $7 million, 10,000-square-foot home in the Hamptons hotspot of North Haven, intending to move into it when they sold their twenty-acre Bridgehampton estate, which they'd put on the market for $26.5 million. Then, in 2006, the tabloids erupted with news that the forty-seven-year-old Cook was bedding a nineteen-year-old intern from his office. Keil leaped into the fray with news that Cook was using the vacant North Haven home as his "love shack" for their assignations, "[making] full use of its six bedrooms . . . [where] no prying eyes could spy the caddish Cook creeping inside with his petite paramour." Sex and real estate—is there any *Post* reader who didn't relish every word?

There was a time when Keil felt a little uneasy describing himself as a gossip columnist. He's quick to point out that he can also write a smart nuts-and-bolts business story about, say, mortgage rates. But in a world where newsstand sales of *Us Weekly* and the *Star* far exceed those of the *New York Times*, he's comfortable with what he does—and he's convinced that America's celebrity-obsessed readers give him a measure of job security few business reporters enjoy. "I've always been a naturally nosy person, so this sort of goes hand in hand," he says. "They're two of the basic human needs: shelter and gossip." And whether the real estate market goes up or down, the need for both will likely remain constant.

Keil's brand of journalism satisfies a distinctly twenty-first-century appetite, but long before Americans became so fascinated by celebrities, they were obsessed by homes. So-called "shelter magazines" like *House & Garden* have been around for a hundred years, and for nearly that long newspapers have devoted space to Sunday real estate sections. These sections have given rise to their own peculiar weekend ritual: Many people read the home listings even if they're not contemplating the purchase or sale of property. They're reading, quite simply, because when it comes to houses, we tend to be curious.

During the last decade, however, the way the media satisfies—and tries to profit from—that curiosity has undergone a dramatic shift. Newspapers and magazines are still relevant, but lately the biggest breakthroughs have come on television and online. Click on your cable dial and you'll find no shortage of shows with titles like *Flip This House, Designed to Sell,* and *Buy Me* that constitute an entirely new genre of reality programming: real estate television.

On the Internet, meanwhile, a host of new Web sites have been created to capitalize on people's desire to learn more about the value of their own home—and those of their neighbors, friends, and coworkers. At the top of this class is Zillow, a Web site that's nominally designed to estimate the value of your home—but is more often used by millions of Americans to get the inside scoop on other people's houses and get a better sense of how they stack up financially with their peers.

The creation and surge in popularity of these media outlets is yet another sign of the hold homes have on the national consciousness. In the first chapters of this book I've described manifestations of House Lust that are distinctly active pursuits. Building a gigantic home, designing a home from scratch, or doing a large-scale renovation are activities that take lots of time and lots of money; there's nothing recreational about any of them. In this chapter, in contrast, we'll explore a more passive and widespread manifestation of House Lust. It's hard to label something an obsession nowadays unless you can spend countless hours watching it on TV, or waste an afternoon clicking online. Thanks to the shows on HGTV and Web sites like Curbed and Zillow, House Lust now has a year-round hold even on people who aren't actively buying, selling, or building anything.

At the simplest level, house-focused TV shows and Web sites provide basic entertainment. They capitalize on the fact that we're a nation of lookie-loos who enjoy seeing the insides of other people's houses. These shows also cater to a population that's increasingly distracted. Unlike with *Lost* or *24*, it doesn't really matter if you miss an episode of *National Open House*; indeed, these shows are designed for grazing, so you can jump in midepisode while channel surfing. And like most reality shows, real estate programs are reasonably cheap to make, leading channels like HGTV to be able to flood the dial with them and still turn a profit.

But the entertainment value of these shows is only part of the explanation for the popularity of real estate programming, both on television and on the Internet. Part of the reason so many of us are watching is that amid swollen house values and declining savings rates, real estate has become a key piece of so many Americans' financial futures—and often an asset that we've borrowed heavily to finance. Even as the real estate boom has ended and home values have receded, Americans remain keenly interested in following the ups and downs of the market; indeed, since the boom turned to bust, the ratings of many of HGTV's real estate shows have only gone higher. In the same way that thousands of stock investors stayed glued to CNBC during the dot-com boom, hoping to amass tips that would make them rich, much of our twenty-first-century fondness for watching shows on house flipping and room makeovers is driven by a sense of financial self-interest.

There is a third factor driving us to these new forms of information—and it is, arguably, the most powerful. We're nosy. We're voyeurs. We want to see things we shouldn't be seeing. And when it comes to catching a glimpse of the assets and liabilities of our friends and neighbors, houses offer wonderful windows.

It's a phenomenon Shira Boss knows well. A newly married journalist living in New York, she and her husband owned an apartment in a building where people—themselves included—seemed keenly interested in one another's finances. "The most prized fruit of [the building's] grapevine is which apartment is being sold, and for how much," Boss recounts in *Green with Envy*, a wonderful book recounting her exploration of Americans' fascination with one another's money. When a couple their age moves in next door, Boss is fascinated to learn that they bought the apartment without a mortgage. One day the neighbor asks Boss to recommend a cleaning service—a luxury Boss and her husband could hardly afford. They wonder: Where *does* this couple get their money? "We live in an ultraopen culture that freely shares our most intimate concerns—but rarely when they involve money," Boss writes, citing psychologists' fondness for calling discussions of finances "the last taboo." (She's right: I know more about my closest friends' sex lives than I do about their finances—a state of affairs that is probably pretty typical.) In my favorite tidbit from her reporting, she cites a survey showing that twice as many Americans would be embarrassed if a friend saw their pay stub as would be ashamed if their friend found a vial of Viagra in their nightstand.

The evolution of these shows and Web sites reflects the shift in how Americans think about homes. Until a few years ago, TV shows that took viewers inside homes focused only on the most upscale properties. In the 1980s Robin Leach hosted *Lifestyles of the Rich and Famous*, and in the 1990s MTV launched *Cribs*; both shows offer fast-paced tours of the homes of celebrities, rock stars, athletes, and the superrich. But in recent years real estate television has become remarkably democratic: HGTV mostly avoids showing celebrity homes, and instead mainly focuses on middle-class homes that are within reach (or only slightly beyond it) for its average viewers. By doing so they're acknowledging that one of the key draws of these shows is that they allow viewers to compare themselves to people like them, which is in line with psychological research showing that people are most interested in comparing their own habits to a "reference group" made up of people of similar status. Indeed, people who watch lots of HGTV have told me they usually change the channel if the homes on the screen are far nicer or shabbier than theirs, and they get most excited by watching programs about houses that are comparable to or only slightly nicer than their own.

Lately these shows have also become much more open about the prices of the houses they feature, which is another defining characteristic of the new wave of real estate programming. Emily Post might roll over in her grave if she were to watch *My House Is Worth What?*, a cable program in which homeowners go on camera to talk about how much they paid for their house, and then hear a Realtor reveal its current value and what renovations they might do to boost its worth. The rules of etiquette still forbid these kinds of discussions of money. But in a country where real estate has emerged as a full-fledged spectator sport, that's fast becoming a rule that's made to be broken.

Just after 8:00 one evening, Annabella Gualdoni and Jeff Webb are sitting in the living room of Annabella's remodeled Craftsman home just west of Boston, with plates of take-out Chinese perched on their laps. The television is tuned to HGTV. They're watching *House Hunters*.

The show is the highest-rated program on the HGTV cable network—a fact that's remarkable when you deconstruct its simple premise. *House Hunters* follows along as a family shops for a home. It sounds pretty prosaic, but viewers are hooked.

In this episode, a young San Francisco couple hopes to trade up from their cramped 700-square-foot house into something roomier. Gualdoni and Webb cringe as the camera pans the couple's current living room, which is awash with clutter. "What you need is to not have *two giant dogs* in your 700-square-foot house," Gualdoni says to the screen. Blissfully unaware of the insults viewers like Gualdoni might hurl their way when the show airs, the San Francisco couple looks at three homes, ranging in price from just over $500,000 to nearly $800,000. Gualdoni is skeptical. "There's just no way someone has that wide of a budget," she says.

The first home they visit is older, with a small, outdated kitchen. The second is a little larger with a big, unfinished basement. The third home is much more spacious—the living room is almost ballroom size—but it needs serious renovation work, and it's nearly half again as expensive as the first house. "They should probably go for the first one, but I don't think they will—they'll probably go for the second," Webb says. Gualdoni mulls over the choices. "I would go for the third if budget is not a concern," she says. As the show enters its final commercial break, viewers are left wondering: *Which house will they choose?*

Shown in prime time five nights a week, *House Hunters* routinely garners hundreds of thousands of viewers, outperforming much of its competition on the cable dial. And it's just one of the shows, on HGTV and other channels, that are feeding—and feeding off of—America's House Lust. On A&E Network, viewers have watched developers buy dilapidated old homes, execute quick rehabs, and sell them for big profits on *Flip This House*. On Bravo they've tuned in to watch Malibu real estate agents joust for clients and their seven-figure properties on *Million Dollar Listing*. And on ABC they've watched hottie carpenter Ty Pennington lead a do-gooder team of contractors and designers on *Extreme Makeover: Home Edition* who find a needy family, demolish their house, and rebuild it into the stuff of dreams—for free, in just seven days. For people who are really into houses, programmers now offer something to watch seven days a week.

For some people these programs are merely a place to pause while channel surfing. Others consider them worth watching only when there's nothing more compelling on. Then there are people like Gualdoni and Webb, self-proclaimed HGTV addicts for whom these shows are appointment television.

I ask Annabella and Jeff exactly how much real estate television they watch. Gualdoni has been busy lately, so she's logging only ten hours a week. Webb, however, has been home caring for a sick relative, and HGTV has become his constant companion. He watches thirty hours of home shows each week. "That's so embarrassing," he says, later asking me to downsize his estimate to twenty-eight hours.

Watching HGTV with serious fans like these, it turns out, is a bit like watching an NFL game with guys who wear team jerseys and paint their faces before kickoff. They routinely talk back to the television and second-guess the participants' decisions. If it was possible to bet on the outcome of real estate shows, Gualdoni and Webb might be tempted to wager.

Gualdoni, thirty-eight, works at a real estate office, occasionally assisting clients but mostly keeping an eye out for investment properties to buy herself. In addition to her renovated Craftsman, she owns four rental apartments, along with a three-family home she's currently rehabbing to flip. Webb, forty-three, shares her fascination with houses. When he was a child his family spent weekends visiting model homes. Today he pores over the Sunday real estate listings. In a typical year he visits dozens of for-sale homes during weekend open houses—never to buy, just to look. Annabella and Jeff met when they worked in a hospital together a decade ago. They're not a couple—in fact, during our HGTV marathon, Annabella's husband, Vito, sits in an easy chair in the corner, wishing we'd let him watch sports instead.

The commercial break is over, and the *House Hunter* couple returns. The narrator repeats the question, ratcheting up the drama: "Which house will they choose?"

As cliffhangers go, this isn't exactly "Who shot J.R.?" But as their Chinese food grows cold, Annabella and Jeff are on the edge of their seats.

If, like Gualdoni and Webb, you've ever found yourself sucked into watching a few hours of HGTV, you're enjoying a genre of TV that owes its origins, strangely enough, to an omelet.

In the early 1960s, Boston's public television station aired a series called *I've Been Reading*, in which a literature professor chatted on camera with authors of newly published books. One day the show featured a cookbook called *Mastering the Art of French Cooking*. Before she went on the air the book's then-unknown author, Julia Child, asked for a hot plate and some eggs. Instead of just talking about her book, she wanted to do a demonstration by cooking an omelet on live television.

The audience loved this funny, eccentric middle-aged lady, so WGBH assigned a young producer named Russell Morash the task of creating a regular show to feature her. In those pre-Emeril, pre–Rachael Ray days, there were no cooking shows; America was still in the era of overcooked pot roast, Campbell's soup–based casseroles, and jiggly Jell-O molds. But *The French Chef* caught on with the public, and eventually ran from 1962 to 1973, establishing Child as the country's über-chef and earning producer Morash a unique title: the Father of How-to Television.

As *The French Chef* wound down, Morash moved out of the kitchen. First he launched a how-to horticulture show called *Victory Garden*. By the mid-1970s, Morash, the son and grandson of carpenters, had begun toying with ideas for a show about home renovation, his own nights-and-weekends passion. The timing seemed right. With the 1976 Bicentennial looming, America was on a historical kick, and there was growing interest in finding ways to save older homes rather than bulldozing them. The country was also gripped by the energy crisis, and rising fuel costs had people learning to install insulation and make their drafty old homes more energy efficient. Another factor that made the idea appealing: The 1970s were a boom time for real estate, thanks partly to the rampant inflation that was driving up the price of everything.

So in 1975 Morash hired a local contractor named Bob Vila to host a pilot in which Vila toured local houses that had undergone major remodels. That first show didn't turn out very well. Showing completed renovations didn't give viewers any sense of the process— it was sort of like a cooking show that featured only completed·

dishes, but no actual cooking. So four years later Morash spent $12,000 to buy a crumbling house in Boston. He hired a local contractor named Norm Abram to do a top-to-bottom renovation while a camera crew captured the scene. Vila acted as the show's host, interviewing the carpenters and plumbers and providing play-by-play commentary. Lots of people thought Morash was nuts—including his father. "You're making a show about a carpenter?" he asked, incredulous. One of Morash's supervisors figured the show—which Morash called *This Old House*—would die off quickly.

The boss figured wrong. Today *This Old House* is a multimedia franchise with spinoff TV shows and a monthly magazine. Morash is now retired, living in a nineteenth-century home (with kitchen cabinets he built himself), his bookshelves lined with Emmy awards. As I visited with him one evening, he poured us tea and described why, despite colleagues' initial skepticism, he thought the show's wide appeal was so obvious. "A house is the single most expensive thing a family will ever own, and it's fragile. It's always wearing out—even a new one. You worry about your biggest investment, and along comes a TV show to make those worries more manageable," Morash says. "That's why the show works."

Morash wasn't the only one who thought so. During the 1980s, while *This Old House* was busy rebuilding old homes, Ken Lowe was building his career as a programming executive at E. W. Scripps, the Cincinnati-based newspaper and media company. His career required him to relocate to new cities every few years to take bigger jobs, and at each stop he'd move into a house that needed work. But when it came to home improvement, he felt ill-equipped. Lowe recalls: "I was constantly griping to my wife, 'Why doesn't somebody do more television programming in this area?'" Where Russell Morash saw a niche suited for a single public-television show, Ken Lowe had a grander idea: building an entire cable network around home improvement.

By the early 1990s, after years of toying with this brainstorm, Lowe was ready to pitch the idea to his bosses. He used several props to demonstrate how he'd execute it. One was a diagram showing a house, describing how each room could inspire its own program. At another point in his pitch, Lowe held up a newspaper and described how nearly every section had already formed the basis for a successful cable network. The news section inspired CNN, the sports pages inspired ESPN, the business section inspired CNBC, and the food section inspired the Food Network. Then he held up the home and real estate sections. No cable network—not yet anyway. His bosses thought he was onto something, and backed him with $25 million to get the network on the air.

Lowe moved to Knoxville, Tennessee. He picked that location largely because of its low home prices: He thought it crucial for his young production team to be owners, not renters, to make them simpatico with their fledgling audience. The team's toughest task would be creating so many new shows from scratch so quickly. While networks like the History Channel and the Golf Channel—both launched the same year as Lowe's network—could buy up existing programs to fill airtime (World War II documentaries, say, or coverage of last year's U.S. Open), home-related programming was so scarce that Lowe's team had to get production companies to create it. In the first two months after Scripps committed to HGTV, Lowe's team green-lighted twenty-three new series.

When the network launched, on December 30, 1994, it reached just 6.5 million homes. But in a viewer survey by *Broadcasting & Cable* magazine, HGTV ranked second out of twenty new networks in terms of audience interest. HGTV's early shows mimicked the how-to flavor of *This Old House*; although its shows depicted smaller, craft-oriented projects instead of whole-house renovations, many of them consisted largely of the same sort of step-by-step instruction.

But after a few years, executives realized the how-to format was wearing thin. That sentiment grew in mid-1997, when HGTV hired Michael Dingley, a young programming executive from the Discovery Channel. Dingley aimed to get away from the step-by-step formula; he wanted shows to be more entertaining, even for people who had no plans to pull out a glue gun or a jigsaw. Inside the network, Dingley began talking about how every HGTV program should contain the Three I's: Information, Ideas, and Inspiration.

Dingley's first big success was *Designing for the Sexes*, in which an interior decorator mediates between a couple who have conflicting views of how to redo a room. The show did contain lessons on interior design, but it was more story driven, with real people as its stars. For most viewers, the show's biggest payoff came in looking at the before-and-after views of the rooms. Makeover shows like these became a craze after *Trading Spaces* launched in 2000 on TLC. *Trading Spaces,* in which neighbors switch houses and redecorate each other's rooms, was based on a successful British show called *Changing Rooms*; it became the first in a number of successful reality shows (most notably *American Idol*) that were imported to the United States. The show was a huge influence on HGTV shows that followed it. The key moment in all these makeover shows is the "reveal," in which the host dramatically unveils the made-over space and cameras catch homeowners' reactions—whether they're joyous or disastrous. "It's a great visual, and people love the payoff of the results," Dingley says. By 2003, the cable dial was cluttered with home makeover shows— there were more than thirty of them on the air, by one count. But by then Dingley and his colleagues were busy creating shows in which real people buy and sell property.

It's an idea that was sparked when Los Angeles–based television producers and cofounders of Pie Town Productions Jennifer Davidson and Tara Sandler decided to buy a home. During the 1990s the couple had worked with Dingley to produce the Discovery Channel shows A *Baby Story*, which follows a pregnant woman into the delivery room, and A *Wedding Story,* which chronicles the joys and pains of wedding planning. Dingley hired the duo to create *Designer's Challenge,* and when that show began doing well, Dingley made it clear he was open to new ideas.

As the women rode the emotional roller coaster of trying to buy a house in the hot Southern California market, they realized how perfect the process would be for television. "We were freaking out," Davidson says. "We were trying to make a decision whether we were going to put an offer on a house, and it was very dramatic. It had a lot of the dynamics and storytelling we'd been using with A *Baby*

Story and *A Wedding Story*. We recognized that there was as much potential drama in searching for houses as there was in watching people give birth." At around the same time the seller accepted their offer to buy a house in Studio City, Sandler and Davidson called Dingley and pitched the idea for a show called *House Hunters*. He quickly ordered up twenty-six episodes. The first one aired in 2000.

Within a couple of years *House Hunters* was the network's hottest show, fueled largely by the public's increasing fascination with real estate. And inside HGTV the race was on to find new ways to capitalize on America's obsession with homes.

Beth Burke is sitting in her Midtown Manhattan office, talking into her speakerphone. Burke, thirty-eight, used to be a producer at VH1, where she helped launch *I Love the '80s*. In 2005 she jumped up the cable dial, becoming a director of original programming at HGTV. In this job Burke oversees a handful of the network's real estate shows, coordinating the network's dealings with the independent production teams that do the actual filming. Her most important job is to work with producers to make each show as compelling as possible. She looks at rough-cut edits of each episode, offering notes on how to improve them. It's her job to keep channel surfers from clicking away.

When she first joined the network, she was assigned to work on *House Hunters*. She'd seen the show before, but she was amazed to learn it was the network's biggest hit. "It's literally a couple looking at three different houses—does that sound to you like a hit show?" she says, still incredulous. As the daughter of a real estate agent, Burke is familiar with the small dramas involved in buying and selling homes, but she's still amazed that her employer was able to turn them into a commercially successful program.

Burke has since moved on from *House Hunters*. Today there's a whiteboard in her office listing the shows she's supervising. Near the top is a new program called *Get It Sold*. The show features a family that's been trying to sell their home, but hasn't had any luck. So the host and a real estate agent work together to stage the house—reducing clutter, moving furniture, and doing very cheap cosmetic fixes. *Get It Sold* sounds quite similar to another HGTV show called *Designed to Sell*, in which a designer and carpentry team spend a few thousand dollars to fix up a for-sale home, in hopes of boosting its sales price. The difference, apparently, is in the scale of the makeover, with *Get It Sold* involving much lighter lifting. Still, the similarities are evidence of the popularity of this new genre: Viewers have such an appetite for real estate shows that HGTV has little concern about airing two different shows with such similar premises.

As I sit in Burke's office, she's on the phone with *Get It Sold*'s top producer in California, along with a field producer in Washington, D.C. They're talking about the home of Paul and Naomi Cummings of Arlington, Virginia, whom producers are considering for an upcoming episode. Burke has seen photos of the inside of the family's home, and she's not convinced they're right for the show.

"The house looks *kind of* a mess?" Burke asks the field producer.

"It's a total mess," the producer says, describing how Mrs. Cummings is a packrat who holds on to everything. "It's not like they're shabby, but she just has this collector's sensibility—they just can't declutter." The couple has already lowered the price, but they've still received no offers.

Burke probes further. "I just really want it to look like a mess inside. It looks pretty bad in the pitch, but is it as bad as it looks?"

After a few minutes of back-and-forth, Burke is convinced the couple needs her show's intervention. She approves the Arlington house for the next episode of *Get It Sold*.

It's a brief exchange, one of dozens of decisions someone like Burke makes during the course of the day. But it illustrates how the network cultivates what it calls "the Oops Factor," which it understands to be one of the reasons home shows are so appealing to viewers.

Casual viewers may assume all these shows appeal mainly to house voyeurs, and that the main appeal is catching a glimpse inside someone else's house. The voyeuristic appeal of these shows is one reason the entire genre has been derided as "real estate porn"; back in the 1990s, Harvard professor Marjorie Garber wrote a book called *Sex and Real Estate* exploring this meme. But, in fact, there's a far more complex set of forces at work when we watch these shows—and it's a set of emotions the folks at HGTV have become skillful at exploiting. In the *Poetics*, Aristotle deconstructs how playwrights create effective tragedy, leaving viewers with a complex mix of pity, fear, and epiphany en route to climax and resolution. Sitcoms, action movies, and news shows all have similar dramatic conventions, aimed at heightening their emotional appeal.

And if you spend enough hours watching home shows, talking with devoted fans, and watching over the shoulders of the people tasked with producing them, you start to understand a few of the keys to their appeal.

The Oops Factor: When Burke frets over whether the Cummings home is truly a design disaster, she's acknowledging a requisite element of home improvement shows: To be effective, the "before" scenes in the before-and-after transformation have to be compellingly offensive, the equivalent of a home-design train wreck from which viewers can't avert their eyes.

This emotion is exploited most obviously on personal makeover shows, like *Queer Eye for the Straight Guy* or *What Not to Wear*, in which the hosts dress down their premakeover subjects, ridiculing their clothing, haircut, and other flawed fashion statements. The same emotions explain the appeal of the audition episodes of *American Idol*, in which producers showcase some of the worst singers, holding them up for ridicule. Our mothers may have urged us not to laugh at the misfortunes of others, but nowadays there's no shortage of TV shows that have found ratings gold via schadenfreude, by letting us laugh at people who are lousy singers, can't properly dress themselves, or don't know where to put the sofa in their family room.

At HGTV there's an aversion to the obvious nastiness displayed by hosts like *American Idol*'s Simon Cowell. While staffers exploit the fact that their viewers enjoy catching glimpses of their neighbor's bad taste, on the air they require hosts to deal with the subjects' shortcomings with diplomacy and kindness. At HGTV the prevailing attitude is that no matter how bad one of the houses might look, viewers should be laughing with participants, not at them.

Back in Massachusetts, HGTV addicts Annabella Gualdoni and Jeff Webb are acutely aware of this element of the shows' appeal. Just as some fans watch NASCAR races hoping to see a nasty crash, they love to see houses decorated so badly they can't be sold. "You want to see something really ugly, to be able to go, 'Man, those people have bad taste,'" Gualdoni says. Their favorite part of the "staging" shows like *Designed to Sell* is when a hidden camera captures the pre-makeover reaction of potential buyers, who are secretly taped as they tour the for-sale home. "They're ripping apart the house—'It smells like dog in here'—and that's kind of fun," Gualdoni says.

The Getting-smarter Factor: HGTV has come a long way from the days when every episode featured step-by-step instruction. But the people creating these shows still believe that viewers long for a takeaway—a tangible reward and a new set of skills they earn in exchange for the thirty minutes they've spent watching. Even without an obvious how-to formula, producers aim to bake in a lot of implicit instruction.

Gualdoni is convinced she's profited from the time she's spent parked in front of home shows. As we walk through her home—which she and Vito renovated themselves—she points to rooms that were inspired by shows like *Trading Spaces*. When Gualdoni looks at homes for sale, she feels better equipped to weigh the homes' strengths and weaknesses because she's taken virtual tours of thousands of homes from the comfort of her living room by watching these TV shows. Now she can actually visualize what a prospective purchase will look like when she's finished working on it. "That definitely comes from watching these shows," she says.

Webb sees signs that Gualdoni isn't the only one learning from this genre of programming. When he visits open houses these days, he's grown accustomed to seeing properties that look far more put-together than the ones he saw a few years ago. He attributes that mostly to the public's embrace of the concepts taught on shows like *Designed to Sell*. People are more aware that walls should be bathed in neutral paint colors; that countertops should be barren; that too many family photos will turn off potential buyers; and that Dad's beer-cap collection belongs in a box in the basement, not on the coffee table. Before these shows caught on, most Americans simply vacuumed and tidied up before letting potential buyers wander through. Now, Webb says, many sellers seem to be using the knowledge they've gained from HGTV to conduct their own extreme makeover before they call a real estate agent.

The Game-show Factor: When producers at Pie Town first pitched HGTV on a show that follows couples as they hunt for a home, programming czar Michael Dingley suggested they try a format similar to the one used on *Designer's Challenge*. One key to that show's appeal is that viewers are left guessing (or even talking among themselves during commercials) about which of the three decorators the homeowner will (or should) choose for the assignment. Likewise, Dingley suggested that *House Hunters* should play up the suspense surrounding which property the house hunters will choose. "It's such a simple format, it sort of lulls you into submission," says Pie Town's Sandler. "It's *Goldilocks and the Three Bears* over and over. 'This house is too big, this house is too small, this house is just right.'"

Shows that let viewers play along at home have a long history of success. Game shows have held a place in the American consciousness for a half century, and one key to the *American Idol* phenomenon is that show's ingenious method of turning viewers' passive preferences into an active element in the show, by letting them vote on the winners via text messages and toll-free calls.

Few people play along at home with HGTV shows as much as Jeff Webb. During the cliffhanger moment in *House Hunters*, Webb tries to answer three questions himself: Which house *will* they buy? Which house *should* they buy? And which house would *he* buy? Even for a guy who watches many hours of these shows, he's found he has a hard time predicting the house hunters' choices, and he suspects that's intentional. "I think the producers are editing buyers' comments so they'll throw us off the trail," he says. The more likely explanation is that people just behave unpredictably regarding such an emotionally charged issue as which home to buy.

The I-know-what-your-house-costs Factor: When Beth Burke began working on *House Hunters*, one element of the show really irritated her. While the host gave a vague sense of the buyer's price range, viewers weren't told exactly what each of the houses cost, nor what the buyer ended up paying. She called the producers to ask about the obfuscation. "They said, 'People don't really like to say the price of the house,'" Burke recalls. "So I said, 'If they won't say the prices of the houses, they won't be on the show.' And you know what? People would rather be on television than not say the price of their house." As soon as episodes that disclosed the prices began hitting the air, the show's ratings began rising. Those ratings provide numerical proof of a concept most of us know intuitively: We're endlessly fascinated by other people's finances, and knowing what someone paid for their home can offer a delicious look into their pocketbook.

Once producers saw how discussing the real prices of homes seemed to bump ratings, HGTV began creating entire shows built around the concept. In *What You Get for the Money*, producers pick a particular price point—say, homes worth $350,000—and visit four or five different cities, showing viewers exactly how big and how nice a home they could buy if they relocated. In *National Open House*, producers pick four different price points (perhaps $300,000, then $600,000, then $900,000, then $2 million) and present faster-paced looks at how those price levels compare in a few different cities. These shows seem particularly appealing to people whose homes appreciated during the boom, since some of them fantasize selling their pricey home, moving somewhere more affordable, and banking their profits. It's a practice some have begun calling "real estate arbitrage," and these shows help fuel that dream.

Even on HGTV's existing shows, there's a lot more discussion of home prices than there was in the past. "That's the big trend on all the networks," says Davidson. "These shows are now playing up what these folks spent on their houses, how much their renovations cost, how much their house appreciated. Money, money, money—it's a big component."

Back at HGTV's Manhattan office, every day around 3:30 p.m. the staff receives an e-mail containing the ratings for the previous night's shows. After its arrival you'll sometimes hear jubilant yells up and down Burke's hallway. Some offices will stay silent. Ultimately these ratings are the bottom-line measure of just how well Burke and her colleagues have done mixing these various elements to make shows that viewers can't bear to tune out.

While HGTV's ratings have held solid—and even improved—as the housing market cooled, the advertising community still sees room for improvement. The average HGTV viewer is a woman in her early fifties, and ad buyers would be happier if the shows attracted a younger audience and more males. Ad buyers I spoke with suspect most people watch real estate shows only when there's nothing better on. "The older demographic suggests that these shows are filler programming, not something you really choose," says Kristi Argyilan, executive vice president at Arnold Worldwide, a Boston-based ad agency.

Still, advertisers do see some positives about the new genre. Because the shows are about design and home improvement, they're an ideal spot to place ads for appliances, Home Depot, or paint; the theory, backed up by research, is that since viewers are watching the show to pick up tips on making their home better, they're naturally more amenable to watching ads for products that serve the same function. And even if, for many of us, shows like *House Hunters* or *Flip This House* are programs of last resort, something to gaze at when it's just too early to go to sleep, the ad buyers see an advantage in that. Unlike destination television, which many viewers set for recording on their TiVo (or other digital recording device), many people seem to be watching real estate programs live, and not skipping through the commercials.

At HGTV they're aware their viewers are too old, but there's only so far they're willing to go to fix that problem. "When I first came in from VH1, I was like, 'We've got to shake things up and make it a little bit crazy,'" Burke says. "But you know what? That's not really what people want out of this network. Yes, we can get some cute young hosts and freshen things up. But people just enjoy it because it doesn't get too crazy, and it doesn't change too much."

When Annabella Gualdoni began selling real estate, one behavior annoyed her more than all others: when friends declined to let her represent them because they didn't want her to know how much they were spending on their house.

Gualdoni scoffs at their naivete. "I'm [thinking], 'When we hang up the phone I'm just going to go into [the Multiple Listing Service, a real estate database] and see how much you paid for it; then I can go into the Registry of Deeds database and see what your mortgage is,'" she says. "Some people are really secretive about price, but it's out there—anybody can figure it out. I don't have any special powers. I just know where to look."

Strictly speaking, it's still considered a breach of etiquette to disclose the price you've paid for a house or to ask someone the value of theirs. To confirm that, I called Peter Post, Emily's great-grandson and a modern-day etiquette guru. Post tells me it's okay to talk in very general terms about one's financial hits and misses—to say you closed a really big deal at work, or have done really well owning a certain stock. But even if the price you paid for a house is easily available online, Post says it's still impolite to talk about it. "It makes people uncomfortable when other people start talking dollar numbers, even if everybody could go look it up," Post says. The subtext of any of these conversations, he believes, is "My house is worth $450,000, and yours is only worth $300,000." It's a subject that well-mannered people would just as soon avoid.

The money taboo remains firmly in place when it comes to talking about one's earnings. But in many places it's become slightly less scandalous to talk about home values. For evidence of the shift, look to HGTV, which now requires the people on many of its shows to disclose this information—and is still flooded with aspiring guests. This shift in mores is partly a function of the market boom we've gone through, and partly a function of the Internet.

This is, in many ways, one of the *less* revolutionary behavioral changes produced by the Internet, which is creating a new openness about all aspects of life. A few pages away from Braden Keil's *New York Post* real estate column, the *Post's* gossip pages often contain items on Joe Francis, the guy behind *Girls Gone Wild* who's made millions by convincing tipsy coeds to lift their shirts for his video camera—a business model that, one suspects, wouldn't have been so successful in more innocent, pre-Internet days. In Hollywood, aspirant celebrities now routinely leak homemade sex tapes in what's becoming a well-choreographed career strategy to raise one's stature in the public eye.

Compared with these exhibitionist behaviors, disclosing what you paid for a house seems rather tame, but it's still a sensitive area for some. Online one day I met a woman who calls herself Madame X. She runs a financial blog with the subtitle "An Anonymous New Yorker Tells the World How Much She Earns, Spends and Saves." When we talk by phone she declines to give her name. But even though she anonymously discloses to the world her income (which, including her bonus, should hit $100,000 in 2007), in her off-line life she's told only a handful of people—perhaps four or five close friends and a few family members—how much she just spent for her first home, a Brooklyn condo purchased for just over $300,000.

Madame X says it's not uncommon for people in her circle to commiserate about the cost of their homes. She sees the behavior as part of a proud tradition of New Yorkers complaining about the expense of everything, the same way Los Angelinos complain about traffic and Bostonians kvetch about the weather. But Madame X also attributes some of this increasing openness to the Internet. "Some of the information may have been in the public record before, but who was going to go look it up at City Hall?" she asks. "Now things are much more Google-able and searchable, so people are more curious and start poking around."

Still, even a woman who bares her finances online remains a little shy about money in real life. "I wouldn't come right out and ask someone what they paid for their apartment—it would just feel kind of weird," she says. "But if they started to talk about it and offered the information, it'd certainly be interesting."

Lockhart Steele understands the appeal. In May 2004, after a few years of toiling in the new-media trenches, Steele launched the blog he calls Curbed. "In New York City it all comes back to real estate, rent, and the neighborhoods we inhabit," he wrote, laying forth his vision for Curbed to become "the center of the virtual conversation about real estate in Manhattan, Queens, and beyond."

Home prices are not Curbed's focus. But in reporting on celebrity transactions, the latest marketing plans by condo builders, and the skirmishes between the city's big brokers, property values are a key ingredient in the stew of real estate information that makes Curbed so compelling. Truth be told, Steele is more interested in urban planning than what Ethan Hawke and Matt Lauer paid for their brownstones. "I don't get out of bed every morning and say, 'Oh, my God, I can't wait to look at the real estate listings today," he says, noting that at age thirty-two, he still rents his third-floor walkup apartment. "The reality is my obsession is about neighborhoods—I love chronicling how they evolve and change." Still, he realizes that most of the 25,000 daily visitors to his blog are real estate nuts, so a considerable number of his postings are aimed at satisfying readers' appetites for insight into the homes other New Yorkers are buying and selling.

One regular feature is called Floor Plan Porn. It's a graphical element that shows the layout and dimensions of lavish Manhattan apartments for sale. On Wednesdays real estate appraiser Jonathan Miller posts charts and other wonky statistical analysis of the market. In a typical installment he calculates that two-bedroom co-ops have been gaining value more than other apartments, and that the average price differential between a two-bedroom and a three-bedroom apartment now stands at around $2 million. Curbed's take on that factlet: "Your guests will have to sleep on the couch."

If you live in New York and care about real estate, Curbed can be downright addictive. But it's not national, and it contains only limited information on any one property. That's why, for online home enthusiasts, there have become far more popular places for online home snoopery.

The first is Realtor.com, which lists every home for sale by a real estate agent in the United States. In an average month it attracts around seven million unique viewers. According to the site's research, half those visitors aren't really considering buying a home. They're just browsing. "Some are pure voyeurs, recreational users who have no intention of moving," says Alan Merrill, the Web site's executive vice president. Some are just ogling high-priced homes; others are keeping tabs on listings in their neighborhood. I understand the appeal: I'm far more likely to kill a few minutes window-shopping on Realtor.com than I am on eBay or Craigslist.

For home browsers who really want to drill down, though, the prime destination is Zillow. The site, created by an Internet mogul who was himself frustrated when he tried to find information on homes in his neighborhood while preparing to list his own property, went live in early 2006. The day it opened the site crashed under massive traffic; in its first month of operation it attracted millions of visitors. TV news shows pounced; *Fortune* magazine put it on the cover. In creating a case that millions of Americans have a burning interest in other people's houses, Zillow's popularity is the smoking gun.

On the surface, Zillow's mission is to help you estimate your home value using a proprietary algorithm and public property data it's aggregated from hundreds of county tax offices and real estate listings. Many users claim its estimates are wildly off base, but no matter: Most of them keep clicking to the site anyway. And while just about everyone checks on the value of their own home, most users also check out the values of other people's houses, too. During the site's first month of operation, the average visitor spent twenty-one minutes per visit at Zillow—far more time than is required to look up one's own house.

Just months after the site's launch, tales of these voyeuristic expeditions were already plentiful. At Zillow headquarters, workers heard stories of people who went through their Christmas card lists, Zillowing the names of everyone they knew. Some companies began using the site to get a sense of job applicants' net worth. Writing in the *Los Angeles Times*, Meghan Daum admitted to a drunken, post–2:00 a.m. Zillow binge in which she targeted the homes of "at least twenty friends and neighbors, not to mention a handful of crushes, colleagues, former professors, former bosses . . . a number of exes, their exes and the women they dated after they broke up with me." (She admitted to gloating upon learning that some of her exes apparently couldn't afford to buy a house yet.) Daum concluded that Zillow offers something far more than a private glimpse of someone's net worth. The site, she writes, "offers an intangible yet extraordinarily revealing window into our aspirations."

Within days of its launch, Zillow was being used as a verb, just like Google. People used to Google someone before going on a blind date. Now they could Zillow them, too. Less than a year after Zillow's launch, the *Wall Street Journal* reported on a postwedding party where the discussion of home prices became so intense the entire gathering migrated to the host's computer, fishing out address books to do a group Zillow of everyone they knew.

For Bobbie Conti, a Seattle data analyst, the site became, for a time, an almost daily stop. On her first visit she looked up her own house, of course. Its valuation was nearly spot-on—just $4,000 different from a professional appraisal she'd recently had done. She Zillowed her neighbors and ex-boyfriends, and began to visit the site five or six times a week, for perhaps ten minutes at a time. Is this habit becoming . . . a problem? "I'm not an addictive personality," she says. "I just like data a lot." Her biggest surprise regarding Zillow isn't that a group of Americans has found a new hobby in looking up the value of one another's homes—it's that some aren't shy about it. One friend readily admitted to Zillowing Conti and her parents. "It wasn't this sheepish thing after half an hour of discussion," Conti says, describing how the friend owned up to it immediately and unabashedly. "I would have waited awhile to admit it . . . but I guess it's okay to do."

Peter Post and his better-mannered brethren may look down their noses at such behavior. But along with giving us etiquette-busting abominations like the e-mailed thank-you note, the Internet has changed everything—and for many of us, ogling our neighbors' homes on the Internet is a guilty pleasure that's here to stay.

Back in the Gualdonis' living room, the San Francisco episode of *House Hunters* has reached its climax. Will this couple choose the undersize home with the outdated kitchen, the midpriced property with the unfinished basement, or the upscale fixer-upper with the ballroom-size living room? As Annabella Gualdoni and Jeff Webb watch intently, the announcer throws them a twist. Apparently this episode was filmed when the San Francisco market was still red-hot. Even though the couple has offered $40,000 above the asking price for home number two, theirs wasn't the highest of the multiple offers. To give them an advantage, however, their real estate agent has written a heartfelt letter to the seller, explaining why this couple deserves the house. The letter so moved the sellers that they passed over the higher bidders and awarded the home to the lower-bidding *House Hunters* pair.

"That's crap," Gualdoni yells at the screen. "That's crap."

"I don't believe that," Webb says.

"That letter puts you at an advantage on an equal offer, but there's *no way* the seller is going to accept a lower offer," Gualdoni says. "No way."

"I don't believe that either," Webb says.

The show fast-forwards one year, revisiting the couple after they've settled into the home. Upstairs they've done a ton of redecorating, and the kitchen and their new home office look fabulous. Downstairs they've turned the unfinished basement into a lavish master bedroom–and–bathroom suite. Webb and Gualdoni grow quiet, murmuring approval. "Oh, man, nice," Webb says, eyeing the new bathroom and laundry. Outside they've done a massive landscaping project that lowered the backyard by several feet, enhancing its private feel, and added a deck. "I want to know how they're getting all their money," Gualdoni says.

As *House Hunters* ends, another real estate show—this one called *Buy Me*—comes on. Annabella's husband would still prefer to be watching ESPN, but we stay tuned to HGTV.

As shows like these have grown in popularity, critics wondered whether real estate television might be experiencing its own bubble. Observers opined that these shows would inevitably suffer their own version of what's commonly called the "CNBC Effect," which refers to how ratings for the financial news channel tend to rise and fall with the stock market. When home sales flattened out, skeptics predicted, shows like *House Hunters* and *Designed to Sell* were doomed to fade away, too.

So far there's no evidence of that. In fact, HGTV programming czar Michael Dingley is convinced just the opposite phenomenon will take hold: The more people worry about the value of their own home declining, the more inclined they'll be to watch shows that can teach them the tricks to protect their investment. Russell Morash, the man who dreamed up the genre more than three decades ago, is convinced he's right. "I think these shows are bulletproof for a simple reason," he says. "The subject is so fundamental: *shelter*."

So if you feel a momentary pang of guilt while Zillowing your exboyfriend, take heart: Your prehistoric ancestors would have done the same thing with their neighbors' caves, if only they'd had the right tools.

CHAPTER FIVE

SEARCHING FOR CASH FLOW:
POCATELLO, IDAHO

How Run-down Rental Property Became the New 401(k)

On a sunny July afternoon I'm driving south on Foothills Boulevard
in search of house number 77. To my right lies the Bannock moun-
tain range, and in front of it, up a small embankment, sits a row of
working-class houses. I find number 77, a two-family home purchased recently by a man named Edi Stocker. Out front is a pickup
truck sitting on the gravel driveway.

I pick up my cell phone and dial Stocker's number. When he answers, I inform him that I'm parked in front of his new duplex. He's
intrigued. "How does it look?" he asks. "How's the neighborhood?"

These may seem odd questions for a new homeowner to ask
about his property. But like a lot of people who've been buying
houses here recently, Stocker has never been to Pocatello. In fact, the
California resident has never even been to Idaho. And though he's recently purchased real estate in Alabama, Tennessee, and Florida, he's
never visited any of those homes, either.

Stocker, a computer systems manager at a technology company, is
an unlikely property magnate. But like a lot of middle-class people
burned by the dot-com stock crash, he decided to pursue a different
strategy. One weekend that quest took him to an investment boot

camp, where a real estate expert tutored him on why houses trump stocks as a route to riches. The guru pointed Stocker—and hundreds of other people—to markets like Pocatello, where low prices and strong demographics add up to a can't-miss proposition. At the end of the seminar the boot camp organizers put attendees in contact with real estate agents in these faraway cities to help them find the perfect parcel. Many bought in, hoping that it would only be a matter of time before Donald Trump has to watch his back.

The Foothill Boulevard apartments that I'm checking out represent a pretty typical deal. Stocker purchased the building with help from a Pocatello agent who specializes in selling homes to out-of-state investors. The entire transaction took place via e-mail, telephone, and FedEx, with the broker e-mailing photos and inspection reports, and Stocker overnighting signed offers and wiring down payments. So if Stocker's apartments stay occupied, the rental income he receives should more than cover the costs of the mortgage, taxes, and insurance, leaving him with "positive cash flow"—the holy grail of this new breed of property investors. And over time, as the mortgage balance goes down and property values go up, Stocker should be left with a valuable addition to his net worth.

Buying houses over the Internet is a decidedly twenty-first-century behavior. But there's nothing new about people buying property with an eye toward investment. In medieval Europe feudal lords lived off the rents paid by their serfs. In nineteenth-century America one of the nation's largest fortunes was built by John Jacob Astor, the German-born fur trader who bought big swaths of undeveloped land in New York City. Before his death Astor remarked: "Could I begin life again, knowing what I know now, and had money to invest, I would buy every foot of land on the island of Manhattan."

But during the early part of this century investing in property became a far more democratic pursuit—pursued not just by the Astors and the Trumps, but by thousands of middle-class people, too. Some of them, like Stocker, were buying low-priced rental homes, which they intended to hold for the long term. Others hoped to do quick rehabs they could "flip" for profits, an activity celebrated on new television programs like *Flip This House*. And in the hottest markets, like Phoenix and Miami, people found a novel way to profit: They'd put down payments on new-construction homes, which they'd often sell before they were even ready for occupancy, capitalizing on fast-rising prices.

For generations most Americans had been content investing in a single house—the one they lived in. Suddenly some people were collecting homes the way elementary school boys collect baseball cards.

It's hard to measure exactly how many Americans began buying houses to flip, rent, or rehab during the recent boom, but most data suggests it's a big number. In 2004, according to one Wall Street analyst's calculations, the percentage of homes bought by investors reached 14.5 percent of all residential real estate transactions, double the average from 1978 to 2002. By 2005 one real estate economist figured, 27.7 percent of the seven million houses that changed hands were bought by someone with no plans to live there or use them for vacation homes, but simply to try to make money off them.

In a memorable cover story published at the height of this speculative boom, *Fortune* magazine's Grainger David reported on characters like Zareh Tahmassebian, who'd place small deposits on preconstruction homes. "See this wood?" he said, pointing to the frame of a half-built Phoenix house he'd agreed to buy. "This wood made money for me! I don't own it, but I own the rights . . . and it's already gone up $45,000. What a country!" Grainger encountered one middle-class couple who'd bought so many investment properties so quickly they couldn't recall whether they owned eight, ten, or twelve residences. (The correct answer, it turned out, was twenty.)

Back in Pocatello, a few blocks away from Edi Stocker's new house sit the apartment buildings recently purchased by Judy Peterson, fifty-nine, a California special-education teacher. After her son attended a real estate seminar, Peterson liquidated her retirement accounts (paying a steep tax penalty) and bought a three-family house in Pocatello. Then she bought another property. And another. By the middle of 2005, when I first visited Pocatello, Peterson owned eight apartments there, which were all rented out. "I have friends who say,

'You did *what*?' But I think this is a better risk than the stock market," she says. "You can't find investments like this in California."

You can't find them in Massachusetts, where I live, either. So, after spending a lot of time talking with people like Edi Stocker and Judy Peterson, I decided to join their party. Before I knew it I was the proud owner of a couple of run-down Pocatello apartments myself.

If you hang out in business schools, you'll hear finance professors describe the many reasons why the stock market is, for most people, a smarter investment than real estate. Stocks are more liquid, meaning you can buy and sell them in an instant, paying only tiny brokerage commissions. In contrast, selling a piece of real estate can require months and consume thousands of dollars in commissions and closing costs. Historically, stocks outperform houses in terms of investment returns over the long term. It's easier to diversify with stocks, spreading your bets across a variety of companies in a wide array of industries; with real estate, you're betting a bundle on a single piece of property whose fortunes are tied to one local economy.

But during the housing boom, a lot of people began to question that wisdom. Many opted to invest in homes instead of—or in addition to—stocks and mutual funds. It was a shift in investor preference driven by at least a half dozen factors.

At the top of this list is the dot-com meltdown. Nearly everyone I met who began investing in real estate in the early 2000s lost money when technology stocks collapsed. For many people it was a searing experience, one that soured them on stock investing in general. Housing prices in many areas had begun rising sharply, so after being burned by stocks, people sought refuge in property.

In explaining the appeal of this different asset class, many of them cite a key attribute: Unlike stocks, real estate is tangible. The fact that people can see and touch property gives it an aura of security lacking in other modern investments, which exist primarily as only blips in our online accounts. As one Pocatello investor put it to me: "People don't *need* GE stock—GE stock could go down to zero. But no matter what happens with the market, everybody needs a place to live." After watching stocks like Enron actually go to zero, some people found that logic compelling.

The third factor driving investors' frenzy for houses is the easy financing. Just fifteen years ago, getting a mortgage could be an ordeal: Borrowers had to have solid credit and fill out mountains of paperwork, their finances and character carefully assessed by local bankers. During the 1990s that changed, as computerized credit scores, the securitization of mortgage debt, and the emergence of "no-documentation" and subprime loans made it possible for many marginal borrowers to get money to buy houses. Access to capital is a key element of any boom; easy money from venture capitalists drove the tech bubble, and low interest rates and easy credit have been prime drivers of the private equity craze. In the same way that easy credit allowed people in previous chapters to build supersize homes or finance mammoth renovations, it also allowed people like Edi Stocker—and eventually even me—to borrow to buy investment properties.

The fourth key to people's fondness for real estate investing is the leverage it offers. There is nothing new about leverage, but during the recent boom more people came to understand its magic. While the bravest stock investors can buy securities "on margin," most stock players invest only money that's actually theirs. In contrast, the vast majority of people buying real estate—whether it's a house to live in or an investment—put up only a small slice of the price in cash, and finance the rest. That leverage acts as a magnifier of returns. If you put $10,000 down on a $100,000 property that appreciates by 10 percent in a year, your $10,000 investment has doubled in value. Of course, leverage can also work in reverse, magnifying your losses.

The fifth element of the appeal of this way of investing is the cash flow it can provide. When you invest in a 401(k), you're required to let your employer suck out a portion of each paycheck, and no stranger is going to make that payment for you. In many real estate investments, in contrast, once you pay the up-front costs, you're hoping the ongoing monthly expenses will be paid for by tenants to whom you rent the property. You can also tax-deduct many of the costs, including depreciation on the property and interest on the mortgage, boosting your cash flow even further. Sure, there are huge risks to this way of investing—if the property lies vacant or tenants trash the place, you could lose big. But if all goes well, your property increases in value without requiring you to lay out cash every month—and if you're lucky, the rental income may exceed your monthly expenses, giving you positive cash flow. What's not to like about that?

The last explanation for why so many people jumped onto the property bandwagon is the reason so many of us do dumb things: We're following the herd. And in the same way that people bragged about owning Netscape or Amazon during the dot-com era, during the housing boom there was a cachet to being able to brag about property ownership. Simply put, buying property became cool.

On the surface, Pocatello seems an unlikely place to explore the phenomenon. Shouldn't I be visiting Miami or Phoenix, the usual datelines for stories of irrationally exuberant real estate investors? In fact, I ended up in Idaho because one morning my *Newsweek* editor noticed a small chart in the *Wall Street Journal* that showed the ten housing markets where investors made up the biggest percentage of recent mortgage applicants. The table consisted largely of towns in California, Arizona, and Florida—predictable places where boom-era speculation was rampant. But the third-ranking city on the list was Pocatello. "Why are so many people buying investment property in a place like that?" he asked me. I started calling Pocatello real estate agents, who said they'd suddenly become inundated with calls from out-of-state folks looking to buy rental homes there. The chief attractions: a moderately strong economy and superlow home prices. In 2005, when I visited, the average home in Pocatello was selling for just $98,000.

As I drove around the city, looking at the shabby little homes people were buying over the Internet without even walking the property, part of me thought: "This is nuts." But the more I looked at the numbers, the more I found that, with the right property, the right tenants, and the right person to manage it, this might be an investment that makes sense. And before I knew it I owned a Pocatello property all my own, with all the upsides—and downsides—that go with it.

Like most of the people who wind up perusing Pocatello property online, my journey began in a hotel ballroom, at a real estate seminar.

It wasn't hard to locate one. During the real estate boom, all you had to do was open your e-mail in-box, channel surf to a late-night TV infomercial, or open a newspaper to find experts touting surefire ways to make a bundle investing in housing. "How to Make Money in Any Real Estate Market," read the headline in my local paper one morning. "You Haven't Missed Your Chance." Midway down the left side of the page was a photo of a grinning man named Carleton H. Sheets. "Over the past 35 years, and through every market imaginable, I've bought and sold more than $20 million in real estate," read the caption. "I personally guarantee the skills you can learn from my Real Profit$ Active Learning Method can sharpen your senses and take you through any market condition."

The following Sunday afternoon I find a seat in a hotel conference center. At the front of the room is a large projection screen. The room darkens, and Sheets, in a blue blazer, grins down from the screen. He's standing in the foyer of a lavish home with a fancy dual staircase, a little like the Goldbergs' home I described earlier in the book. "Because of the soaring popularity of this program, I'm sorry I can't be with you personally today," he tells us. "I've sent a trusted associate of mine." The video turns off, the lights come up, and Karl Noons takes the stage. The fact that Carleton himself isn't here already has me feeling a little bit like the victim of a bait-and-switch, but I decide to stay.

Noons is broad-shouldered, forty-nine, and wears a sports coat and an open collar. He says he grew up in Rhode Island—not far from today's seminar—and was an unspectacular student. "I was no different than anybody else in this room," he says. After high school he spent time as a painter, then moved to Hawaii and worked in construction. His life changed, he testifies, when he began studying with Sheets seventeen years ago. Within weeks he'd done his first real estate deal, netting $12,000 in profits. After lots of one-on-one training, Noons says he emerged as a top student and close friend of the guru. Today Noons lives in Sugarland, Texas. He says he's bought and sold more than 300 properties, and cleared well in excess of $1 million in profits. He puts a stack of tax returns on a table and offers to let us examine them. (The effect is a little like if your college professor carried copies of his degrees into class.) On the projection screen he shows photos of the luxury home in Hawaii where he spends half the year.

By now there are thirty-one students in the room. Noons's assistants keep bringing out more chairs to accommodate late arrivals. The group includes six women and four African Americans, but the average attendee is a middle-aged white guy. Asked to raise their hands, about half say they're currently renters; half own their homes. Six have previously purchased investment properties. All but four say they've seen Sheets's infomercials on television.

For the next two hours Noons repeats a lot of the same catchphrases. He emphasizes over and over that he's no smarter or better than any of us—he's just gotten "professional training." He talks repeatedly of his closeness to Sheets, saying that "Carleton wanted me to tell you . . ." He offers up the fact that seven in ten millionaires make their fortunes in real estate. The difference between them and us, he says, is the professional training they've received that enables them to "take it to the next level."

The next level, it turns out, is a $3,995, three-day intensive session. What we're getting today is simply a preview of the professional training he's offering—the way a drug dealer will offer buyers a taste before money changes hands. During today's seminar Noons doesn't really teach anything: He's merely telling us what he *will* teach us if we sign up for the three-day class.

Thirty-five minutes into his shtick, Noons removes his jacket. He begins explaining the benefits of leverage and no-money-down purchasing, and how it's possible—even in high-priced markets like Boston—to find investments that will yield positive cash flow. "I've cash-flowed in Hawaii. I've cash-flowed in California," he says, his voice rising. "Out of 300 properties, I've never not positive cash-flowed. Why? It's because of my professional training."

Instead of just bidding on regular houses, Noons says students who "take it to the next level" will learn how to purchase foreclosed homes and other distressed properties at big discounts from home-owners in financial crisis. On the screen images of nearby homes quickly flash by: 59 Hooper Road, 7 Dale Road, 27 Lincoln Avenue. To help with financing, Noons will even give students the phone number for his personal lender, Waleed. And to really learn how to discover good properties, on the third day of the professional training seminar we'll board buses and tour listed houses.

With fifteen minutes left in the two-hour session, Noons is speaking loudly and more quickly, shifting into high selling mode. The dates for the three-day seminar flash on the screen. If we're worried about our ability to get financing to make a real estate investment, he says, bring in the listing for a good property the first day, and he'll go in halvesies with us, splitting the profits. On the screen, under the heading "Invest in Yourself," the original price—$3,995—is slashed to an "Action Discount" price of $2,995. "That's just $8 a day for the next year," Noons tell us, utilizing the trusty Save-the-Children-style math. If we attend the seminar and aren't happy after the first day, we can get a full refund. If we do a real estate deal and don't make $3,000 in prof-its, Sheets will give us our money back. "The only way you can lose here is if you go back out those doors and do nothing," Noons says.

After his session ends, a handful of students begin registering for the three-day class. Other students crowd around Noons. One asks for Waleed's number. (Noons declines to hand it over.) I check out the tax documents. They appear to be capital gains schedules for various Hawaiian property deals, bearing the names of several companies. Noons's name isn't on any of them. Later, when I check online databases for anyone named Noons who lives in Sugarland, Texas, I find none listed.

I loiter near the door. Across the hall, in another ballroom, a modeling company is talking to a roomful of teenage girls about how to take the first steps toward Hollywood stardom. While I don't stick around for their whole pitch, it's a safe bet that it, too, involves some pricey professional training.

Afterward I describe the seminar to John T. Reed, who runs a Web site that tracks and rates the teachings of various get-rich-quick real estate gurus. The Sheets seminar I've just experienced is typical of the genre, he says. "You could go to ten different seminars by ten different real estate gurus and hear those same phrases," he says. "It's cookie-cutter."

Reed became interested in real estate investing while a student at West Point in the late 1960s. Disenchanted with military life, he found a magazine article saying that most millionaires achieve their riches by either starting a business or investing in real estate. After graduation, Lieutenant Reed owed the army five years of service, and military regulations prohibited officers from operating an after-hours business—but he was allowed to buy investment real estate. Within a year of graduation he'd bought his first rental property—a $14,000 duplex in Collingswood, New Jersey. Over the next few years he read everything he could about how to succeed in real estate.

By the late 1970s Reed had been discharged from the army, graduated Harvard Business School, and purchased more than a half dozen properties. And he'd read every real estate advice book he could get his hands on. Most of the books—particularly William Nickerson's *How I Turned $1000 into Five Million in Real Estate in My Spare Time*—offered sound wisdom. That changed, Reed says, in

1980, when a man named Robert Allen published a book called *Nothing Down: How to Buy Real Estate with Little or No Money Down.* While previous real estate experts advised that people buy property the traditional way—by making a down payment and financing the rest—Allen suggested investors try to cajole sellers into lending them part of the purchase price, alleviating the need for up-front cash. "His book was total bullshit," Reed says, alleging that all of the techniques Allen advocated involved fibbing (or worse) to lenders to obtain financing. Nonetheless, the book became a runaway best seller, and Allen became a fixture on the real estate seminar circuit.

The hucksters' next big innovation came thanks to cable television. As channels proliferated, programmers had big blocks of late-night time to fill, and in 1984 networks began selling half-hour segments out to companies that created long-form advertising. Behold: the birth of the infomercial. Alongside abdominal workout machines and poultry rotisseries, real estate gurus flocked to infomercials to tout their "courses"—typically a book or two, augmented by cassette tapes that rehashed the information contained in the book. By 1986, according to *Money* magazine, at least eighteen real estate experts were touting their courses on television, with Carleton Sheets listed among the industry's top half dozen players. Over time many of Sheets's rivals fell on hard times. Some went bankrupt or faced tax-evasion charges; at least one went to prison. But Sheets had remarkable staying power. By 2004 Sheets remained among the nation's biggest buyers of infomercial television time.

While the infomercials mostly focus on selling books and tapes, the gurus' most lucrative line of business is the seminars. Reed says if I'd attended Sheets's $3,995 professional training, they'd likely have tried to sign me up for another course . . . and another. Reed says some people refinance their house to pay seminar tuitions.

Whether on TV, in hotel ballrooms, or on the Internet, the gurus' pitches rely on a few standard tricks, which Reed highlights in his self-published "The Real Estate B.S. Artist Detection Checklist." They emphasize their luxurious lifestyle, showing themselves in lavish locales like Hawaii surrounded by women in bikinis. They claim to do dozens, hundreds, or even thousands of these deals themselves. They emphasize that anyone can succeed in this line of work, no matter what their background. (Remember Karl Noons's line: "I'm not different than anybody else in this room"?) To better illustrate this, Robert Allen publicizes how he's pulled people off unemployment lines, and within days they're successfully buying profitable properties. To entice people with bad credit that will limit their ability to get financing, the gurus will offer to partner up and invest alongside you in properties. They rely on words like "fool proof" and "risk-free." They offer lots of testimonials—usually from people who won't give their last names. They print their books using extremely wide margins and lots of blank pages, to make the volumes seem hefty.

"Financial scams all revolve around the following phrase: 'I'm going to tell you how to get rich quick, without risk, without effort, without any experience, and without any cash,'" Reed says. "That's the format for all of them."

Over the years Reed has investigated several of the gurus. One tactic is deceptively simple: When a self-proclaimed expert starts touting the big profits he made on a real estate deal, Reed asks him to hand over the address so he can look up the property records himself. In several cases Reed has concluded that gurus misrepresented the facts of the deal, but most of the time, Reed says, the deals don't even exist. Regulators periodically go after these promoters, but it's a tough pursuit. Reed says that even if the techniques they teach are illegal, there's no law against teaching them—only doing them. Beyond the legalities, the gurus' biggest sin is exaggerating the ease and effectiveness of their systems, misrepresenting their own success, and charging outrageous prices for tips that are usually available for free online or at the public library.

After talking with Reed, I called both Robert Allen's and Carleton Sheets's organizations to let them respond to Reed's criticisms.

Allen's representative, Joe Kilsheimer, says: "Robert Allen offers a wealth of traditional information on how to buy and sell real estate and how to profit from it, and he has a fantastic track record of doing this. I'll leave it at that."

Sheets's representative, David Dulumaris, said that Sheets has trained tens of thousands of people since 1983, that Reed's criticisms are aimed at garnering attention for his own books, and that the company had stopped offering seminars and was shifting to a business model in which it offers material for free over the Internet and generates revenue from advertising and selling one-on-one personal training, which he compared to a personal trainer in a health club. "We've helped tens of thousands of people, and we feel very good that what we're providing is meaningful and has helped change tens of thousands of lives," Dulumaris says.

In fact, some people do cite Sheets as a positive influence on their life. Maura Hennigan spent most of the 1980s and 1990s as a Boston city councillor, a prestigious municipal post, but even after decades of service her government income topped out at $75,000. Boston is a high-cost city, so "I was really struggling," she says. Then one night she watched Carleton Sheets's infomercial. "All of a sudden I just thought, 'I have to try something,' so I tried it," Hennigan says. "I bought the book and the cassette." The cost was a bit less than $100.

A year later, utilizing Sheets's advice, she borrowed to buy a $135,000 three-family home. A short time later she bought a second, four-unit building for $180,000. "Carleton really showed me how to do it," Hennigan says. "A lot of the advice is very sound." Her properties cash-flowed, but more important, she'd purchased them just as Boston's real estate market began to soar. Eight years later the value of her two properties stood at triple what she'd paid for them. Looking back, she feels her infomercial encounter with Carleton Sheets may be the most important event in her financial life. "I worried, 'I'm going to lose my shirt; I'm going to lose my home,'" she says. "But I was very careful, and the market took off, and I was very, very fortunate." However, Hennigan points out that she learned everything she needed by making a minimal investment in a book and some cassettes. "I've heard of people who've gone to these seminars where they want thousands of dollars from you, and they promise you're going to make it all back, but the average person probably won't," she says.

When it comes to the actual techniques of the get-rich-quick crowd, most of their lessons have been around for years. But there is a twenty-first-century twist that caught on during the boom. It's the one preached by guys like Tim Owens, one of the gurus responsible for sending hundreds of investors to Pocatello.

Owens, a former finance manager at California-based Del Taco, tells an up-from-the-bootstraps story similar to the ones told by most real estate gurus. In 2000, unhappy in his corporate career, he sold his beloved '65 Mustang and used the $12,000 proceeds for a down payment on a $200,000 home in San Juan Capistrano. As it appreciated he refinanced it, pulled out cash, and began buying more real estate. Owens claims that within two years he'd bought twenty-four properties and accumulated $1.4 million in equity—all from that original $12,000 stake. By 2004 he began teaching others how to mimic his success.

Owens, along with several other boom-era real estate advisers, focuses on geography as his competitive advantage. Instead of telling newbie property investors to search for real estate in their own backyard, as Sheets does, Owens suggests they focus on undiscovered and undervalued cities across America. "What I'm looking for are towns that are a little less known," Owens told me. "College towns, military towns, major transportation corridors—something that would show good growth." He offers a simple shorthand for the kind of town that appeals to him: He likes to see a newly built Home Depot, but he likes to begin buying before Starbucks moves in.

In 2004 and 2005, Owens gave seminars throughout the Los Angeles area, pointing investors to places like Kingman, Arizona; Cedar City, Utah; Cheyenne, Wyoming; and Pocatello, Idaho. Unlike gurus who charge thousands of dollars for seminars, Owens priced his sessions at just $295 for ten weeks of training. It was hardly an act of charity: Owens made most of his money from referral fees paid by real estate brokers in cities like Pocatello, where he'd direct buyers. During 2004 and 2005, Owens says, his clients purchased as many as 300 properties in Pocatello, all from the same real estate broker, and Owens collected a 1 percent referral fee on the sales price of each home. Those fees probably exceeded $300,000—and Pocatello was just one of several cities where Owens profited by steering investors.

Clients like Ethan Chang say they're happy with the strategy Owens laid out. Starting in early 2004 Chang purchased six properties in Florida, Alabama, Arizona, and Indiana. Like Edi Stocker, Chang has never seen any of these homes. At the seminars "they pretty much tell people that this is armchair investing—[they] have the property managers lined up for you, and good, honest agents lined up for you," Chang says. Despite his growing portfolio, one thing Chang doesn't have is cash flow. The carrying costs of most of Chang's properties exceed the rents he's collecting, so he's currently laying out nearly $2,000 per month to cover the extra costs. "But they're appreciating," he says confidently.

While the real estate seminar business will never be recession-proof, the new focus on guiding people toward obscure markets does create opportunity. Housing is a local phenomenon, so there will usually be at least some places where prices are rising. Even in 2007, as housing prices were falling in many markets, several Texas cities—Austin, Houston, Dallas—remained hot. The night before I spoke with Reed, the San Francisco Real Estate Investment Club hosted a woman from Arizona who gave a talk entitled "Is Phoenix Still the Place to Realize Your Real Estate Investment Dream?" As Reed observes dryly: "She sure as hell didn't come all the way from Phoenix to say, 'No.'"

When an out-of-state investor wants to buy property in Pocatello, real estate agent Greg Johnston will e-mail them some listings, but he strongly urges them to come out for a visit. He'll greet them in the parking lot of the Holiday Inn, which is where he meets me one morning during the summer of 2005, just as the national real estate frenzy is hitting its peak. He points me toward the passenger seat of his cinnamon-colored Chrysler 300M, and begins to show me the city.

Johnston is twenty-seven years old. He's dressed in khakis and a cream-colored golf shirt, and wears a large Realtor pin with his name on it. He's been selling real estate for six years. His father, Jim, is the town's most successful Realtor, having been in the business for thirty-five years.

We drive through a series of working-class neighborhoods filled with small bungalows and drab multiunit dwellings. Periodically Johnston points to a property he's sold to an out-of-stater, like this four-unit apartment building bought by a client two years ago. She paid $168,000, and has put about $12,000 into improving it. Today she could get $220,000 for it, he estimates. But the rentals are providing a nice cash flow, so she's in no mood to sell.

Pocatello sits in a river valley, 150 miles north of Salt Lake City, that was once home to the Shoshone and Bannock Indian tribes. The city takes its name from a Shoshone chief who granted the railroads a right-of-way through Indian territory. Originally inhabited by fur trappers, the region attracted a large number of white settlers after gold was discovered in Idaho in 1860, but Pocatello's real growth came in the years that followed, as it became a railroad way station for goods and people moving west on the Oregon Trail. Even today railroad tracks bisect the downtown, which features nineteenth-century brick buildings. Today the area's economy has mostly shifted to light industry and agriculture. If you've eaten french fries at McDonald's, there're reasonable odds they grew in soil not too far from Pocatello.

The city owes its newfound status as a hot spot for real estate investors to a strange mixture of factors. The metro region has a population of around 80,000, and it's the home of Idaho State University, whose 14,000 students form a solid base of renters. Some of the area's biggest employers offer steady jobs, but don't pay well enough for workers to buy their own homes, boosting the pool of renters. Compared with other states, Idaho's laws are landlord-friendly, offering swift recourse if a tenant turns into a deadbeat. Even geology plays a role. Because of the area's low water table, homebuilders typically dug deep basements, and over the years many homeowners turned those big basement spaces into apartments that they rent out. The result is a community where lots of people are accustomed to being landlords, and where even normal-looking one-family homes often have a rental unit hiding underneath.

Johnston stops the car in front of a small bungalow. The previous owner ended up in foreclosure, and a new buyer has contracted to buy it from the bank for $45,000. It's in rough shape, Johnston admits, but still represents a good investment. If the new buyers put in $10,000 to repair it, they'll wind up with a decent four-bedroom house that they can rent for $700 or $750 a month. The mortgage on the property will be less than $400 per month. After paying taxes and insurance, the buyer will be left with a couple hundred dollars a month in positive cash flow. We drive on.

In addition to selling property, Johnston also manages dozens of rental apartments that his family owns here. As we drive through town, we pass FOR RENT signs with Johnston's name and phone number on them. The rental market is pretty tight, he says, particularly for inexpensive one-bedroom units. "In the fall you won't see a single FOR RENT sign here," he says as we drive through a student neighborhood. "Everything rents out."

As we get closer to the local university, the homes get nicer. The lawns are better maintained. Three thirtyish women walk by with babies in strollers. "This is a professors' neighborhood," Johnston says. We pass by the Idaho State president's mansion, a large, Georgian-style prewar building that would look right at home in an older part of Los Angeles. It's among the nicest homes in the area, but even upscale properties like this provide a sort of reverse sticker shock to people used to high-priced markets. Johnston recalls one of the nicest homes he's ever sold, a 3,600-square-foot home on four acres of land, with a three-car garage and a central vacuum system. The sales price: $311,000.

When dealing with out-of-state investors, Johnston urges caution. When they're looking at rental properties, he tells them to not overestimate their ability to raise the rent. If a unit is currently renting for $450, don't expect you can suddenly jack it up to $500 to make the numbers work, he says. And just because you live in a place where home values are growing at 18 percent, don't expect that to happen in Pocatello. "The thing that Pocatello offers is steady 4 or 5 percent appreciation, and a lot of investors are happy with that," Johnston says. Sure, you can make more than that investing in Treasury bonds, but the leverage and tax deductions can make a real estate investment with a 4 percent return perform a lot better than it may sound.

Johnston stops the car in front of a building on South Eighth Street, about a block from the university. It's a four-unit building his family owns; two of the apartments are vacant. We open the door. Inside conditions are ripe for a keg party: earth-colored carpeting, lots of linoleum, a Nixon-era bathroom. "This is the average condition for an older unit," he says. "You don't want to make them too nice." When a unit goes vacant, the owner will usually just fix anything that's obviously broken, repaint, and recarpet, spending perhaps $2,000. Since the owners will never live here themselves, there's no economic incentive to do a *This Old House*–style major renovation. At another vacant unit we look at, Johnston calls his maintenance guy on his cell phone, instructing him to tighten up the handrail, replace the shower curtain, and clean off the door, which has been egged. Back in the car we drive to another neighborhood, stopping once so he can replant a Greg Johnston FOR RENT sign that's fallen over.

As we drive around the city I can't help but think about how its aesthetics are affected by all these absentee landlords. Renters have little incentive to improve a property they don't own, and landlords are similarly cold-eyed in calculating improvements, doing just enough to prevent vacancies and keep the rents increasing. Owning a home offers clear financial benefits for people in the form of tax benefits and wealth accumulation—but there are benefits for society, as well, which is why the government has spent nearly a century promoting the idea of homeownership and providing incentives so people can buy houses. Research by Robert Dietz of Ohio State University summarizes these benefits, showing that children of people who own their homes perform better in school; that homeowners vote more frequently than renters; that people who own their home are generally happier and more satisfied with life than renters; and that property values generally rise faster in neighborhoods with higher rates of homeownership.

According to census data, Pocatello's homeownership rate is only slightly less than the national average. But clearly there are downsides to the influx of out-of-state landlords. I call the city's mayor, Roger Chase, to ask him about this. Although local landlords aren't perfect either, Chase says they've had to browbeat several out-of-state investors to properly maintain their rental homes, or to make repairs to comply with the building codes. "It's much more difficult to deal with those who are out of town," Chase says. On the whole, however, he's happy to see people investing in Pocatello.

For local brokers dealing with out-of-state investors, the biggest problem can be locating a decent property that's available to sell them. "I can't find hardly any," says Larry Herrud, president of the Greater Pocatello Association of Realtors. His father-in-law sold off two apartment buildings to an out-of-stater a few months back, but lately prices have been rising so solidly, he regrets the sale. Herrud says the area's popularity isn't just a function of investor interest. "If I were to attribute it to anything, it's the lifestyle," Herrud says. "We're slow-paced, and we've got the mountains. It's two hours to Salt Lake or Yellowstone or Sun Valley. It's not crowded. There's less crime. It's just a great place to live."

Pocatello is a place where investors try to make their money slowly and steadily, holding properties for at least a few years, collecting rents, and hoping for appreciation.

But when it comes to real estate investing, there are far faster ways to make a buck. And that's what lured Chas Carrier out of his suit-and-tie corporate job and into working-class Dallas neighborhoods. Carrier is a forty-seven-year-old Wharton MBA. Just a few years ago he was the CEO of a medical equipment company. But now he has a new calling: flipping houses.

Carrier and his Wharton roommate co-own two Dallas franchises of a company called HomeVestors, which bills itself as the McDonald's of house flipping. The company was started in the late 1980s by a Dallas real estate agent named Ken D'Angelo. His aim was to buy run-down houses at deep discounts from owners who found themselves in financial straits. To locate potential sellers he began putting up billboards with a simple message: WE BUY UGLY HOUSES. Underneath the headline was a phone number.

By 2006 there were 260 local branches of the company buying more than 7,000 houses a year—making this company the largest buyer of homes in America. Franchisees pay an up-front fee of $49,000 and receive a two-week training course, along with access to easy, short-term financing to buy homes. They pay for their own advertisements, which route calls from potential sellers to their offices. Nationally, the We Buy Ugly Houses team receives 200,000 calls a year from people who want to unload a home.

Carrier bought his first ugly house a few days after setting up shop in April of 2006, paying $71,000 to the owner, an older woman who didn't feel like doing the repairs necessary to get a good price for it. Carrier hired a contractor to do some light cosmetic improvements, and sold it ten weeks after he bought it for $20,000 more than he'd paid. It's just one of the fifty homes he purchased in his first six months in the business. Within a couple of years he expects to be buying more than 100 homes annually. So far he hasn't lost money on a single transaction, and has earned an average of $10,000 per house.

The key to making the system work, franchisees say, is buying only the right properties at the right price. Nationally, HomeVestors reps buy homes at an average price of around $100,000, and their aim is to pay just 65 percent of what they think a house is worth. Once they've bought a property, they can do one of three things: fix it up and rent it out, renovate and resell it to someone who will live in it, or quickly sell it as-is to another investor, a technique they call "wholesaling." The public perception—created largely by shows like *Flip This House*—is that flippers mostly rehab homes and sell them to people who will live there. But as so many people have become interested in real estate investment, HomeVestors franchisees have spent much of their time wholesaling homes—often to people who've attended a Carleton Sheets seminar. "They say that something less than 3 percent of people who go to a real estate seminar ever buy a property, but so many people are going to seminars, that still leaves a lot of investors," Carrier says.

In Washington, D.C., Joel Pulliam got into the ugly-house business a few months before Carrier. Pulliam, a forty-two-year-old with an MBA from the University of Virginia, worked as the vice president for product marketing at America Online before he ditched the Internet to pursue real estate. He's had a rockier go of it. In his first year and a half as a franchisee, he's made as much as $55,000 on a single home, but he's also lost money on some. At one point he owned eight houses, and he figured they showed paper profits of $350,000. But before he could finish rehabbing them the market softened, and by the time he unloaded them all his profit had dropped to just $100,000. "I'm not going to sit here and say I wasn't disappointed," he says. "Two hundred and fifty thousand dollars—poof." Like Carrier, Pulliam is now focusing less on rehabbing properties and more on quick flips to other investors.

Some people have moral issues with the techniques house flippers use. Says John Hayes, HomeVestors' current CEO: "It just doesn't seem possible to most people that anyone would sell their house for a 65 percent discount." Indeed, more than a few people—including several state legislatures and attorneys general—worry the sellers are being taken advantage of in these transactions. Not so, the HomeVestors folks say. "For consumers who need to get out from under a mortgage, who inherit a property that's three states away and they can't keep up with it, we offer a solution," Hayes says. Some observers compare it to the decision a car owner makes to trade in a used vehicle to a dealer before they buy a new one. Everybody knows the dealer will pay less for a trade-in than the owner could sell it for himself, but he's doing it for the convenience.

For new franchisees the other big surprise has been how fascinated their friends and neighbors are by their profession. So many people have seen a few episodes of shows like *Flip This House* that they're intrigued by the practice. "The programs don't show the reality of the business in terms of all the risks that are inherent," Pulliam says. Nor do the big profits shown at the end of each episode account for the financing costs or commissions involved in buying and selling the properties. Still, there is a sense that they're in a hot profession, one that people love to talk about at cocktail parties. "It seems to fascinate everybody," Carrier says.

And even after the boom ended, interest in this business continued. In mid-2007 I attended a HomeVestors seminar for potential franchisees in Massachusetts, a place where home prices were falling and the inventory of listed homes had soared. To potential home flippers, these conditions represented a buyer's market—and a great time to scoop up bargains. The room was filled with people interested in making money by buying ugly houses.

By now real estate investing fascinates me, too. If you spend time with the get-rich-quick crowd, you can't help but want a piece of this action. I ignore it for a while, but slowly it gnaws at me. I decide to take it to the next level. It's time to buy some investment property.

I call Greg Johnston, the Idaho real estate agent. I'd first visited Pocatello during the summer of 2005, and written about it for *Newsweek*. After that article appeared, prices there continued to rocket upward. But by the time I call him in September of 2006, things have cooled off a bit. Some out-of-state investors have sold their property, and the influx of newbies has slowed. Still, the low prices remain attractive, and the rental market remains strong. I ask Johnston what I can buy.

He e-mails me a listing for a house in an older neighborhood near downtown. It's one story, with two side-by-side one-bedroom apartments. It was built in the 1930s, but Johnston says it's structurally sound, with a good roof and newer vinyl siding. At $65,900, it's the cheapest duplex for sale in Pocatello right now. Johnston says he manages a lot of similar one-bedroom apartments in Pocatello himself, and there's a solid market for them. "You get a lot of single people, young couples—there's always a lot of demand for these inexpensive places," he says. Both apartments are currently rented, he tells me, giving me the number for Jenny, the property manager, who can tell me more.

I call Jenny. She's a former real estate agent who manages apartments for the current owner, a local investor who owns fifty-two units. He's selling this building, she says, because he wants to reduce his debt load. She describes the two current tenants. Bob has lived in his apartment for fourteen years. He's sixty-four years old and lives on government assistance with a girlfriend. "He's never going to move out," she says. "When something breaks, he fixes it himself. He treats it like it's his own house."

The other tenant is James, a divorced dad with a steady job who has weekend custody of his child. James has no current plans to move, Jenny says, but the child sleeps on the couch during visits, and sooner or later James will probably want to move to a two-bedroom place. If he does, the unit should rerent quickly. "Those apartments go really fast because they're right in town," she says. The combined rent on the two apartments is $615. Jenny says she's willing to continue to manage the property, taking 10 percent of the monthly rent.

My next call is to a Pocatello mortgage broker. We talk about interest rates, monthly payments, taxes, insurance, and closing costs. If I buy the home slightly below the asking price, I'll face a monthly payment of about $500, including insurance and taxes. Add in Jenny's property management fee, along with the water bill, and the carrying costs will just about equal the $615 monthly rent. Any big maintenance expenditures would send me into the red. Still, I'll be scoring tax deductions, and the home should increase in value over time.

I call Johnston, the Realtor. I tell him I'm thinking of making a bid of $60,000. He says the property has already gotten one bid in that range, and the seller rejected it out of hand. He suggests I bid

$63,000, halfway between the list price and the lowball figure I'm considering. I agree and fax him the paperwork. By midafternoon the seller counters at $65,000.

There is a certain excitement to this back-and-forth, a competitiveness that's led more than a few eBay auction bidders to wildly overpay for merchandise. Buying stocks or mutual funds lacks this negotiation element, and it's one reason why certain people find real estate more exciting. I want to buy this duplex, but I'm determined to avoid getting caught up in the frenzy. I counter at $63,500, contingent on my lining up financing, the house passing its inspection, and the existing tenants signing new one-year leases. "With one-year leases, I think this will be a safe investment," Johnston says. If the seller doesn't accept my counteroffer, I tell myself, I'll walk away. An hour later Johnston tells me we have a deal.

At some point before I actually made an offer on the house, I mentioned to my wife—casually, in passing—that I might use part of my book advance to make a down payment on a rental property in Idaho. She's not very enthusiastic. She'd prefer we invest in something more tangible—like the house we live in, which could use some renovations. I tell her that our new tenants, Bob and James, will be paying most of the costs of the Idaho property. I tell her about the tax deductions—and that we can now tax-deduct part of the costs of a ski trip to Idaho if we visit to check on our property. (She reminds me that she doesn't ski.) After some discussion, she tells me she won't sign any mortgage papers, so if I go ahead with the purchase it will be entirely my responsibility. I agree to this arrangement. For the next few months, whenever we discuss money—say, if I politely ask what she spent during a trip to the mall—she offers a simple, conversation-killing response: "A lot less than you spent on that house in Idaho."

My offer is contingent on the home inspection, and a few weeks later the inspector's report shows up via e-mail. On the front cover is a photo of the place. It has a big tree in the front yard, and two satellite dishes hang from the right corner of the house. The inspector writes that the roof looks good, as does the siding. The windows and a porch badly need new paint. The faded linoleum kitchen floors are in tough shape. The attic contains no insulation and prewar wiring. In one photo, showing an impossibly cluttered bedroom, the camera catches an older gentleman with no shirt on. It's Bob, the longtime tenant. I call the inspector to talk about his findings. "I felt like I needed a shower after I got out of there," he says. Mechanically the house is sound, if unattractive. Still, I tell him what I've agreed to pay for it, and he sounds amazed. He invests in local apartments himself, and he's sold similar properties for far more.

Weeks pass as the mortgage broker and I dicker over a loan package. At a real estate convention I run into Jim Johnston, Greg's father and Pocatello's biggest broker. We talk about the property I'm buying. "It's not what I would have chosen," he says, citing the busy street. He also remarks upon how the Internet has changed the whole home-buying experience, since it's made it more possible for people to buy properties without even seeing them. I ask him if he's trying to say that if I'd seen this house in person, I'd have been afraid to buy it. "Exactly," he says. I'm starting to feel really uneasy. But then he adds: "But the numbers work nicely, and it should do well for you." I keep thinking of his son's e-mail: "I think this will be a safe investment." God, I hope so.

A few weeks later a UPS truck pulls up to my house with a thick stack of mortgage documents. It feels strange to be signing to buy a house I've never actually seen, so I click on Google Earth and punch in the address. My duplex is hidden by trees, but I do get a better sense of the neighborhood, which is a few blocks from Pocatello's train tracks.

Before I sign the papers I call Jenny, the property manager, just to check in again. There have been some changes, she tells me, sounding upbeat. James, one of my tenants, violated his parole and has been sent to jail for six months. The good news is she's quickly rustled up a new tenant named Chris, whose references checked out nicely. She's also raised the rent. Meanwhile, my other tenant, Bob, has been allowing local vagrants to hang out and drink on his porch. Jenny is planning to read Bob the riot act about this. I agree, and we hang up.

By now I'm more than a little nervous. The town's biggest real estate broker has told me he wouldn't buy the place—and that I wouldn't, either, if I'd actually seen it in person. One of my tenants has gone to jail. My wife would prefer I not spend the money. And now I have substance abusers loitering on my deck.

I decide to plunge ahead anyway. I take the stack of documents to a notary. I scrawl thirty-two sets of initials and sixty-one signatures (ten of them notarized). I wire money to the title company. Including inspection costs, insurance, closing fees, and the down payment, I've dropped nearly $7,000 on my new duplex. But as Carleton Sheets told me (via his good friend Karl Noons), it takes money to make money. And like Edi Stocker, Judy Peterson, and a growing number of would-be Trumps, I've finally taken it to the next level.

At long last, I have cash flow.

In Richard Ford's Pulitzer Prize–winning *Independence Day*, the novelist tells the story of sportswriter–turned–real estate agent Frank Bascombe. He's a divorced dad with a troubled teenager, a lackluster love life, and a big dollop of middle-aged angst. In addition to selling homes, Bascombe also owns a couple of investment properties himself, located in a slightly run-down part of town. "It might seem unusual that a man my age and nature (unadventuresome) would get involved in potentially venal landlording, chockablock as it is with shady, unreliable tenants, vicious damage-deposit squabbles, dishonest repair persons, bad checks, hectoring late-night phone calls over roof leaks, sewage backups, sidewalk repairs, barking dogs, crummy water heaters, [and] falling plaster . . . often eventuating in lengthy lawsuits," Bascombe tells readers. "The quick and simple answer is that I decided none of these potential nightmares would be my story."

In the days after I close on the Pocatello duplex, I share Bascombe's optimism. Jenny mails the first few months' rent right on time. There are no maintenance headaches. The winos have apparently disappeared from my front porch. And thanks to depreciation and other tax deductions, my property investment saved me around $650 in income tax in 2006.

At first the most disconcerting element of my shift from homeowner to landlord involves home improvement. I'm frugal in parts of my life, but since my home is an investment, it's a realm in which I've tended to put aside my cheapskate tendencies, choosing upscale appliances and stone countertops. To me, home improvement is a virtue, and I always feel a small thrill when I've made my home a little bit nicer or more functional. It's only natural I'd want to do the same with my rental property.

But as a landlord that philosophy is a problem. The key to maximizing my investment is to spend as little as I can improving my Pocatello duplex. As Greg Johnston told me during my visit, "You don't want to make it too nice." Shortly after the closing I call Jenny, my property manager. I tell her the inspector said there's no insulation in the attic. On the day I call her it's fifty degrees outside my house, but just 9 degrees (with a driving wind) in Pocatello. My tenants pay their own heating bills, so I won't save any money by insulating the attic. But I care about global warming, and the thought of my tenants wasting energy to heat their uninsulated dwelling pains me. Insulation is cheap—why not put some in their ceilings?

Jenny argues against it. My tenants are paying just $70 a month for gas and electric combined, she says, which is very low. They aren't complaining about the heating bills. If it isn't broken, why fix it? I feel guilty about it, but she's right. If I'm going to turn a profit on this investment I need to skimp on making improvements my tenants won't care about. I can't make it too nice, even if I want to.

Within a few months, however, the uninsulated attic is the least of my concerns. For the first few months I'd owned the place Jenny had collected the rent and mailed it off to my bank for deposit. But in March the money never arrives. It must be lost in the mail, she tells me. I'm concerned, but I believe her. To prevent this from happening again, I open an account with a bank that has a branch right in

Pocatello, so Jenny can make deposits in person. In early April we talk on the phone. She tells me she's collected the rent and will deposit it that afternoon. It's the last time I ever speak to Jenny. The deposit never materializes.

I spend the next few weeks leaving Jenny voice mails and e-mails. She responds by e-mail a couple of times, blaming her lapse on a family member's illness, and promising to get me the April rent soon. (She continues to maintain that March's rent is lost in the mail.) She never does. By May I've hired a new property manager, who seems more reliable. After visiting the duplex he tells me that Chris, who replaced the tenant who went to jail, says Jenny has been charging him $375 rent—but she's been paying me only $350. The new tenant has also been complaining to Jenny for months that his refrigerator is broken, to no avail.

The two months' lost rent has cost me nearly $1,300, and I'm ticked. I could sue Jenny, but there's too little money involved to hire a lawyer, and it'd be extremely hard to sue her myself (without a lawyer) from out of state. I could also file a criminal complaint against her, telling police I believe she's embezzled my money. In mid-May I send Jenny registered letters letting her know that if I haven't heard from her by June 1, I'm calling the authorities.

In early June, after several more unreturned calls and e-mails, I call Jenny's boss at her day job. He tells me Jenny still claims the March money is lost in the mail, and that she deposited the April rent. (No, she didn't.) But he also says that Jenny's own finances—and, indeed, her life—seem to have unraveled in recent weeks. Her brother died after a long illness. She recently lost her house to foreclosure, he says. By the time I get off the phone with him I'm slightly less angry, and just sad. Partly I blame myself for what happened: I'd been too trusting. Although a piece of me wants retribution, I don't have the stomach to call the police on the woman. I resolve to drop the matter and move on.

Seeking solace, I decide to call other Pocatello investors to see if they've done any better than I have. First I call Judy Peterson, the California special-ed teacher. Her real estate investments have been a decidedly mixed bag, she says. In mid-2005 she owned eight Pocatello apartments. But less than two years later she's sold most of them. "I made back what I put into them and a little bit more, but not a lot," she says. In addition to her Pocatello investments, Peterson also spent $6,000 on a real estate course on investing in foreclosed properties, but ultimately she decided against pursuing that strategy. "The reason I didn't do it was because I felt like I was taking advantage of people at their lowest moment," she says. She tried to get a refund from the company that sold her the coursework, and ended up receiving $2,000 after complaining to the Better Business Bureau. That experience helps put her Pocatello adventure into context: Her rental properties haven't exactly performed like Google stock, but at least she didn't lose money on them.

"I don't have any regrets," she says. "I had fun. I think you have to go into it and decide you're going to have fun at it—it's not a lot different than the stock market. You don't put money in the stock market without realizing you could lose some of it."

If only Pocatello investor Susan Kopf could be that optimistic. Kopf and her husband began buying property there in 2002, buying three buildings in all. It was, Kopf says, a disaster. The Kopfs are missionaries who live in Papua New Guinea, in a desolate village with limited e-mail, telephone, or mail service. They return to the United States once every four years. Their remote living conditions left them unable to keep tabs on their Pocatello properties, and Susan claims their property manager horribly mismanaged their units. Apartments were left empty for months. When they were rented, most tenants moved out quickly, and Susan suspects the property manager was pocketing security deposits. Every couple of months the property manager would write to the couple, saying they needed to send $1,000 or $2,000 to stay current with utilities or taxes, or to make repairs. On one bill the Kopfs noticed charges for mowing the lawn, but when they asked another Pocatello real estate agent about the weather, they were told there'd been such a bad drought recently that there was no way the grass needed mowing. "We were at his mercy," Kopf says. During 2006 the couple sold two of their three Pocatello investments. Though the properties had risen sharply in value—one they bought for $68,000 sold for more than $90,000—Susan says they paid so much in expenses over the years that they barely broke even.

Finally I call Edi Stocker. He still owns his rental units in Alabama, Tennessee, Florida, and Pocatello. When we first spoke he'd talked about taking a cross-country motorcycle trip to visit them, but that never materialized. To this day he's seen them only in photos.

Up on Foothills Boulevard, at the duplex I'd visited many months before, one of the units has been vacant for months, he says, after an army family was suddenly redeployed and broke their lease. Before that vacancy, "everything was perfect—it was just bad luck," Stocker says. His property manager has been looking for a new tenant, but has told him that four-bedroom apartments like his can be slow to rent.

Still, Stocker is not discouraged. At forty-eight he's got a long time horizon until retirement. The apartment will eventually rent again, and things should turn out just fine. "All the properties I have are cash-flow properties—if they rent I'm okay," he says. And even if the value of his investments in Pocatello haven't doubled or tripled in his three years of ownership, that's not the end of the world. "I knew it wasn't going to just go up like crazy," Stocker says. "I'm just hanging in."

For now he has little choice. Unlike stocks or mutual funds, which can be unloaded with the click of a mouse, selling an Idaho apartment building could require patience, price concessions, and a sizable real estate commission. As with any illiquid investment, it's tempting to think optimistically and hold on, hoping for the best.

Stocker hasn't gotten rich quick—not yet, anyway—and neither have I. But even as America's real estate boom recedes in the rearview mirror, we're still in the game. We've taken it to the next level. And when the dust settles, we're hoping we'll still have our cash flow.

CHAPTER SIX

WELCOME TO THE JUNGLE:
NEW ORLEANS, LOUISIANA

How a Half Million People
Tried to Turn House Lust into a Career

It's late on a Saturday afternoon and I'm sitting near the back of a big ballroom in a downtown convention center, waiting for a seminar to begin. There are several hundred seats in this room, the majority of them still empty. As I wait, a guy with shaggy hair and glasses sits down in the row in front of me. There's a woman four or five seats to his right—a middle-aged blonde in a floral shirt.

They're far enough apart that neither is under any obligation to even acknowledge the other's presence. If this were a convention of normal people—say, Rotarians or high school guidance counselors— these distant seatmates might give each other the slightest nod or a smile. But this isn't a normal convention. It's a meeting of the National Association of Realtors, and its members belong to a species that often behaves with a slightly different set of instincts from traditional Homo sapiens.

Suddenly, without the slightest introduction, the man pulls out his business card and wordlessly hands it to the woman down the aisle. She reciprocates, also without speaking. He looks at the card, noting her geography. "Chicago—we're practically neighbors," he coos, as they start talking about the markets in their respective towns.

Watching this cards-before-words exchange leaves me feeling like a naturalist observing a strange mating ritual: *Quiet, please, the Realtors are networking.*

Most of the behaviors we've explored so far in this book—buying made-to-order or oversize trophy homes, launching large-scale renovations, spending obscene amounts of time watching HGTV, or perusing real estate Web sites—are decidedly amateur pursuits. For all the time many of us devote to obsessing over our own homes, we're not taking the leap to making a living at it. For the majority of us, House Lust is a pleasurable diversion, like yoga or gardening, a pastime that will never rise beyond the level of a hobby.

But Americans have a long tradition of finding something they enjoy and trying to turn it into a career—of finding ways to convert an avocation into a vocation. Sometimes this works out wonderfully. Does anyone who enjoys golf *not* harbor at least a bit of envy for Tiger Woods? Often, however, the hobby-to-career route proves to be a mistake. In the last two decades thousands of people have gone to cooking school, many of them caught up in the dream of becoming the next Bobby Flay or Emeril Lagasse. Only after they graduate do most of them realize that life in a kitchen usually means terrible pay, horrible hours, and very little glory.

Still, that little voice inside our head—the one that says, "This is fun, and I bet I could make money at it"—can be hard to ignore. As homes have become an all-consuming passion for a certain demographic, it's no surprise that little voice has been telling a lot of people they ought to try to make a living working with homes.

Occasionally the voice offers sound counsel.

Ron Spradlin is an air force veteran who lives in Fort Lauderdale, Florida. In 2001 he was earning $17 an hour driving a city bus. But as Spradlin drove his route, he was doing more than watching the traffic. He was studying the neighborhoods. He was keeping mental lists of the hip-looking cafés and shops along his routes. And everywhere he drove he was checking out the houses.

It's a habit Spradlin began a few years earlier, after he'd bought his first home. "Real estate just got in me—it excited me," he says. "I don't know if you've ever found anything in life that you want to share with your family and friends, that makes you want to scream from the rooftops. Real estate became all I thought about, whatever I was doing. I knew I wanted to be looking at homes, showing homes, or finding the next neighborhood."

Spradlin's passion for houses led him to get a real estate license. And as he drove his bus he laid plans for a career shift. His boyfriend had started buying local homes to rehab and sell, and Spradlin began helping him with these projects. By 2002 he'd signed on at a local real estate firm and was selling houses full-time. Home values were soaring; Spradlin's neighborhood began attracting national attention for its fast-rising prices. By his second year as a real estate agent, his income had doubled. By 2005, at age thirty-six, he'd gone from making just over $30,000 a year as a bus driver to earning more than $140,000 a year selling houses.

When friends saw how successful Spradlin had become, they'd often ask him if they, too, should seek their fortunes in real estate. "There's enough here for everyone," Spradlin typically replied. "Just join the party."

Many of them did. When Dick Clark rang in the new millennium in 2000, the National Association of Realtors had 761,181 members. Five years later its membership had swollen to 1,264,640. That's an increase of 66 percent—and it represents a half million people who decided to bet their future on their ability to sell homes and rake in commissions.

By one count, at the height of the real estate frenzy roughly 1 in every 200 American adults had become licensed to sell real estate.

Every decade has its hot professions. In the 1980s power-tie-clad investment bankers became cultural icons. During the 1990s dot-com employees were the object of envy. In the 2000s there's been a fascination with several professions, including hedge-fund managers and the people founding the companies (like YouTube) that constitute the Web 2.0 movement. But if you measure employment trends strictly by the numbers and focus on regular folks without MBAs or programming prowess, few professions have run hotter during the first part of this decade than real estate.

To understand how selling houses became a calling for so many Americans, I traveled to New Orleans for the annual convention of the National Association of Realtors. There, during the city's first big post-Katrina convention, agents shared a few drinks, exchanged tips on how to survive the slowing housing market—and volunteered at Habitat for Humanity projects to help rebuild houses destroyed by the storm. Back in Massachusetts, I hung around open houses, observing agents in their natural habitat. And to better understand the mind-set and inner workings of these creatures, I became one of them, by going to real estate school and obtaining my agent's license. In all these places, what I found were a lot of super-gregarious people who've done fabulously well during the boom—and are hoping for the best during the hard times that followed.

Every ecosystem has its hierarchy. There are hunters and prey, strong alpha males and weaker betas, apex predators and bottom-feeders. Some animals are stronger than others. Some are faster. Some are smarter. If you spend enough time hanging out with real estate agents, you can't help noticing that many suffer from a special form of anxiety about their place in this pecking order. Most are aware that real estate may make them rich, but it won't make them kings of the jungle.

This is not a new phenomenon—real estate agents have always held a slightly uneasy place in American society. The occupation emerged in the mid-nineteenth century, as home sellers began looking to intermediaries who'd do a better job of selling their house than they could do on their own. Sellers entered into these relationships with a degree of wariness, however: Even back then, according to Jeffrey M. Hornstein, author of *A Nation of Realtors*, the average real estate man was generally looked upon as a "devious swindler." By the early twentieth century, those real estate men had begun creating pre-computer versions of the Multiple Listing Service that let them share listings among themselves—and made them an essential party to most real estate transactions. But this innovation—and the steady stream of commissions it helped generate—wasn't enough for many practitioners of the trade, who wanted recognition as a full-fledged profession. So they worked tirelessly to rally members to join professional associations, engage in continuing education, and burnish their public image. The nation's real estate pros "made a concerted effort to associate real estate with the established professions of law, medicine and less frequently the ministry and engineering," Hornstein writes. Not wanting to be seen as commission-hungry middlemen who are a necessary evil when buying or selling a home, real estate agents sought to portray their typical practitioner as "a visionary artist, exercising his creative will on cities like the sculptor of a block of marble."

This status envy is on full display in New Orleans. Convention-eers in every industry wear name tags, but as Realtors wander around the convention center, their chests bear plumages worthy of a five-star general's, with color-coded flags signifying their status as "Local President-Elect" and "State Executive." In the seminars I attend, sales coaches routinely tell the assembled home sellers to rely more on the marketing tactics used by respected professionals like dentists and ac-countants—and to spend less energy mailing out cheesy refrigerator magnets at Christmastime. As they hand out their business cards—al-ways featuring a smiling color photo of themselves—many of these agents display long strings of credentials after their names. More than half of Realtors lack a four-year college degree, but that doesn't stop them from adding status-boosting designations like "Certified Resi-dential Manager" to their résumés. It's just one more way to try to es-tablish the bona fides of a profession one can enter by completing a few hours of training and taking an exam that some practitioners claim is as simple as passing a driver's test.

To be sure, most of the activity in New Orleans is focused not on status, but on the hunt for customers. On the first morning of the convention, dozens of agents sit in a ballroom while Jeannie Davis conducts a seminar on telephone imagery. She gives them shopworn advice, such as putting a mirror near the telephone to make sure they're smiling when talking to customers, since the person on the other end of the phone will be able to tell the difference in the sound of their voice. She talks about the importance of inflection, repeating the same sentence—"I never said you stole the money"—six different times, emphasizing a different word with each pronunciation; as her inflection changes, so does the meaning. It's a reminder that just as a jazz trumpeter must learn to master his instrument, every good real estate agent must learn to command the sound of his voice to effect sales.

Many of the sessions are led by slick sales trainers whose bios tout their history as supersuccessful agents before they put away their FOR SALE signs to make a living preaching self-improvement strategies. Some hype their achievements in terms that sound more apt for a high school quarterback than a real estate agent. "He has set records in his hometown that still stand," reads one brag sheet.

Many of these trainers suggest that agents practice an aggressive brand of networking that would make even an Amway salesman blanch. At one forum a successful agent tells the audience that the first thing you should do as a new agent is pull out your high school yearbook, regardless of whether you graduated high school a year ago or four decades ago. Write down the name of every classmate. Go to the Internet and locate phone numbers for as many of them as you can. Now call them all to get reacquainted . . . and let them know that you're standing ready when they want to buy or sell a house. Next get out the list of people who attended your wedding and repeat the process.

During one conversation an agent tells me he rarely has a substantive conversation with anyone—a florist he encounters in a store, a dental hygienist who picks at his plaque—without adding the person's contact info into his database. "You're already in my Outlook!" he tells me cheerily during a postconvention phone call.

This manic networking is a defining characteristic of a profession that's become obsessed with the old sales adage, "It's not what you know, but who you know." When I show up at the convention early one morning, I find that one Florida broker has left dozens of business cards on nearly every flat surface in the sprawling lobby. Throughout the convention there's constant talk about how the key to winning more business is to get more referrals. Instead of cold-calling or handing out cards directly, agents are advised to cajole every client or friend (like those long-lost high school classmates) to deliver them several new clients.

For Dirk Zeller, the secret to making a killing as a real estate agent lies in a different tactic: appointments. Zeller wears an immaculate black suit, with slicked-back hair and a yellow tie, as he paces in front of several hundred agents in a packed ballroom. He sounds a bit like Jerry Seinfeld doing a routine in which he points out all the absurdities of the way most brokers do business. Too many agents spend too much time e-mailing out listings to prospects, or engaging in unproductive phone follow-up. "I'm just checking back in," he says in a timid voice, mimicking typical agent patter. Equally pathetic, he says, is the way agents give every client their cell phone and home numbers. "Most of us are selling access: 'Call me anytime!' But do attorneys sell access?" he asks. Of course not. Instead of groveling phone calls and 24/7 standby, Zeller says agents should use firm yet simple techniques to force potential clients to sit down for face-to-face appointments: "Would you like to meet Monday at 1:00 p.m. or Tuesday at 11:00 a.m.?" Accountants, dentists, and lawyers don't allow people to drop by anytime they like, so neither should real estate agents. Above all, resist the urge to try to cement a relationship over the phone. "People perceive professionals to be people they book appointments with," he says. When an agent gets a client alone in a room, he says, simple salesmanship is all it will take to win their business.

As I listen, I'm more than a little skeptical. I hold no grudge against these professionals; my own dealings with real estate agents have always been pleasant. I don't doubt that these techniques might help them increase their earnings, but I'm not sure they will do much to increase the status of their occupation. Some agents make fabulous money and have fun, flexible jobs, but no matter how the industry tries to reposition itself, I'm just not sure many parents will ever dream of their sons and daughters growing up to sell homes for a living.

Still, as I hang out with brokers I do hear hints of how America's fascination with homes has given real estate agents—if not respect—at least a bit of social cachet.

Gerald Germany is a former University of Nebraska football player who lives in Manhattan. Laid off during the dot-com bust of the early 2000s, Germany had to find a new line of work. He'd been impressed by how the brokers he met were able to make so much for doing so little. "All the agents I was meeting, 80 percent of them were dumb, lazy, or a combination of both," he says. "For anyone with any discipline or work orientation, which I have, these are green pastures. These were not sophisticated or smart people, and they were making tons of money. I said, 'I need to get some of that.'"

He got his real estate license and signed on with Corcoran, a powerhouse Manhattan brokerage. Germany focused on selling apartments in the 200-unit building where he lived. "If you're in a pretty good building you can make a good chunk of money every year just selling apartments there," he says. "Then through your day-to-day life you'll pick up a few buyers. You can hustle, network, and work it, and really do a lot of business." By 2005 Germany was selling $25 million in property a year and earning $250,000 annually. Over the next five years he expects his income to break the half-million mark. Beyond the money he's crafted a lifestyle he loves. He sets his own hours, rarely visits his office, and is at the beck and call of no boss.

He's also become very popular at parties. "It happens all the time," he says. "If you're at a cocktail party or a bar, people will hear through whispers that you're a Realtor. Pretty soon you have any number of people asking you questions about the market. You can sort of sit there and hold court, and they look to you as the expert."

That may not make Germany the king of the jungle. But having a job that fuels interesting cocktail party conversation can be a heck of a nice fringe benefit.

During one of the seminars I attend in New Orleans, the speaker asks a crowded roomful of conventioneers—350, by my count—a simple question: "How many of you dreamed of becoming a Realtor when you were in high school?" The crowd laughs. Just a single person raises his hand.

It's a clear indication that for most people, selling houses is a fall-back option, a do-over alternative when plan A fails—or when, to paraphrase John Lennon, life intrudes on their best-laid plans. As one former agent privately put it to me, real estate sales is America's version of the foreign legion: less a calling than a refuge. In a telling moment during the 2007 Super Bowl, a General Motors commercial showed a robot being fired from his car factory job after dropping a bolt. Afterward, to show his life tumbling downward, the robot is depicted working in a fast-food restaurant and—you guessed it— standing in front of a FOR SALE sign, trying to sell a house.

Whether it's a dream job or a fallback plan, sometimes this transition can work out splendidly. Agents don't travel to New Orleans only in search of new sales techniques—they also come for inspiration and affirmation from people who've found success, who serve to show that with a little persistence and luck, they can too.

They go to hear the stories of people like Jessica Horton.

I first encounter Horton in a conference hall after a panel discussion, where she and three other successful young brokers give advice to agents who hope to emulate them. Horton tells a life story that's so compelling that if Reese Witherspoon reads this chapter, I fully expect her to buy the rights to Horton's story and bring it to the big screen.

Jessica's thick Georgia accent betrays her roots in America's peaches-and-peanuts region, in this case a one-stoplight town an hour south of Atlanta. When she was growing up, her family lived in a trailer. Her mother is a waitress; her father worked in a manufacturing plant. Money was tight. In high school Jessica began working at an after-school job, where she met an older boy named Jason. They fell in love. They fooled around. Jessica became pregnant. At seventeen she dropped out of high school, they married, and their son arrived. "The proper Southern order," jokes Jason, who's eight years older. After the baby arrived Jessica worked as a teller at the local bank, earning minimum wage. When she became pregnant with their second child, at nineteen, she told her boss she'd need a raise to cover the rising child-care costs. No dice. So she began looking for work and considered taking a job at McDonald's. Instead she decided to get her real estate license.

Then she started hustling. When she heard the plant where her father worked would be shutting down, she offered him sympathy for his upcoming layoff, then followed up quickly with a question: "What's going to happen to the building?" It would be sold, he told her. So Horton got on the phone to the British-based company that owned it and pitched a vice president on giving her the listing. She practically grew up in the plant while visiting her father at work, she said, so she knew the property inside and out, and could do a better job showing it off to buyers than any other agent in town. Horton got the listing, quickly found a buyer, and earned a $25,000 commission—more than she'd earned in a year at the bank. She used that money to buy a moving truck. On each side she stuck a five-foot-tall photo of her face, and underneath it a simple message: "Buy or Sell a House with Me, Use My Moving Van for Free!" Calls poured in.

At the Century 21 brokerage where she worked, Horton's new-found success angered the more established agents. "They had a fit when I got that moving truck," she says. "I said, 'I can do whatever I want—if you don't like it, go buy yourself one, too.'" When her colleagues remained hostile, she left Century 21 for a brief stint at a RE/MAX franchise, then made a bold move: At age twenty, she borrowed money to open her own RE/MAX office, becoming the company's youngest franchisee worldwide.

As her own boss, Horton hired her husband to do marketing and technology-oriented work, like creating her Web site. After seeing how some buyers seemed hesitant to work with her because of her youthfulness, she hired her mother-in-law as an agent, mostly to have a more mature person around to lend an aura of experience to their nascent operation. And all the while Horton clamored for listings, emphasizing her aggressiveness. "I flat-out tell my clients, 'If I don't sell your house, I can't make my house payment. If I can't sell your house, I can't put food on the table for my kids.'" Around town she put up gigantic billboards with her face on them. Sellers responded. On the day we talk, Horton has 350 listings. It's a number that makes even veteran agents' eyes widen, sort of like a Major League Baseball player who tells you he's batting .700.

At twenty-four, Horton is the top agent in the three Georgia counties in which she works. Her town—Griffin, Georgia—is a place where the average home costs $130,000; like a lot of nonmetropolitan areas, it's missed out on the real estate boom. But despite those low transaction prices, in 2005 Horton sold $20 million worth of houses.

As a result, trailer park living is a distant memory. Today Jessica, Jason, and their two children live in a 3,000-square-foot home on six acres of land, which is worth $350,000. She drives a new Chevy Suburban. Jason drives an Acura. They visit Disney World every year, and routinely stay in five-star hotels. Her success has made many of her town's rival agents despise her, she says. Some tear down or deface her FOR SALE signs. One time somebody attacked one of her billboards with paintballs, which was big news in town. Nonetheless, her face is so visible on billboards that people routinely recognize her while she's shopping in Wal-Mart. "I get stared at," she says. "It's embarrassing." But it's a nice living.

"This is something we got into because we had no other options," she reminds me. And thanks to real estate, now she has plenty.

In *Caddyshack*, Bill Murray plays a maniacal golf course groundskeeper who stalks a groundhog. After a series of ill-fated attempts to snare him, Murray retires to his maintenance shack to fashion plastic explosive bombs and utter the movie's famous soliloquy: "My foe, my enemy, is an animal. And in order to conquer him, I have to think like an animal, and whenever possible, to look like one. I've got to get inside this dude's pelt and crawl around for a few days."

Although I'm not hunting real estate agents, I am trying to understand them—to get inside their heads. Just talking to brokers, I realize, will get me only so far. I must know my quarry better if I'm ever going to truly understand why hundreds of thousands of Americans have quit their jobs to sell real estate. I have to think like a real estate agent, and, whenever possible, to look like one.

Better yet, I shall become a real estate agent.

It's a mission that brings me to the lobby of a suburban Hampton Inn early one Saturday morning. I'm directed to an upstairs ballroom, where a bald man in a white Polo shirt and light-colored khakis hands me a slip of paper. I write down my name, address, and credit card number. He hands me a white binder and a receipt for $199. In Massachusetts the law requires aspiring real estate agents to attend twenty-four hours of classroom instruction before taking the state exam. So I've just enrolled in a weekend real estate course that jams this entire curriculum into two twelve-hour days. If I schedule the exam quickly, by next weekend I'll be licensed to sell houses.

The ease with which a newbie like me can enter the field is one big reason so many people did so during the boom. Economists call real estate a profession with "low barriers to entry." If people could become hedge-fund managers by taking a weekend course, America might suddenly be overrun with them, too.

By 8:00 a.m. I'm one of fifteen people sitting at small tables. At the front of the room the Polo-wearing instructor introduces himself as Bill, and tells us he's been teaching these classes since 1984. Behind him are a podium, two artificial trees, and a whiteboard. Bill begins by telling us the official school rules: No laptops or video cameras are allowed in class. Students cannot be visibly drunk or asleep. No reading magazines during the lectures. During the two twelve-hour days, we'll be given a ten-minute break every couple of hours, and a one-hour lunch at 1:30 p.m. He suggests we abstain from turkey sandwiches, lest we have trouble staying awake.

My classmates are seven men and seven women who appear to range in age from their twenties to their early sixties, with most falling near forty. One man is a bank loan officer, and another is a contractor. One woman is a property manager at a large apartment building. A handful own rental investment properties.

During breaks I talk with a few about their careers and aspirations. Although this is a course designed to teach people to sell real estate, what's most striking is that I don't meet a single student with firm plans to actually sell houses. If you hang out at law schools you'll meet some people who don't intend to practice law; they just see a legal education as useful training that will help them in whatever they pursue. Likewise, most of my classmates have only a vague sense of exactly what they'll do with their real estate license. But at a time when real estate agents are stars of reality-TV shows like *Million Dollar Listing*, and in an era when so many people are obsessed with finding the perfect home or investment property, having a license will make them an insider, they believe, and provide a useful arrow in their professional quiver.

Bill tells us he'll conduct class by reading aloud each page in our binders. Every so often he takes off his reading glasses and steps from behind the podium, interrupting this oratory with war stories, explanatory asides, and questions to ask the class. He rips open a bag of chocolates and periodically throws candy to students who offer correct answers, which makes the proceeding feel a bit like Sea World. As an added bonus, we quickly realize, we get to hear Bill's jokes. The first few times he says the word "assets," he intentionally stutters, to emphasize the first syllable. When that shtick grows tired, "assets" becomes his signal to spank himself. When he uses his fingers to count off the different ways to take title to a property (joint, tenancy in the entirety. . .), he accidentally starts with his middle finger, flipping the class the bird.

In addition to enduring Bill's jokes, to get our license we must pass a two-part multiple-choice exam by answering 70 percent of the questions correctly. The first part is state-specific, and covers a variety of procedural mumbo jumbo and trivia concerning the state's real estate bureaucracy. Who appoints members of the Massachusetts Board of Real Estate? (The governor.) How many times a year must they meet? (Four.) How many days does a buyer have to conduct a lead inspection of a property? (Ten.) The second part features more general questions about real estate transactions, including basic contract law. To do well on the exam, Bill tells us, we should take it within two weeks, while the material is fresh in our minds.

While this technical arcana dominates the lessons, Bill intersperses his lectures with bits of practical wisdom. To avoid getting sued, he says, good agents avoid making specific claims about a property. If a potential buyer asks where a property line is, for instance, we should respond with a three-part answer: "I don't know. The seller says it's by that fence. But you should probably hire a surveyor if you want to know for sure."

By late afternoon on Saturday my classmates and I have the grim look of prisoners. We're obsessed with what we'll eat during our next break, and we spend part of each free period on our cell phones, calling friends on the outside to complain how miserable we are.

There's a rich irony to this predicament. Many people choose to become real estate agents because they crave the freedom of being their own boss, and want a job that lets them come and go from the office at their leisure. But in order to reach that goal, we have to spend a weekend locked in a hotel conference center, subject to a set of restrictions most of us haven't encountered since high school.

On day two Bill arrives wearing the same clothes he wore on day one. Today he periodically interrupts his lectures to make apocalyptic economic predictions. In the months ahead, he expects unemployment to soar, inflation to rise, home mortgage rates to break 10 percent, and foreclosures to run rampant. But as Sunday afternoon turns into evening, he realizes the clock is ticking, so he's quickly back on script. "Okay, let's talk about the Massachusetts Wetlands Protection Act."

Mercifully, class ends. I schedule my exam, and ten days later I'm sitting at a desk in a suburban office park with a small touch screen in front of me. For the next ninety minutes I touch my way through 122 questions. Some of them are drawn straight from Bill's lecture. When does an agent have to provide prospective buyers with a disclosure form? (At the first personal meeting to discuss specific properties.) Some are basic math problems involving commissions, interest rates, and prorated tax bills. I struggle through questions about landlord-tenant law, but by the end I'm confident I've answered at least eighty-five questions correctly, the number that will get me my license. I step outside the test room and am sent to a small waiting room. Two minutes later I hear my name called. "Stand against that wall." A camera clicks. "Did you bring a check?" I did, writing one that brings my total investment in this process (including tuition for real estate school, the exam fee, and the licensing fee) to $413. "Congratulations," they tell me, handing me a small laminated card and a wall certificate.

When my wife tells the neighbors I've gotten my real estate license, one responds dryly: "Will you be having a graduation party?"

After I've passed the exam, a couple of friends ask me, half seriously, if I'd consider helping them with a home search. I politely decline. Like a lot of jobs—law, medicine, carpentry—book learning goes only so far in real estate. Despite my new license, I know nothing about the basic skills of realty: how to set the listing price of a home, how to negotiate a selling price, or how to write up a formal offer. If I actually wanted to learn the craft and practice of selling homes, I'd need to spend long hours under the tutelage of an established broker, who'd show me what it really takes to be a success. Step one, presumably, involves printing up lots and lots of business cards.

If I continued on to an apprenticeship in the real estate trenches, I suspect I'd find it extremely difficult. It's conventional wisdom that as home prices soared during the boom and houses sold faster than drinks at last call, just about every agent was reaping a windfall.

That conventional wisdom, it turns out, is wrong. While some agents and brokers earn a nice living, many don't—and as thousands of newcomers have flooded the field the last few years, many inexperienced agents made very little money. At the very least this suggests a lot of these newcomers failed to do the basic research about how the industry really works—or else they vastly overestimated their own skills and chance of success.

Consider the numbers. In 2004, according to surveys by the National Association of Realtors, the median income for a Realtor was $49,300. But if you pick apart that number, it becomes obvious the distribution is skewed. Some veterans describe real estate as a so-called 80/20 business, in which the top 20 percent of agents earn 80 percent of the compensation. The actual distribution isn't quite that lopsided: According to the latest stats, 26 percent of Realtors earn above $100,000 annually. Still, the numbers show that many agents are earning pay that's only slightly above minimum wage. Among sales agents (who have less experience than full-fledged brokers), 38 percent earned less than $25,000 a year. When you factor experience into the equation, the earnings picture looks even dimmer. Thanks to the influx of newcomers, in 2005, 37 percent of all sales agents had been in the field for two years or less. And the average earnings for those in the field two years or less stood at a paltry $12,850.

That number is especially alarming when you consider that the average real estate agent gets no health insurance or retirement plan, and runs up about $8,000 a year in business expenses. Presumably many of these low earners are working only part-time; many probably have a day job as well. Still, given those numbers, many of the newcomers trying to make a full-time living selling homes would be far better off pulling espressos at Starbucks.

In light of those bleak realities, it's no surprise that some agents don't last long. In 2000 the California Association of Realtors began a longitudinal study to find out how new agents fare during their first years in the business. The association picked 100 people who passed the state's licensing exam that year and began tracking them. Five years later, 57 of those 100 had dropped out of the field. Among the quitters the biggest complaints were lack of support from their brokerage bosses and their inability to make enough money.

Realtor conventions aren't a great place to find these flameouts—the kind of people for whom getting into real estate has proven as singularly unsuccessful as Michael Jordan's decision to quit the NBA to try his hand at baseball. As in most fields, conventions attract the industry's stars—particularly since agents have to pay their own way to New Orleans and ante up for rooms at the city's overflowing hotels.

Still, during my time in New Orleans I hear several stories that give some insight into why so many people take steps to see their smiling photo emblazoned on a FOR SALE sign, only to learn they don't have the energy or chutzpah necessary to earn a living peddling houses.

At a cocktail party one evening I meet a pleasant woman in her thirties who spent eighteen months as an agent in Washington, D.C., and northern Virginia. She has always loved homes, and assumed she'd excel in helping people buy them. But when she began taking young buyers around to look at houses, she found herself growing anxious. Buying a house is a huge financial decision, and it's no surprise that first-time buyers can be a little nervous about the process. But this young agent found *herself* becoming just as anxious as the buyers, obsessing over whether she might lead her clients to buy a house they might someday regret. All sales jobs require resiliency and the ability to lose deals or clients without a lot of angst, but she found herself unable to establish sufficient distance from her clients and their search for housing. Like a young doctor who can't tolerate the reality that some patients will die, this agent found herself stressed out by the crushing responsibility she felt while advising clients in their pursuit of the American Dream.

Adding to that stress, she found the glad-handing, schmoozing, and networking it took to find clients particularly unpleasant. "I wasn't extroverted enough," she says. She hated handing out business cards, and found herself shushing her husband when he'd suggest to friends that they consider letting her list their houses. She ended up taking a salaried marketing position for a real estate–oriented business, and she's much happier.

At dinner that same night I meet a woman who spent seven years as an agent in Alabama—and hated every minute of it. Until you've worked in an office with no guaranteed Friday paydays, where people fight over phone calls for a chance at a commission, you don't know just how much backstabbing can go on, she says. Today she's married to a superwealthy attorney—they pour me a glass of the twenty-one-year-old wine as we talk—and she doesn't have to work. She comes to New Orleans regularly, she says, but never for a real estate convention—thank the Lord.

When I ask veteran brokers about their worst-performing new agents, many of them tell stories about people who flocked to real estate after the dot-com meltdown, and didn't have the skills to sell houses. Back at the convention hall I meet broker Ben Coleman, who runs a Century 21 office in San Francisco. "You had all these people who were dot-goners," he says, who sought a foothold in real estate as their lifeline. But the reality is that there's very little skill overlap between info-tech work and real estate sales, Coleman says. Techies sit in front of a screen all day, with much of the product of their work proceeding from their brain, through their fingertips, onto the screen. It's the antithesis of the work an agent does, which is driven by gregariousness, negotiation, and interpersonal skills. Coleman recalls his biggest train wreck: a former Bank of America tech-department employee who spoke Chinese. Coleman hired him thinking he'd find success selling homes to San Francisco's Asian population. But he couldn't get clients or listings. One day, when another top agent decided to drive his new BMW to see a listing, the newbie agent decided to follow him to the home in his own car. At a stoplight the newbie rear-ended the top producer's new Beemer. Coleman dismissed him, and the last anyone heard from him he was working at Home Depot. "He never sold a house," Coleman says.

One broker points me toward a guy who spent eighteen months selling real estate before packing it in. Now he works at Staples. Like most of the flameouts I encountered, the former agent asks me not to use his name, because he doesn't want his current employer to hear how spectacularly unsuccessful he was at selling houses. "It was a very painful part of my life," he tells me. He'd been successful in other sales jobs before trying real estate, but selling houses was different. There were too many other people plying the same neighborhoods. He hadn't lived in the area long enough to have a deep network of friends and relatives whose houses he could sell. He did make some sales, but it wasn't unusual for him to go three months without a commission check, and he didn't have a cash cushion to make that a viable way to live. If someone considering a move into real estate asked his advice, here's what he'd say: "Do you have friends who are ready to buy or sell, and if so, how many? If you don't have that, and you don't have money [to tide you over between commissions], stay away." Most of the people he saw stick it out were women who relied on their husbands' income for support, who could trudge ahead even if they earned very little money. To hear him tell it, the criteria for success in the field sounds almost oxymoronic, but it's true: To really earn a great living in real estate, you have to have enough resources to be able to withstand periods when you'll make virtually *no* living in real estate.

For some agents that's not a problem—they're in the game mostly for recreation, not to earn a living. That stereotype is especially true of older women. For decades real estate has been an attractive option for women returning to the workforce after years of raising children. Christine Hansen, a broker in Fort Lauderdale, oversees about 125 agents, and she has five who almost never sell anything. Typical is a woman in her early sixties. Her husband is retired, and they're wealthy. "When people ask her, 'What do you do?,' instead of saying, 'Nothing,' she says she's a Realtor," Hansen says—despite the fact that the woman hasn't sold a house in at least two years. That example is hardly an anomaly. In season four of *The Sopranos*, even Carmela Soprano studies for her license, mostly out of boredom. The presence of so many recreationally minded agents is one reason why, in 2004, 13 percent of all Realtors helped facilitate zero transactions, and presumably earned no money.

The numbers also reinforce a common stereotype: that most real estate agents look like your mother. It's true that half of agents are forty-nine or older, but the demographics are changing. Brokers in New Orleans claim they're seeing far more people in their twenties entering the field. For many of these newcomers—most with college degrees, and some with MBAs—real estate is hardly a fallback option, but a true aspiration. "We're seeing a lot more people who have business sense, and a lot more people entering the industry as one of their strategic career goals," says Ernie Brescia, Century 21's training chief. As Manhattan agent Gerald Germany indicated earlier in this chapter, in areas where people talk incessantly about real estate, being an agent can have a real social cachet. Among the indicators of this shift: In 2005 the men's magazine *Details* profiled young Los Angeles agents. The magazine's conclusion: "Successful real estate agents are now suave, hip go-getters."

Along with younger, cooler practitioners, there are other demographic shifts at work. As I hung around Realtors during my reporting, I noticed that more than a few of them are gay men—including Ron Spradlin and Gerald Germany. In a lot of cities it's a clear trend. In 2004 the *Boston Globe* reported that as many as half of the brokers in some Boston neighborhoods are gay. Some pros attribute this trend to the stereotype that gay men have a more sophisticated eye for design than heterosexuals. "It's that whole *Queer Eye for the Straight Guy* phenomenon," agent Joe DeAngelo, who is gay, tells me one afternoon as we drive around Boston in his black BMW X5 with Liz, a tall blonde looking to buy a loft apartment. As we move in and out of apartments, DeAngelo does seem more design-oriented than the average agent. He's not shy about telling Liz how he'd move the walls around in a two-bath apartment to create a full-fledged master bedroom. Some observers say gay men are also better able to relate more diplomatically with both the husband and the wife in a married house-hunting couple, compared to women or straight male agents.

Whether male or female, gay or straight, agents enjoy another big advantage by choosing this line of work, one that might help them overcome the limited average earning potential: They become really smart about property. Many try to use those smarts to maximize their own investment in housing. For some brokers this means buying, renovating, or designing from scratch a really nice residence for themselves. "It's a huge advantage seeing a lot of floor plans, seeing what really works, and listening to buyers' opinions about what they really like in their homes," says Enzo Ricciardelli, an agent at Sotheby's International in L.A.'s Brentwood neighborhood, who used his design savvy to build a 5,500-square-foot Italian-style villa in Pacific Palisades, not far from Steven Spielberg's and Tom Hanks's homes.

For other brokers there is a big advantage in being among the first to hear when a new property hits the market: They can buy it themselves as an investment. Despite the average agent's relatively modest earnings, nearly 40 percent of all Realtors own investment properties. Some industry veterans say that during times when home prices appreciate quickly, it's common for the profits from these investments to exceed their earnings from commissions. Michelle Peppe, a broker in Naples, Florida, cites an old real estate maxim: "You don't make money selling real estate. You make money buying it."

But after talking to veterans about the way this business really works, I'm not sure I could make money doing either—and even though I have a license to sell, I'm thrilled that I haven't quit my day job.

It's one thing to hear sales trainers tell agents how to garner more respect from the public. But to really understand how the public feels about the professionals who help them shop for homes, you need to do field research, to observe these two species in their natural habitat, in the place where they most often cross paths: inside a Sunday open house.

The Coldwell Banker signs guide me in toward the end of the cul-de-sac. I arrive a few minutes early and spy the lady of the house sequestering the family's two dogs into an outside pen. The family depart, and I go inside to meet Deborah Gordon, the agent charged with selling this home.

Gordon has been in the business for nearly three decades. She is one of the more successful brokers in this particular suburb, just west of Boston. The house she's showing today has an open floor plan, four bedrooms, and more than 3,700 square feet. She sold it to the current owners a few years ago, and since then they've done a massive renovation. There's marble tile everywhere, a chef's kitchen, and a bar downstairs. The homeowner has done a nice job of getting ready for today's open house: The counters are cleared, and the place sparkles. "She's a good housekeeper," Gordon says. A few minutes later we open a closet and a giant pile of shoes comes tumbling out, like something you'd see in a sitcom. Okay, so it's not perfect.

For an agent like Gordon, one of the toughest parts of winning a listing like this is getting the seller to agree on a realistic price. During the boom this was no problem, since a home that was listed too low stood a fair chance of attracting multiple bids, which could drive the price up to the correct level. But on the day of this open house, that era is a memory; the Boston market has cooled off, and Gordon, like other agents, now devotes much energy to urging clients to set more realistic prices to avoid having homes languish on the market. There was a time when this family thought their house might command

$2 million. Before Gordon would take the listing, she convinced them to price it far lower, at $1.55 million.

Like most veteran brokers, Gordon has conducted hundreds of open houses, and she has a few rituals she sticks to. She always brings a book or some Sudoku puzzles to occupy her if no one materializes. It's mostly an act of superstition, she says, since whenever she brings along her distractions, attendance seems better than when she doesn't. She always signs a fake name in the first spot of the sign-in sheet by the door. (Today's pretend guest is "David Schulman—New York City.") "If you don't fill in anything, visitors won't fill in anything," she says.

Gordon is pleasant and easy to talk to. But over the years she's become accustomed to seeing buyers who are less and less interested in conversation. She finds herself having to pry names out of thirtysomethings who, to her mind, lack the manners to properly introduce themselves when they walk in the door. Today Gordon has brought along a new agent named Sheila Goddess who will keep an eye on the house while Gordon goes on a showing with another client. At one point a woman in her thirties with glasses and brown hair comes in, and it's just as Gordon has described: The woman refuses to put her name on the sign-in sheet, answers Goddess's questions in a clipped fashion, and is almost hostile in her unwillingness to tell the agent about her home search. It's the kind of interaction to which Goddess, who got into the industry after three decades as an elementary school teacher, has grown accustomed.

"It's hard for me to go from a field like teaching, where you're almost revered, to a field like real estate, where you're almost hated," she says. "The buyers walk right by you." Gordon believes the younger generation spends so much time using services like eBay, Craigslist, and Amazon to cut middlemen out of their lives, they've become less comfortable dealing with anyone whose job involves selling on commission. "The younger buyers don't want to talk to Realtors—if they could buy the house over the Internet, they would," Gordon says. "They have no social skills." An alternate explanation, of course, is that they're sick of being handed business cards, mailed calendars, and winding up on a broker's e-mail list after even the most minimal interaction.

Today's open house is relatively quiet, with just a few potential buyers wandering through. That allows the agents to easily keep tabs on where the visitors are. This is a nice neighborhood, so Gordon and Goddess aren't unduly worried about theft or other shenanigans, but misbehavior can be an occupational hazard. Open houses are one of the few times we readily invite strangers to wander through our bathrooms and bedrooms, poking and peeking wherever they please. Some take advantage of the privilege. At the height of the boom *GQ* reported on a trend called "house humping," in which thrill-seeking couples try to furtively have sex in a quiet corner (or even a closet) of an open house, without the agent noticing. But if any couples get lucky during their walk-through of this stylized home, they're incredibly fast and discreet.

Aside from the homeowner's thorough cleaning job, this home has other things going for it: smart furnishings, flat-panel televisions, and convincing fake floral arrangements. During the boom buyers didn't much care what furniture they saw during an open house, but as the climate has shifted toward a buyer's market, details matter. This house doesn't need a professional makeover, but if it did there's no shortage of helpers whom Gordon could hire to work their magic and make the property sparkle. Over the years they've come to call themselves home stagers.

Staging is another data point in the uneasy relationship between the people who sell homes for a living and those of us who buy them. Over the years agents have come to believe that most Americans are too stupid, lazy, or unimaginative to see past the ugly furniture and hideous wallpaper in a for-sale home, to really evaluate the bones of the home that lies beneath. To overcome that obstacle they've adopted staging, a practice that originated in California but has migrated nationwide. It's been helped along by two of the trends discussed in previous chapters: the spread of well-merchandised model homes in new-home communities, along with the buzz created by HGTV staging shows like *Designed to Sell*. Lately agents and homeowners have co-opted stagers' best-known tricks, but in some markets a lot of agents are still inclined to bring in a professional to oversee the makeover.

Jenny Gibbs got into the staging business after buying and selling several Brooklyn apartments and hearing real estate agents praise her design sensibilities. Staging, Gibbs says, "is sort of like set design—it's not really for living in; it's just for show." The trickiest part is explaining to the home's current owner why their current decorating scheme is sort of . . . atrocious. "You have to be so diplomatic," Gibbs says. "Without impugning anybody's taste, you have to make sellers understand their choices are personal choices, and they're not necessarily right for everyone."

Many of the tactics Gibbs employs have become conventional wisdom for home sellers. She'll repaint the walls an inoffensive beige. (One agent tells me the basic goal of staging is to make every room look like a page from the Pottery Barn catalog.) She'll declutter the space, clearing countertops and making sure there aren't too many personal photographs on display. Sometimes she'll hire movers to remove some of the homeowner's possessions, or bring in some of her own furniture that she keeps in two big storage lockers and rents out to clients. "Sometimes it's as simple as moving the couch—some people have the right things but they're not in the right spot," she says. Oftentimes she'll have to coax clients into purging the stuff that's filling closets and corners. In her line of work she's hyperaware of how much stuff fills the average home. "People really are living with garbage—I shouldn't say that because it's not politic, but there's an inertia for some people and their houses. They can't get rid of stuff. I love helping people pare things back and get back to what they really need," says Gibbs, who describes herself as a "thrower-outer" who's been known to discard her children's toys if they go unused for a couple of weeks.

Mostly, though, her work is about overcoming the limited imagination of the home-buying public. Most buyers get so distracted by bad furniture or messy countertops that they can't focus on the merits of the house that lies underneath. That's especially true in New York

City, she says, where a lot of buyers currently live in rental apartments where they're not even allowed to paint, let alone knock down walls to reconfigure the floor plan. "A lot of people just don't have the spatial and visual imagination," Gibbs says. "They see what could be a third bedroom being used as a dining room, and that's the only way they can see it."

At Gordon's open house, traffic is so light that no amount of redecorating is going to yield an offer on this Sunday. It appears this house will be on the market awhile longer. Which means a couple of Sundays from now, home shoppers will again see a notice in the newspaper that this home will be available for their viewing pleasure. The door will open, and Gordon and her colleagues will deal with a parade of lookie-loos, house humpers, and other would-be home buyers, many of whom won't have the slightest interest in giving a real estate agent the time of day.

Back in New Orleans, much of the convention talk centers on the slowing housing market. In most seminars the fact that so many homes have been languishing on the market is treated as bad news, and the training gurus are pumping up agents by offering new tactics to try to juice sales. But in some of the meetings there's a counterintuitive notion on display, a contrarian wisdom based on a simple premise: In a world in which technology is making a lot of Realtors feel like an endangered species, could the end of the real estate boom be a *good* thing?

It's a sentiment based partly on the experiences of people like Gus Treewater. In 2004 Treewater and his wife, Jill, decided to sell their San Francisco condo. They did a little homework on what comparable homes were selling for, and guesstimated its value at nearly $900,000. Traditionally Realtors want a 6 percent commission, which on the Treewaters' house would total . . . $54,000. It's a staggering sum, far more than my parents paid for the home I grew up in.

And during the boom, when houses in places like San Francisco frequently received multiple offers within days of being listed, it seemed like a lot of compensation for very little effort.

Beyond the money, when Treewater had visited neighbors' open houses over the years, he'd been bothered by the way he'd seen real estate agents behave. Some lacked basic knowledge about the house, like the year it was built. Some were too quick to respond to a potential buyer's reluctance—say they didn't like a bathroom—with an offer to show them a different listing. It's conventional wisdom that agents' primary motive in holding an open house isn't to sell the listing, but to meet potential clients to whom they can sell some property—any property. Those murky motives bothered Treewater. Unlike an agent, Treewater knew everything there was to know about his house; he could show buyers around better than any stranger could. Selling a piece of property didn't look so hard, really—and if he might save $50,000 by doing it himself, why not give it a try? "I felt I could do as good or better a job as a broker could, because I had my best interests above anybody else's," he says.

So he found a real estate agent who agreed to handle all the paperwork once Treewater found a buyer and negotiated a price. The agent would charge a flat fee of $400, and Treewater ended up paying him another $400 to list the home in the computerized Multiple Listing Service. Treewater spent another $1,500 printing full-color brochures and signs. He listed the home on Craigslist (for free), and spent nearly $1,500 on newspaper advertisements to promote a series of open houses, which he hosted himself. All told, he spent about $5,000 out of his own pocket to alert potential buyers to his home.

By the end of the first Sunday open house, more than a hundred potential buyers had wandered through Chez Treewater. By the end of six weeks Gus and Jill had received four offers on their home. They ended up selling it for $860,000, not far off the $890,000 price at which they'd advertised it. Total commission paid: zero. "I'd do it again in a minute," Gus says.

He's hardly the only one fed up by paying high real estate commissions—and taking steps to avoid paying them. For decades the industry has fought off critics who see the fact that every broker wants to charge you 6 percent as something more than a coincidence. As *Freakonomics* authors Stephen J. Dubner and Steven D. Levitt have put it, some observers charge that Realtors "[behave] like a cross between a cartel and a mafia, hoarding access to home-sale databases and harassing competitors who dare to offer discounted commissions." No less than the free-marketeers at the *Wall Street Journal* have editorialized against the "Realtor Racket" and questioned whether the profession engages in price-fixing. Like Dubner and Levitt, the *Journal* looks at the situation as basic economics: Just as the power of the Internet has helped reduce the costs of buying books, stocks, and airline tickets, the day when agents could get away with charging $50,000 to sell a home should be relegated to the history books.

For agents, this is hardly a new concern. For decades a small percentage of homes have been listed by do-it-yourselfers as For Sale By Owner (which the industry calls FSBOs, or "fiz-bos"). And for people who want a modified do-it-yourself approach, two franchised giants, Help-U-Sell and Assist-to-Sell, have been around since the 1970s. These discounted brokers charge a flat fee—say, $2,995—to sell a house, no matter what the sales price. It's a model that makes sense to most people, since the actual work involved in selling a house doesn't appear to vary that much whether the house costs $300,000 or $900,000.

But the do-it-yourself method really caught fire during the boom, thanks largely to the Internet, which made it easy for novices to advertise their own listing. Despite the fact that everyone seems to have met someone who's successfully sold his own home, the industry works hard to dispel the notion that many people are successful at Realtor-free selling. While perhaps 15 percent of American homes typically sell without the aid of an agent, the National Association of Realtors suggests that many of them are sold between family members or friends, so there was no real need to market the property to the wider public. Even since the advent of Craigslist, eBay, and all the Internet-powered vehicles that let home sellers advertise a listing themselves, the majority of people who put a FOR SALE BY OWNER sign out front garner little interest from buyers, they say, and eventually cave in and list the house with an agent anyway. That's not surprising. Buying or selling a home is the biggest financial transaction in most people's lives. Why wouldn't they entrust it to a trained professional, the same way they entrust their health care to a doctor, their tax issues to an accountant, and their legal issues to a lawyer? You know, the kinds of people they make appointments to see.

Historically, consumers' embrace of do-it-yourself real estate tends to be cyclical. "These types of business models prosper in seller's markets," says consultant John Tuccillo. "When the market turns and it becomes a buyer's market, these [alternative players] go back into hibernation." That's why some of the folks in New Orleans welcome the end of the great twenty-first-century housing boom. Good-bye, Help-U-Sell—and hello, Century 21.

But lately some smart folks have been betting this cyclical pattern will be overcome by the power of the Internet. Thanks to technology, the brokers' biggest weapon—the Multiple Listing Service—just isn't as valuable as it was before. Nowadays home buyers can look up homes themselves on Realtor.com, and home sellers can list them for free online. As this information has become more widely available, why shouldn't costs go down? "The traditional, straight percentage-of-sale-price commission does not serve the interests of either home buyers or sellers," concluded a Brookings Institution study. "The traditional commission structure has become structurally unsound and should be rebuilt."

For salespeople whose jobs are upended when customers learn to buy whatever the salesman is selling without his help, there's a tried-and-true tactic of career reinvention: Begin to think of yourself not as a salesman, but as a *consultant*. Indeed, the *Freakonomics* authors, Dubner and Levitt, point to travel agents and stockbrokers as examples of professions that have made this transition; nowadays they call themselves "travel counselors" and "financial planning specialists." In fact, a pioneering group of Realtors has already begun making this shift. They belong to a group called—you guessed it—the National Association of Real Estate Consultants. Instead of the industry's full-service, commission-based model, the home-selling consultants offer à la carte pricing, charging different rates based on whether they'll actually show the house to buyers, advertise, negotiate the transaction, or merely handle the paperwork. Association founder Julie Garton-Good foresees a day when someone selling a home will pay in advance, often by credit card, choosing whether to write the ad himself or ante up for the consultant to do it. By 2014 she hopes that half of the homes in America will be sold by an agent working off a menu of prices, instead of a commission based on the home's value.

Her work has made her understandably unpopular among most of the nation's agents. "It has not been the most politically correct thing to do," Garton-Good says. "I call it the holy grail of the percentage commission—a lot of agents feel it's their birthright to get their full commission." She says these traditionalists overestimate the lure of à la carte pricing. Once consumers are told how much work is really involved in selling a house—about fifty hours, on average, she estimates—many decline to take on the work of showing the house themselves, and instead pay an agent to do more, not less. Still, she thinks folks who've jumped into real estate should be more willing to embrace the industry's changes, and more interested in working with consumers to better meet their needs. She characterizes the average agent's attitude this way: "We know the system is broken, we know that customers don't like it, but let's keep it a secret long enough to be able to retire."

So if these nontraditionalists' grand visions come to pass, there will still be plenty of real estate agents—er, *consultants*—to attend Rotary luncheons and sponsor Little League teams. Even as a price-conscious public and the power of the Internet change their business, many will adapt and survive.

On a Saturday night near the end of their convention, the assembled real estate pros don green T-shirts, masks, and beads. Clutching their drinks, they lead a boisterous parade down Bourbon Street. The spectacle is less bawdy than the usual Mardi Gras scenes, but since the average agent probably bears a strong resemblance to your mother, that's not a bad thing.

The celebratory atmosphere might be a bit surprising, since this convention takes place during what some observers have begun calling the worst housing recession since the Great Depression. Indeed, it's tempting to look upon the brokers' festivities as part of the city's tradition of throwing jazz funerals, and to see their march through the French Quarter as a final act of jubilation in honor of having lived through some of the best times to sell a home in the country's history.

But in between the partying, there's a quiet buzz throughout the convention focused on a couple of questions: Just how many agents will survive the downturn? And how many of those half million people who tried to turn House Lust into a way to make a living will admit defeat and seek their fortunes in another field?

Realtors are a perennially optimistic bunch, so it's no surprise, perhaps, that they've found a way to put a positive spin on the prospect that their ranks will thin. The attrition will be a good thing for everybody, most brokers say. The real estate world has become overpopulated with agents, and many look forward to the winnowing effect the slowdown will doubtlessly have. When the Realtor lobbying group's chief economist, David Lereah, predicts in a convention-hall speech that the number of people selling homes will decline as home sales fall, the crowd roars its applause. (Later he tells me the population of agents could drop by as much as 100,000 in the next year.) Sure enough, just a few weeks after the convention ends, the *Wall Street Journal* runs a story featuring agents who've left the industry to open a dog-training school or join a Web start-up—the latter example offering proof that what goes around, comes around.

Even newcomers who reaped small fortunes during the fat years aren't above rethinking their career plans during lean times. Among the people engaged in this introspection is Ron Spradlin, the bus driver–turned–agent in Fort Lauderdale.

After watching his income soar, Spradlin has now watched it

recede just as sharply. In his peak year, 2005, he earned more than $140,000. When I spoke to him in late 2006, he guessed his income for the year would be just $25,000. Part of that drop is a result of the general real estate slowdown, but Spradlin also suffered because a series of hurricanes damaged some of the rental property he'd bought for himself. Working to repair these homes took away from the time he had to work with clients.

In his own office he's seen agents growing discouraged and leaving the industry. "I would be totally lying if I said those thoughts hadn't come into my head," he says. The dismal numbers on his tax returns aren't the only reason. As he's gotten older he's become more aware of the value of the benefits that come with more traditional jobs—particularly pensions and 401(k) retirement accounts. "I may have to look at corporate America," he says, not sounding wild about the idea. But he still loves homes, he says, and he will never leave the industry entirely. "Even if it's only part-time, I will still be in real estate—there is no doubt in my mind," he says.

No matter how long the current housing bust lasts or how far it falls, there is one thing that's certain. This bust will be followed, someday, by another boom. And when it does, thousands of new people will begin dreaming of cashing in by selling homes for a living.

If history is any guide, most of these next-generation newcomers will learn a simple lesson: It's a jungle out there.

CHAPTER SEVEN

DOUBLING DOWN:
NAPLES, FLORIDA

It's Great for Getaways, but What's the Cost per Night?

If you ever find yourself talking to market researcher James Chung, you may be surprised to learn the question on his mind: Are you monogamous or promiscuous?

No, he's not interested in your sex life. Instead, Chung, the president of Reach Advisors, who makes his living using survey data and focus groups to better understand what we buy and, more important, why. He uses this framework to describe the way twenty-first-century Americans think about their vacations.

Monogamous types are happy going back to the same vacation spot year after year. They prize comfort, convenience, and familiarity over novelty and adventure. They're the kind of people who are more likely to reorder something they've previously liked at a restaurant or to buy all their clothing at a single store, rather than try something new. And when it comes to real estate, if they've got the money, they've traditionally been the people most likely to buy a vacation home, since they see no drawbacks to visiting the same treasured spot time and again. Besides, these rational types argue, owning a vacation home can be a good investment and make sound economic sense. Even monogamous types who can't afford to buy a vacation home find ways to stay true to their favorite getaway by renting the same lakeside cabin summer after summer, or by becoming regulars at the same hotel or resort.

Promiscuous types, on the other hand, want adventure and variety. They have trouble remaining loyal to the same getaway year after year. If they're less affluent, they're the kinds of folks who take elaborate driving vacations, spending each night in a different bed. If they're affluent, they might flit between posh hotels in Europe, luxury resorts in the tropics, and perhaps even exotic African safaris. Owning a vacation home has typically held little appeal for them, because who wants to go back to the Hamptons or Cape Cod every year when you can go to Bali one year and Costa Rica the next?

But as in our love lives, often people's attitudes toward vacation homes change over time. We get older, less adventurous, more willing to compromise. We ditch our randy past and get the urge to settle in for the long haul.

It's a life-cycle shift that Audrey Heckaman understands well.

Heckaman is a forty-year-old pharmaceutical salesperson who lives in Cleveland. As a single woman she's taken some fabulous vacations over the years. But over time, as she watched her friends settle into more routine vacation lifestyles, she started to feel a little jealous. Then one of her bosses bought a place in Naples, Florida, which sounded idyllic; he'd boast that his family had a place waiting for them whenever they wanted to get away, and they never had to think too hard about where to go.

Their move also made financial sense. This boss was constantly bragging about how his vacation home had soared in value. Meanwhile, Heckaman's stock portfolio had been offering scant returns, so she was looking for alternatives. "I don't want to put my money in the stock market," she says. "Real estate is more tangible, and I can enjoy it."

So after years of promiscuous vacationing, Heckaman traded in her brief flings with travel books and tour guides and decided to settle down. During a trip to Naples she made an appointment with a real estate agent. Together they drove to a condo community called

Forest Glen, a few miles inland. After looking at a model, she agreed to pay $221,000 for a two-bedroom, second-floor condo being built on the fifth fairway of the community's golf course. It was the beginning of a beautiful relationship.

Since closing on her vacation home in 2004, Heckaman usually flies south a half dozen times a year. To help pay the mortgage, sometimes she rents her condo out, charging up to $3,500 a month during the height of the winter season.

Today she has only one regret: that she didn't buy a getaway home even sooner.

The American love affair with vacation homes was once a privilege reserved for the affluent. When we think of summer homes, we may still envision the palatial, Gilded Age mansions of Newport, the rustic Great Camps of the Catskills, or the Gatsby-esque estates of Eastern Long Island. Or, in these celebrity-obsessed times, perhaps we imagine having a second home in the places where today's A-list goes to relax: a penthouse condo in Miami's South Beach, a pied-à-terre in Greenwich Village, or a ski chalet in Aspen.

But in fact, today you don't need a record deal or Google stock options to own a second home. According to a 2006 survey by the National Association of Realtors, the typical vacation-home owner has yearly earnings of $102,000—not pocket change, but not exactly a Bill Gates–size paycheck, either.

And while real-estate gossip columnists like Braden Keil regularly report on celebs who've dropped tens of millions on Hamptons estates, the average vacation home is far more modest: In 2006 the average buyer spent only around $200,000.

As second homes have migrated down the socioeconomic food chain, interest in them has grown. During the real estate boom, as many as 40 percent of the homes sold each year were being bought by people who already had a primary residence—and even as the housing market slowed in 2006, Americans were still buying vacation homes at a record pace, with 1.07 million changing hands that year. By 2006 Americans owned 6.8 million abodes where they could escape from their daily rat race.

Twenty-first-century Americans are hardly the first to want a place to get away from it all. Two millennia ago wealthy Athenians and Romans kept country residences. (Wouldn't you need a break if your day job involved inventing concepts like democracy and philosophy?) For centuries affluent Parisians have escaped to their châteaus. And British royals have long split their time between palaces and castles whose names are familiar to anyone who reads *People* magazine: Buckingham and Windsor, Kensington and Balmoral.

While an unheated pondside cabin may have little in common with these royal retreats, they do share the quality that is the essence of a vacation home. "Defined not by location, architectural style or size, a summer house—or cottage—represents a psychological destination," Amy Willard Cross writes in her exploration of the appeal of vacation retreats. "It provides refuge from a wearying world . . . where the demands and routines of normal life recede from memory."

Part of the modern-day allure of a monogamous relationship with our vacation homes stems from the real estate boom, of course, which sent home prices in plenty of resort areas soaring. But beyond that short-lived price spike, there are other factors—both economic and sociological—that are driving our desire to own a home away from home.

In places like Florida, discount airlines are a key part of the equation. Thanks to Southwest and JetBlue, people can now routinely fly halfway across the country for $200 or so—less than the average round-trip train fair from Boston to New York. The discount carriers didn't exist prior to the deregulation of the airline industry in 1978, and it was only during the 1990s that Southwest and its imitators began to have true national reach. Owning a vacation home beyond driving distance was once impractical for the middle class, but the spread of cheap airfares—along with Internet sites like Travelocity, which help us find them—now gives us the option of keeping second homes on opposite coasts, even on different continents.

The changing nature of professional jobs is another key factor. Unlike the rich folks who once summered in Newport, most of today's vacation-home owners are still working, but they're likely to have more freedom in how—and where—they do it. Compared with our parents' generation, more Americans are self-employed today. That frees them from counting the number of vacation days they take, and gives them more flexibility to sneak away for long weekends or declare the office closed between Christmas and New Year's.

For those of us who remain on somebody else's payroll, technology and new ways of working are making many jobs far more portable. If you hang out in a resort setting, you'll find a lot of people who are staying in their vacation homes but aren't really on vacation. Thanks to BlackBerries, e-mail, and cell phones, many of these workers needn't even tell clients they're working from poolside instead of from their usual Aeron. Those who can't work remotely find ways to fit visits to their vacation home into a regimen of heavy business travel. And with so many businesspeople on the road so much, some companies don't really care where they spend their weekends. In fact, for someone based in Chicago who has to spend the week working in Atlanta, it might actually save the company money in airfare if he heads to his Florida bungalow before resuming the business-travel grind on Monday. For evidence of how prevalent this lifestyle has become, drive to the Fort Myers airport early Monday morning, and you'll find no shortage of husbands and wives dropping one another off for a business trip, while the remaining (lucky) spouse stays behind at the vacation home for the week.

Technology isn't just allowing people to work from their vacation homes—it's also making it simpler to locate one, buy it, and manage it after the purchase. In the last decade the emergence of real estate Web sites and e-mail-ready digital photos have made long-distance home shopping far more convenient. In places like Naples, brokers get a lot of their business from Web sites like VacationHomes.com, or by setting up their own sites like NaplesRealEstate.com. Once you've bought a getaway home, the Internet makes it a lot easier for those who choose to rent it; Web sites like Craigslist make it a snap to find tenants, eliminating the costs of relying on an agent to act as middleman. The Internet also allows second-home owners to manage their home's upkeep from afar. Some resort-home owners I met get weekly e-mails from a caretaker, letting them know the temperature of their pool water. Another one routinely uses a remote Webcam to see the view from his back deck hundreds of miles away.

Aside from these rational factors, fans of this lifestyle cite two big emotional factors that drive their purchases.

The first is the pressurized nature of twenty-first-century professional work. For too many of us, our jobs are no longer a 9:00-to-5:00 gig, but a 24/7 obsession—one that's become harder to turn off. And while it's great that our bosses let many of us work from home for part of the workweek, the side effect is that our homes are becoming an extension of our offices, which can make it harder to relax there. To cut the cord, more of us need to change the scenery a little—and a vacation home makes that so much easier.

At the same time, the sharp run-up in home prices during the boom made a lot of people begin to worry that if they didn't buy a vacation home soon, they'd never be able to afford one. In relationship terms, it's an anxiety that's similar to the one women used to feel that if they didn't marry before age thirty, their marital "stock" would plummet. If you talk to brokers and their clients in resort locations, this sentiment comes up repeatedly: "I felt like it was now or maybe never."

The media has only served to amplify this feeling. Each Friday in its Escapes section, the *New York Times* writes about city dwellers fortunate enough to be buying second-home getaways, making single-home denizens (like me) feel like we're part of a dwindling, left-behind population. As second homes have become more common, the newspapers have begun to highlight even more extreme vacation lifestyles. "The Third Home Comes Within Reach" read one recent *Times* headline. For people for whom a mere vacation home is not sufficient, the paper recently presented another option: "The Allure of Buying Your Own Private Island."

While reading those stories can instill a dose of vacation-home envy, there's one event that can really turn us green: when someone from your social circle takes the plunge.

Consider one example: Each summer during the 1990s a former

colleague of mine rented a beach house with his wife and two children on Prince Edward Island, on Canada's eastern edge. They'd been visiting the island for years, and they'd always talked about buying a place of their own there. During one summer visit they heard lots of anxious talk about how developers were starting to buy up vacant land, and how prices of island properties were likely to spiral out of reach over the next few years. At the same time the Canadian dollar had recently dropped, meaning a buyer using American dollars could save even more by buying then.

On a whim they began looking at land. When they returned home, my colleague called to tell me about their purchase. For around $30,000 they'd gotten an acre and a half of waterfront property, paid for with their home equity line on their primary house. They had no plans to build immediately, but hoped to erect a cottage there someday.

Someday arrived quicker than they expected. Soon they hired a carpenter to put up a simple three-bedroom cottage with a large porch and expansive water views. When it was finished his family's summers magically evolved into a luxurious, Cheever-esque routine. The first week of July they'd load up their car and make the long drive from suburban New York City to their new island home. After a week of lobster and windsurfing my friend would fly home, leaving his wife—a teacher who has summers off—on the island with the kids. He'd live a carefree bachelor lifestyle for the rest of July, eating takeout and working late. Then he'd return to the island for two weeks of August vacation. At the end of his stay they'd ready the home for winter, then drive back to New York, rested and restored, in plenty of time for school to begin.

I don't begrudge my friend's summer-home lifestyle—indeed, he's been quick to offer to let me use his place sometime. But I do envy the simplicity of the routine it creates. For someone who enjoys the monogamous vacation lifestyle, vacation-home ownership provides a default option. Owners have no need to weigh dozens of options, fight for a reservation, or waste time looking for a beachfront rental (which may not wind up being as nice as it looked in the advertisements). In the same way that Netflix helps take the stress out of DVD rentals—*Look, the movie I wanted to see just magically showed up in my mailbox!*—having a getaway home seems to uncomplicate the vacation selection and planning process.

True, returning to the same bed again and again may not be as exciting as sleeping in a new one every night. But if you walk down Fifth Avenue South in Naples, the city's main drag, you'll find no fewer than eight different real estate offices, each with a front window covered with photos for getaway homes available for purchase. And most nights you'll find at least a few people huddled out front, ogling the listings.

Monogamy, apparently, can be pretty appealing.

Some of the people who decide to embrace this lifestyle will find themselves, as I did one morning, in the passenger seat of Lana Butsky's orange Hummer H2.

Butsky is a blond, Bosnian-born former model who arrived in Naples in 1999 and began selling real estate. When I meet her, she's wearing a stylish green dress and expensive sunglasses. Like many agents in places like Naples, she focuses her business almost exclusively on the out-of-town crowd. Instead of advertising in local newspapers, her ads run in the *Chicago Tribune* and the *Toronto Star*. And she relies on Web sites like escapehomes.com to send her a steady stream of referrals from all over the country.

When new clients fly into town, Butsky often picks them up at the airport and takes them on a driving tour of the area. Like most brokers, she has a standard route she follows, with standard tour-guide patter. During a would-be buyer's first visit, agents say the goal isn't so much to sell them a house as it is to sell them on Naples itself.

She begins in the city's southernmost tip, a neighborhood called Port Royal. "It's the most exclusive part of Naples," she says. "You have properties here between $3 million and $30 million." As we drive past enormous beachfront homes, one is so large I ask if it's the town library. "No, that's one house," she says, then points toward the neighborhood where Shania Twain and Tom Cruise's mother each own homes.

Naples has attracted America's affluent class for more than a century. Northerners first began eyeing the region as a winter resort in the 1880s, when promoters printed brochures declaring the nascent city to be a paradise where "invalids can escape the chilling blasts of winter and semitropical fruit can be grown for profit." Soon these speculators had divided the downtown area into 1,000 lots, which sold for $10 apiece.

The region remained sparsely settled until the 1950s, when the advent of air-conditioning and jet travel made it more comfortable and accessible. Every couple of decades a hurricane comes and flattens things, reminding people that living in this paradise carries its own set of risks. But over the past few decades Naples has emerged as southwest Florida's most attractive city, with a renowned philharmonic orchestra, an absurd number of golf courses, and countless upscale restaurants. Back when most vacationers drove to Florida, northerners from the East Coast followed Interstate 95 to Palm Beach on the Atlantic side of the state, while midwesterners took I-75 and ended up in Fort Myers or Naples. Today, even as more people fly to their vacation spots, those regional-cultural preferences continue.

As Butsky heads north, into slightly less pricey parts of town, she ticks off regional advantages that go beyond the wonderful weather. She mentions the state's zero income tax. She explains how homestead laws allow people to file for bankruptcy and still keep multimillion-dollar homes. That's why O. J. Simpson lives in Florida, she says—he owes millions as a result of the civil judgments against him, but he still lives in a very nice home. "No one can touch him," Butsky says.

Butsky sees a steady flow of Americans from cold-weather states who want to buy Naples property. But in the last few years the city has emerged as an international destination as well. "A few years ago it was the Germans," she says. "Now it's the British." Like Americans, they too are drawn by cheaper airfares and by the sense that the money they invest in a home may just outperform their stock portfolios.

There are no gangs in Naples, but as Butsky drives through town, she points out the different cultural territories. Kind of like a high school cafeteria, every vacation spot has its own lines of demarcation, its informal system of who lives where—and why.

On Cape Cod, by long-standing tradition, Provincetown attracted gay vacationers, Wellfleet and Truro were favored by psychiatrists, while African Americans migrated to Oak Bluffs, on Martha's Vineyard.

In the Hamptons the long-standing rule, recited by the writer Steven Gaines, has been that "Southampton was for the sporting rich (inherited wealth); Bridgehampton for the nearly rich (working on it); and East Hampton for the really rich (a meritocracy of the self-made)." Within each community, there are further dividing lines: in Southampton, for instance, the tennis players belong to the Meadow, the beachgoers favor Southampton Bathing, and golfers join Shinnecock or the National.

Naples, too, has its own dividing lines, each drawn on the basis of class and preferred leisure-time activity: golf, boating, or the beach. Boat people want to be on property where they can dock their vessel, usually on one of Naples's networks of canals. For people who are desperate to be close to the beach, developers have constructed high-rise beachfront condo towers on the city's north side. Golf people tend to live farther inland, in one of the scores of condo communities that have sprung up around new golf courses. Until the boom of the early 2000s, these places tended to be quite affordable, and the destination of choice for upper-middle-class northerners buying their first vacation spot. "They say, 'I want to get a foot on the ladder while it's still affordable,'" says Tom Doyle, a real estate agent who relocated from Minnesota and has come to specialize in selling golf-course condos to northerners.

Butsky steers her Hummer over to Third Street South, the city's artsy restaurant neighborhood. "Nightlife is not that well developed here," Butsky admits. "Most of the people in Naples tend to go to sleep by nine o'clock. But that's changing. We're getting younger people who made big money during the dot-com era coming down." Naples will never be Miami, but slowly it's shedding its image as a place filled mostly with people who eat dinner at 5:00 p.m. and like to show off photos of their grandkids between games of bridge.

For people stretching to buy a vacation home, one tried-and-true strategy has been to buy a place and rent it out during the high season of January to April. The standard rule of thumb is that those four months of rental can pay the property taxes, condo fees, and all the maintenance on the property for the year, leaving the homeowner only the mortgage to contend with. Still, even some people who buy a place with that math in mind find themselves reluctant to share their getaway with anonymous tenants.

Colin O'Neill runs a snow-removal business in Minnesota, so if anyone deserves a bit of winter sunshine, it'd be him. In late 2003 he bought a golf condo in Naples, intending to rent it out to cut the costs. "I always thought that's how we'd make it work," he says. But once his wife finished decorating, he couldn't stand the idea of strangers messing it up. "You know what? We're not letting anyone stay here," he told her. "We can afford it, so let's just keep it our little escape."

Today the O'Neills visit eight to ten times a year, spending as many as sixty nights a year in Naples. "We have no regrets whatsoever," Colin says.

Still, that leaves their house empty more than 300 nights a year. So like many seasonal residents, the O'Neills hire a home-watch service that sends a rep to visit their house each week. These services abound in areas like Naples. For $25 a visit, someone checks the locks, makes sure the fire alarms are working, flushes the toilets, briefly runs the dishwasher and washing machine (to keep the watertight gaskets resilient), and checks for bugs. If your getaway is a full-fledged house—front yard and all—these caretaker services will mow the lawn and trim the hedges. And if you are willing to pay a bit extra, some services will even spend time getting the house ready just before you arrive: cranking up the air-conditioning, stocking the fridge, and getting the pool to the right temperature. After all, what good is a vacation home if you have to spend your whole weekend sweeping up dead bugs or waiting in lines at the grocery store?

Like any resort area, Naples's employment base depends on tourism—but here more than most places, a lot of that employment revolves around these getaway properties. If you add up all the people who perform these "home-watch" services, along with the thousands of construction jobs required to build these homes and the brokers who help them buy and sell, a substantial portion of the population here owes its economic well-being directly to people's desire to own a retreat. Agent Tom Doyle points out that Naples has no other big industries aside from tourism, so real estate really is the region's major economic driver. Says Doyle: "If it weren't for second homes, Naples wouldn't exist."

After Butsky drops me off, I spend some time wandering around downtown Naples. It's a really nice town, but I feel like I don't fit in. Most of the people here seem far more affluent than me. In general, when it comes to the second-home crowd, I feel like an outsider.

That's hardly surprising. Growing up I had only one family friend with a vacation home—and it was hardly a fabulous Hamptons-style manse. Instead, this family bought a plot of land in Vermont, a few miles from a ski area. One summer they arranged for a group of their friends—my family among them—to drive up to the lot, each armed with tents and camping gear. Waiting there was a huge load of lumber. For the next week the fathers, mostly attorneys, dentists, and insurance agents, climbed ladders and lifted hammers, together building a simple A-frame chalet. Meanwhile, the mothers cooked over Coleman stoves and tried to keep the kids away from the power tools. By the end of the week the walls and roof were finished, and after this army of free labor left, a plumber, electrician, and carpenter arrived to finish the job. In return for their toil, each family that helped build the house was invited to use it for a week each winter. During one February week the following year, I learned to ski.

This do-it-yourself route to vacation-home ownership may sound ridiculously quaint, a remnant of commune-style, hippie-era 1960s living. But in fact, as I began exploring how the second-home crowd lives, I found plenty of evidence that it's just one of the many creative and affordable ways to join the vacation-home-owner club.

Take Bill Sands, whom I met on an airplane one evening. Sands is forty-four years old, and a real estate broker who lives near Reading, Pennsylvania. During our flight we begin talking about houses. In addition to his primary residence, he tells me, he owns three vacation homes. (In the worldview sketched out by market researcher James Chung, this makes Sands a vacation-home polygamist.) "When I tell somebody that, their eyebrows will rise," he tells me. "They'll say, 'Wow, you bought a place in the south of France?' They associate that with being fabulously wealthy." But in fact, while Sands is no pauper, he bought his vacation homes on the cheap, often using the profits from one to finance the next. And he's been able to find some amazing deals, thanks to the many hours he invests in shoe-leather research and on the Internet.

Sands bought and sold a couple of vacation properties—including a condo at the Jersey shore—when he was still in his twenties. Among the three vacation homes he owns now, he's held one—in St. Thomas in the U.S. Virgin Islands—since the early 1990s. While on vacation there, Sands turned his attention to property. At the time the island's economy was depressed after a recent hurricane, and real estate prices were low. Sands zeroed in on a condo community whose steel-and-concrete construction made it less vulnerable to hurricane damage. Sands found condos priced as low as $30,000. Poking around and talking with locals, he discovered why: The condo association was racked with infighting, and the dissension was scaring off buyers. Undeterred, Sands bought a unit for $37,000. Inside he made minor improvements using paint, better lighting, tropical-print furniture, and a space-saving Murphy bed. He also joined the board of directors of the condo association, and over time helped quell the quarreling, which boosted the complex's reputation—and the values of its condos. In 2003 he sold his original studio unit for $114,000, and traded up to a larger one-bedroom condo in the same complex.

These days Sands checks online airfares to St. Thomas nearly every day, and often takes spur-of-the-moment trips there, leaving on Thursday and returning on Tuesday. In an average year he spends thirty nights a year in St. Thomas.

By the early 2000s, after having several vacation-home purchases turn out profitably, he was open to new possibilities. One day he saw a listing online for a condo in the south of France, halfway between Cannes and Nice. Priced at around $55,000, it seemed like a good deal, so he hired a French attorney to investigate. When everything checked out, Sands bought it sight unseen. A few months later he nervously paid a visit. "It turned out to be very lovely," he says, with a huge deck overlooking the Mediterranean. He rents that unit out only to friends, and spends a few weeks a year there himself.

In early 2006 he uncovered another diamond in the rough, a waterfront home on Moon Lake in Pennsylvania, about an hour north of his primary residence. The two-bedroom home appeared nice enough, but what most intrigued Sands was that the property had three distinct pieces—a main house, a guesthouse, and a big barn—that were all served by separate utilities, and could be easily subdivided. The place was listed at $150,000. He offered $135,000. The sellers accepted, and before the closing Sands found a friend who agreed to buy the guesthouse for $70,000, reducing Sands's out-of-pocket cost to $65,000. For that, he now owns a 1,500-square-foot waterfront home. "I like to find these sleeper properties," Sands says. Since his newest vacation home is just an hour's drive from his regular home, he's begun staying at his lake house 100 nights a year, often entertaining friends. All told, he stays in one of his vacation properties at least one out of three nights every year.

Sands admits his lifestyle wouldn't work for most people. "If I had kids I wouldn't be able to do this—I'd be busy with Little League," he says. And even though he's spent less to buy most of his homes than some people spend on luxury cars, the carrying costs do add up. But since he's managed to make money on nearly everything he's owned so far, Sands mostly shrugs off concerns about the ownership costs. Like a lot of people, he feels his frequent getaways are a necessary antidote to his high-stress professional life. Yes, it might be cheaper to rent vacation homes, but he puts a premium on convenience.

"I want the feeling of comfort and familiarity, and that empowers me," he says. "When I work as hard as I do when I'm in town, I need to go someplace and recharge." As much as he loves his primary Pennsylvania residence, work has a way of intruding there, and it's hard to unwind. "When I'm away I can really clear my mind," Sands says. "I believe your mind gets cleansed when you go to these different destinations."

For Norm Jagger, a single destination works just as nicely. Jagger is forty-seven years old and runs an asphalt-and-aggregate company outside St. Paul, Minnesota. In early 2004, utilizing a stock-option windfall he'd earned at a previous job, he decided to shop for a lake home within driving distance of St. Paul. He hoped to pay less than $400,000 for a newer property on the lake within a two-and-a-half-hour drive of the city.

It took him eighteen months of searching, and he had to make some compromises. The home he purchased was thirty minutes farther than he'd hoped to drive, but he finds the three-plus-hour Friday-afternoon drives soothing. "I almost need the drive to decompress, to be able to relax and get into a state of mind to enjoy the weekend," he says. In return for the extra drive time, he got a 1,600-square-foot home on a beautiful lake for $399,000, a hair under his price limit. His wife and three teenagers (each bringing friends) go up almost every summer weekend. They're hardly alone: As their family drives north each Friday, the roadways are filled with thousands of other people heading to weekend lake houses. "It's just an exodus," Jagger says.

With the baby boom generation in its preretirement years, buying a vacation home to use as a weekend home now, and a semipermanent home later, has become an increasingly common form of retirement planning. Many of these buyers intend to turn their vacation home into their primary residence once they retire, and some even find they like their getaway so much, they decide to make it permanent far earlier than they expected.

Leslie Turruellas and her husband lived in a large colonial in Annapolis, Maryland. They loved warm weather, and regularly vacationed in the Caribbean. Then they discovered Naples, and the urge for monogamy kicked in. Though still in their early forties, they decided to buy a second home in Naples as a vacation spot for now and a potential retirement home for later. Thanks to cheap airfares, they found themselves spending more and more time in Florida. So in 2005 they opted to trade in those Maryland winters for year-round Florida sunshine in a beachfront, ninth-floor condo. Leslie's husband still commutes to a job at a software company in Washington, D.C., flying out on Monday mornings and returning to Naples on Thursday nights. But that lifestyle is hardly unusual among younger Neopolitans.

Often people think of resort areas as having predominantly older populations, since retired people are the ones who have the most time to enjoy themselves there. That's especially true in Florida, of course, which has long been known as heaven's waiting room. But Turruellas says they've been pleasantly surprised by how many younger people like themselves are making Naples their home, thanks to the flexibility to telecommute or travel to jobs up north. "It's really changing," she says. "And as all these elderly people pass on, there's going to be a whole new wave of young people here." Usually second-home owners like the Turruellas are treated as out-of-towners by longtime residents. But since the Turruellas have sold their Annapolis place and converted their second home into their first-choice home, they enjoy a new status in Naples. Nowadays they're locals.

As I drove around Naples with Lana Butsky, I couldn't help but notice that many of the beachfront homes have shutters over their windows. At night most of the houses are dark. They're vacant, she says, estimating that the average Naples vacation-home owner uses the place just two months a year.

This vacancy factor is the biggest problem with the monogamous vacation-home lifestyle. There's something unsettling about a home that sits empty for so much of its life. The inefficiency of it strikes some people as wasteful. That's why Bill Sands's friends tease him about his underutilized French condo, and why one Naples home-owner I met admitted that if you divide the costs of his winter home against the nights he actually uses it, he'd probably save money by staying in a suite at the Ritz-Carlton.

The unused-vacation-home phenomenon is hardly new, but a few decades ago some smart folks came up with a way to take advantage of it. And in doing so they created a way for people who are not at all affluent to have a taste of what it's like to own a vacation home.

It's a lifestyle I aim to experience myself. So when I arrive in Naples I don't check into a hotel. Instead, I arrange to stay at the Charter Club Resort, overlooking Naples Bay. The resort is a series of three-story yellow buildings. Out back are a pool and a small outdoor bar. Inside my second-floor unit I find two large bedrooms, two bath-rooms, a spacious living room, a clean and efficient kitchen, and a large screened deck with a view of the water.

My first evening at the Charter Club I visit the small clubhouse over the office. There is a bar, a table with an oversize chess set, some old furniture, and a long row of paperback books. On a coffee table sit three pizzas. Behind the bar is a man named Bill Shook, serving drinks.

Charter Club is a time-share, and this is the weekly cocktail party for visiting owners.

The concept of time-sharing was invented in the 1960s at resorts in the Alps. Instead of selling someone a condo that's exclusively theirs 365 nights a year, a time-share developer would divide ownership in the condo into fifty-two one-week segments. Then he'd sell those one-week increments to buyers, who'd pay a small fraction of the unit's total value, plus a yearly maintenance fee, for a perpetual right to use the unit a specific week each year. In addition to the purchase price, time-share owners would pay an annual maintenance fee of a few hundred dollars. The result: Suddenly even working-class people could own a tiny slice of a vacation home.

The time-share concept took off in the United States in the 1970s, with mixed results. Thanks to a glut of condominium building in Florida, developers began creating tons of time-share units, and to peddle them they hired superaggressive salespeople. They offered prospective buyers free vacations on the condition they sit through a ninety-minute sales presentation. Once inside the room salesmen often turned on the hard sell, utilizing a slippery patter and the underhanded closing techniques familiar to anyone who's ever seen *Glengarry Glen Ross*. "Sometimes people would buy because they were really uncomfortable," says Howard Nussbaum, president of the American Resort Development Association, the industry's lobbying arm. "We have a colorful past."

Over time legislation forced the industry to rely less on high-pressure sales techniques. Big players like Marriott and Disney entered the time-share business and raised standards. The old system in which a time-share owner had the right to only a single week at a particular resort evolved into a more flexible system in which owners routinely trade units and accrue points, exchanging, say, a February week in Florida for an October week in Hawaii. As these trading schemes proliferated, time-share owners became a bit like couples who swing: On paper they have a monogamous relationship with one locale, but in reality they have the option of tossing their keys in the fishbowl each time they go away in hopes of finding something a little more exciting and new—even if it's only for a night or two.

A lot of people who don't know much about the concept—

including me—remain leery. But the industry insists it's cleaned up its act and is now selling a product that makes economic sense. You don't buy an entire pizza if you want just one slice, so why would you buy an entire vacation home when you'll use it only a few weeks each year? "The fact is that people who buy our product love it and buy more of it," Nussbaum says. More than three million U.S. families own a time-share, and each year Americans spend roughly $8 billion on them, with the average week costing $15,800. Industry surveys show 85 percent of time-share owners are satisfied customers, and one in five owners becomes a repeat buyer. "I think this is the future of the way people want to vacation," Nussbaum says.

Munching pizza at the Charter Bay owners' party, I meet several folks who are among that satisfied majority. Chief among them is a seventy-three-year-old woman named Pamela. She's visiting with her husband, her adult daughter, and three grandchildren.

"Are you an owner?" Pamela asks, coming up to me. No, I say, telling her that I'm just looking. We spend much of the next hour chatting, but these folks are uncomfortable speaking to a reporter, so I agree not to use their full names.

This family lives in Orlando, and has been vacationing at the Charter Bay Club for five years. They were unfamiliar with time-shares until about a decade ago, when they were driving around Marco Island and one of them needed to use the bathroom. They stopped at a time-share resort. The salesman told them they could use the restroom if they listened to his sales pitch. Intrigued by the concept, they bought a unit. Today they own more than a half dozen time shares, all in Florida.

They are unusually savvy about managing them, mostly because their daughter took an all-day seminar designed for time-share sales reps that explained the finer points of how the various trading schemes operate. This family now puts tons of energy into accruing trading points, finding the best deals, and working to leverage as many nights of travel as they can out of their time-shares. In an average year this family spends seventy-one nights at time-share resorts.

Over drinks and pizza they explain their strategies to me.

Instead of buying time-shares at resorts they actually want to visit, they focus on buying units at distressed resorts at low prices, then try to use the points they gain from owning those units to trade for stays at more desirable locations. "Buy a dump and trade it," Pamela tells me repeatedly. I tell her I'd be uncomfortable buying a time-share in Florida, since the costs of getting my family back and forth each year would add up. If I were going to buy a time-share, I tell her, I'd want a summer week on Cape Cod. Pamela grows increasingly frustrated with me—in her view I just don't get it. It makes no difference if I want to stay in Hawaii or Cape Cod; the smart strategy is to find a low-cost time-share, regardless of its location, that I can trade for the vacations I really want.

They even get specific, whispering conspiratorially about particularly good deals at a place called Fisherman's Village in Punta Gorda, where owners are practically giving away time-shares to avoid paying their annual maintenance fees. If I'm going to take my kids to Disney World, they insist I need to stay at the Liki Tiki Village Resort, preferably in building 800 or 1200. I should also try the Sea Watch in Fort Myers, but avoid units 1, 2, 3, or 45, 46, or 47, which are too close to a noisy biker bar. Charter Club, where we are tonight, is a nice adult destination, but there are too few families with small children, so my kids would probably be bored here, they say.

I try to follow what Pamela is telling me, but I understand only pieces of it. The truth is, time-shares are a bit like rotisserie baseball leagues. People who are involved in them can be almost cultlike in their passion, but to the uninitiated it just seems really confusing. Time-shares have their own language, with special calendars of red weeks and gold weeks and different networks (Interval International or RCI) through which you can exchange vacations with other owners. Pamela admits it takes some effort to learn to manage time-shares the way her family does, but she says it is well worth the investment. "This is the cheapest way to take a vacation," she says.

As Pamela's family heads off for dinner, I chat with Bill Shook, the sales rep for Charter Club, who's dispensing drinks from behind the bar. He's been selling time-shares for decades, and he recalls the early days when the sales tactics were pretty slimy. Shook says most of the riffraff left the industry in 1981, when Florida required anyone selling time-shares to obtain a real estate license. Shook has a Jimmy Buffett–style, it's-all-good air about him, and it's hard for me to imagine him strong-arming people to make sales. He says he doesn't have to. After spending a night here, many people are immediately sold on the place. The result: He sells sixty or seventy units a year without trying very hard.

Technically, someone who buys a time-share is purchasing a piece of real estate. They are given a property deed, the same as if they bought a home. But buyer beware: Unlike traditional real estate, time-shares typically do not appreciate in value, and people who buy in hopes they will make money when they resell it generally wind up disappointed. Bill Shook may sell you a $15,000 Charter Club vacation week; if you decide to resell it, you may get just a fraction of that value back. While it's tempting to look at a time-share as an investment—and folks like Pamela do fancy themselves as "owners"—it's more like a prepaid expense than an asset. It allows you to lock in your vacation plans years ahead of time, hopefully at a lower cost.

Still, in the same way people turn unlikely things like baseball cards or Beanie Babies into vehicles for profit, a few brave souls do make money by investing in time-shares. Online, I meet a guy named Jon Hassel. He owns four time-share weeks at Charter Club, but he's never actually seen the place. Hassel has a day job as an insurance salesman, but he spends ten hours a week acting as a sort of time-share day trader, trolling Web sites and looking to buy low and sell high.

At the time of our conversation he owns thirty-eight times-shares in Florida, Colorado, Nevada, and Arizona. He'll use only five of these vacation weeks himself. The rest he tries to rent out or flip for profits. "I don't look to get greedy; I just try to make a little bit," he says, describing how he'll buy a time-share for $2,000 and try to quickly resell it for $3,000. In the last twelve months Hassel has sold fifteen time-shares, and sometimes he'll own one for just a couple of weeks. He claims he's made money on every transaction.

Hassel believes that as the costs of resort homes soar ever higher, time-shares will only become more appealing to the vast majority of nonaffluent families. "If you want a condo on Marco Island, it will cost you every bit of a million dollars," Hassel says. "So do you lay out a million dollars, or do you lay out $7,000, which will get you a week on Marco Island every year for the rest of your life?"

For a guy like me, without a million dollars to spend, it's pretty compelling logic.

Even for a man with many millions, it's an intriguing bit of math.

As the founder of America Online and later chairman of AOL Time Warner, Steve Case has a net worth that *Forbes* has estimated at $900 million. And in keeping with his mogul lifestyle, he's owned multiple vacation homes over the years. At one point, in addition to his primary residence in Virginia, he owned getaways in Florida, Santa Fe, and San Francisco. But the economics of these homes always bothered him. "You have this dynamic where you feel guilty you're not using them more," Case told me, sitting in his Washington, D.C., office one afternoon. "When you do have vacation time, you figure you might as well go there because you're paying for it, and it's kind of crazy not to, even if you maybe want to go somewhere else." He pauses. "It's an odd dynamic."

When Case tried to take his family to destinations where he didn't own a home, he had mixed results. In particular, he recalls renting a home in Hawaii that he'd found online. The digital photos he saw were great, and the house did have six bedrooms, as advertised. But what he couldn't see when he'd booked the house online was its funky layout: The only connection between the upstairs and downstairs was via an outdoor stairway, and Case's small children weren't wild about sleeping in bedrooms that would require them to go outside if they wanted to get to their mom and dad's room in the middle of the night. "We ended up using only four of the bedrooms, and the two youngest kids were sleeping on the couches in the living room," Case says. Between the slight remorse he felt over his own vacation homes and the less-than-stellar experiences he'd had arranging stays elsewhere, Case sensed an unmet need. "I had enough experience with vacations to know there had to be a better way."

Then in May of 2003 Case saw an ad in the *Wall Street Journal* for a company called Exclusive Resorts. The company had been founded a couple of years earlier by a Colorado entrepreneur who aimed to create a vacation experience that would be a cross between a time-share and a country club. Wealthy members would pay a large up-front initiation fee (as much as several hundred thousand dollars), followed by annual dues in the $20,000 range. In return they would get the rights to use sprawling, ultraluxurious homes in resort destinations for up to forty-eight nights a year. The deal would be different from time-share resorts because members wouldn't have an ownership stake in the real estate. Instead, as with high-end country clubs, members would get back 80 percent of their initiation fee when they resigned from the club.

Case called the toll-free number in the ad, gave his name and address, and asked for a brochure. Back at Exclusive Resorts headquarters, the company's founder, Brent Handler, saw the name on the call sheet. "I wonder if that's *the* Steve Case?" he wondered, picking up the phone to call him. When they connected, Case told Handler he might be interested in more than just becoming a member. A week later the two men met for breakfast. After an hour of discussion Case offered to buy half the company. "This was a great concept, and it's only a matter of time before it becomes more mainstream," says Case, whose holding company, Revolution LLC, now owns Exclusive Resorts entirely.

When I visited with Case in late 2006, Exclusive Resorts had 2,500 members and owned homes in forty locations, from Telluride to Los Cabos and Grand Cayman to Scottsdale. It was picking up new members at a rate of more than 100 a month. The company wasn't yet profitable, and it wasn't the only player in the burgeoning "destination club" industry. But analysts who follow the sector agree it's alone at the head of the pack. "They are so dominant that it's going to be really difficult for anybody else to catch up to them," says Dick Ragatz of Ragatz Associates, a market research firm that specializes in the resort industry.

A big part of the appeal of destination clubs is the economics. Even folks like Case with bottomless bank accounts hate the inefficiencies of watching their vacation homes sit empty most of the year, and they hate the inconvenience and upkeep required to maintain them. Atlanta physician Mark Feeman used to own two vacation properties, one at the South Carolina beach and one in the mountains of North Carolina. Over time he concluded that they were more trouble than they were worth. If he went to one of his homes for a long weekend, he'd typically spend at least one full day shopping for groceries, making small repairs, or attending to the demands of the property. "While my kids went hiking and my in-laws got to stay for free, I'm waiting for Billy Bob the gravel guy to show up," he says. When you took into account taxes, insurance, repairs, and the mortgage expenses, he figured he was spending anywhere from $35,000 to $60,000 per year on each of his two vacation houses.

So he sold them and joined Exclusive Resorts instead. For $20,000 in annual dues, he's staying in luxury homes—located all over the world—where he needn't worry about a thing. The staff, who Feeman insists are on par with Ritz-Carlton employees, will stock the refrigerator and arrange tee times, massages, private chefs, and theater tickets. As an Exclusive Resorts member, Feeman won't see his investment-gain value if the real estate market goes up, but he doesn't mind. "I can make money other ways with a lot less headaches," he says.

Lately other industries have been finding ways to tap into people's desire to have polyamorous relationships with luxury goods. In the last few years companies have begun offering dues-based memberships that give affluent people temporary use of exotic cars, high-end fashion, artwork, handbags, or jewelry. Some of the clubs—like those that lend out automobiles—work on the same model as Exclusive Resorts, with members paying for so many days of usage per year. For others, including some of the clubs offering jewelry and handbags, the model is more like Netflix, in which members are allowed to keep a handbag or bauble until they tire of it, and then they mail it back in exchange for a replacement.

For someone like Feeman, a destination club allows him to travel to Beaver Creek one month, and Bonita Springs, just north of Naples, the next month.

While in Naples I drove north to check out the Exclusive Resorts homes in Bonita Springs. In all, Case's company owns fourteen upscale properties here, many of them arrayed around a large cul-de-sac. The homes average 5,000 square feet, and they're lavishly furnished, Florida-ized versions of the kinds of homes Toll Brothers builds in Potomac View. They have soaring, coffered ceilings, acres of tile and granite, giant TVs, pro-style kitchens, and large, screened-in pools.

Inside one of the homes, concierges Angie Welday and Shalia Satter show me around. They say their guests run the gamut, from older moneyed types who fly down in private planes to younger, low-key entrepreneurs. Some are high-maintenance: When one guest clogged a toilet in the middle of the night and the concierge suggested she plunge it, the guest refused to operate the plunger and insisted the concierge come to the home to do it. But most of the guests are gracious and more reasonable in their demands. Welday and Satter are periodically reminded of just how privileged a life these people lead: When they tried to show one guest how to operate the elevator in one of these waterfront homes, the guest waved them off, saying she'd had the same elevator installed in her regular house.

As I walk around the Bonita Springs homes, the Exclusive Resorts system seems idyllic to me. The homes are so large—most have at least four bedrooms—that it'd be easy to bring extended family or groups of friends on vacation. Out back is a canal leading to the gulf, making the house ideal for boaters. If I close my eyes I can imagine spending spring break here with friends, our kids happily splashing in the pool, while a private chef prepares our dinner.

Still, no real estate relationship is perfect. One of the problems with destination clubs is that lots of members want to use the homes during the same peak weeks around holidays and school vacations. To dole out weeks fairly, the clubs use computerized systems that allow members so many far-in-advance reservations, along with a number of short-notice take-what-you-can-get trips. For people whose vacations are tied to school calendars, being flexible about where you'll visit seems to be a must.

But Case says that downside is becoming less of a problem as the membership ranks grow. As with America Online or eBay, destination clubs enjoy a network effect: The more people who join, the more homes the club is able to buy, increasing the number of new places to visit.

It's also no coincidence that as the real estate market weakened in 2006, Exclusive Resorts' membership rolls only grew longer. When Case first bought into the company in 2003, his friends were skeptical. Most of them were watching their vacation homes appreciate sharply in value. Why would they give up these profitable investments for membership in a club that can't go up in value? But as homes stopped appreciating—and in some places began falling in value—the risks of ownership have become more apparent, and the (potential) benefits of vacation-home ownership easier to forgo.

"Three years ago people felt any idiot could buy resort real estate and make money, and for a brief period of time it was true," Case says. "But it's not so true today. People are a little less bullish, which makes it easier to see the benefits of Exclusive Resorts. Before, not having appreciation was one of the potential negatives, but now maybe it's a positive. They're not playing the market here—they're making a lifestyle choice for their family."

Market researcher James Chung, who consults with resort companies, says the average American is far more optimistic about the potential to make money on a vacation home than they should be. Historically, he says, the appreciation is anything but steady. "You only make money if you happen to buy it low and happen to sell it high," he says. "That's not an investment strategy—that's luck. If you look at performance over the long term, vacation homes are not one of the better classes of real estate to own, if you're looking at it as an investment."

For Bill and Susan Finnegan, there's another benefit of membership. Before they joined Exclusive Resorts, they'd take their children skiing in places like Beaver Creek, routinely spending more than $1,000 a night for two hotel rooms to accommodate them all. Bill always loved those trips—until checkout time. "I'd always be grouchy, because we'd see this huge bill at the end of the trip, and that sort of ruins it for me," he says. With Exclusive Resorts they're staying in far nicer places, and the costs are easier to swallow. "It's a lot easier to make a payment at the start of the year; then it's done," he says.

Listening to Exclusive Resorts members rave about their vacations, you can't help but feel at least a little bit envious. Maybe monogamy is overrated.

When it comes to real estate promiscuity, there's a new lifestyle emerging in places like Naples. To see it up close I drove to Tiburon, a high-end golf course community a few miles off the water on the city's north side.

The homes, surrounded by gigantic palm trees, spiral out from the Ritz-Carlton hotel and Greg Norman golf course at its center. The homes themselves range from low-rise condos to large stucco residences costing more than $1 million. The developer of this community is WCI, a major Florida homebuilder. While doing market research to figure out how to sell homes here, the company stumbled upon an interesting trend.

Behold, a new type of polygamous homeowner: the "splitter."

WCI, which came up with the label, says splitters are different from the typical "snowbirds" who spend winter months living in warm climates and return north for the summer. Splitters are generally younger, nonretired people who are still working, but who migrate fluidly—and frequently—between two or more residences, to the point that terms like "primary home" and "second home" are becoming irrelevant to them. "They've made a life decision not to have a primary single residence," says Bill Jacobs, the market researcher who helped WCI understand the "splitter" lifestyle. Instead of the primary-home/vacation-home designation, splitters maintain separate-but-equal residences. One isn't necessarily nicer or bigger than another. To frame this in terms of relationships, think of this as a *Big Love*–style approach to real estate.

Many splitters are utilizing technology and professional flexibility to cut the cord. As one example of that, they're often ditching landline telephones—friends never know which house they'll be at, so most simply try their cell phone first. They keep dual wardrobes, and often keep two sets of doctors. According to Jacobs's research, some of these splitters migrate between homes as much as eighteen times a year.

They're an elite bunch, to be sure: It takes oodles of wealth and an unusually flexible career to make a splitter lifestyle work. But for companies building homes in resort areas, it's a demographic that could form a new base of very attractive buyers.

Keith and Kim Ferrari are classic splitters. The couple owns a large, historic home just south of Nashville, which used to be their primary residence. Keith, fifty-one, happens to be a nephew of Enzo Ferrari, who created the namesake sports car, but Keith wasn't born into wealth; instead, he acquired it himself by running several businesses, including a medical-device company and a real estate development firm. But in recent years he sold off the medical company and put his oldest son in charge of the real estate operation. So while Keith still works—as does Kim, thirty-eight, who's an accountant—both have enough flexibility that they're no longer tied to one place. So in 2005 they bought a 5,000-square-foot home at Tiburon. From their backyard pool you're a chip shot off the fifteenth fairway.

If you ask them which is their primary home and which is their vacation home, you don't get a simple answer. Says Kim: "In the beginning Tennessee was home, but now they're both home."

It'd be a seamless back-and-forth lifestyle were it not for one complication: their three children, ages seven, five, and two. For several years, to accommodate their splitter lifestyle, they enrolled their older children in preschools in both Tennessee and Florida, and migrated back and forth. But for kindergarten they felt obligated to choose a single locale, so now they spend the school year in Florida, with Keith visiting Tennessee frequently. "Most of the people who do this don't have young children," Kim says. Still, on the day I visit they're preparing to leave Thursday for a long weekend in Tennessee.

A few blocks away, Luis and Guadalupe d'Agostino are building a fairway home that will complement their existing residence in a high-rise condo in Miami, a ninety-minute drive away. When they made the decision to build the Naples home, they designated it for use on weekends and holidays. But as workers scamper around the roof one afternoon while Luis and Guadalupe watch from the street, they say they've already begun thinking of how they could split time between their residences more evenly. "I would like to get some work over in this area," says Luis, a forty-three-year-old real estate developer. Guadalupe, who sells telenovelas for Spanish-language television, does tons of work by phone and e-mail, so perhaps they'll wind up spending most of their nights in Naples, not Miami. "It could go either way," Luis says.

The average vacation-home owner spends just thirty-nine nights a year in his second property, according to research by the real estate industry. For splitters, the best way to rationalize that investment isn't to opt instead for a time-share or a destination club—it's to forge a lifestyle that pushes that number far, far higher.

On my last morning in Naples I wake up early, buy coffee and newspapers, and drive to the beach. I sit on the sand, watching the waves and scanning the headlines. The breeze is warm. The sunlight feels magnificent. I sip my coffee and watch a solitary jogger move down the beach. When I dip my toes in the gulf, it's warmer than any ocean water around Massachusetts.

I've enjoyed my time here, but as I drive down Fifth Avenue South on the way to the airport, I don't stop to gawk at the real estate ads in the office windows. The fact is, property here is just too pricey for me. Even if I had a lot of money, I wouldn't want a second home that required boarding an airplane to visit. The cost and inconvenience of the travel would keep me from using it very often, and then I'd probably obsess over how much I was spending to maintain a vacation home that sat unused.

After talking with many different vacation-home owners, I've had a chance to think about how my desire for a vacation getaway compares to theirs. I've noticed that I crave vacations less than many of them. Perhaps my workaday routine is less draining than theirs, or I like my one-and-only home a little bit more than they like theirs, so I don't consider it something from which I need to escape. While I do enjoy a couple of days at the beach, over the years I've also enjoyed vacations that don't involve leaving my house, taking a respite from work and visiting close-to-home amenities—the neighborhood pool, the local ice-cream stand, our backyard—that I visit too rarely during the workweek. I'm hardly alone in this: Someone even coined a name for these stay-at-home getaways: "staycations."

I've also found all of the economic arguments against buying a vacation home—the ones offered up by fans of time-shares and the folks marketing Steve Case's destination club—to be pretty compelling. When it comes to vacation homes, I could happily abstain from the pleasures of ownership.

Still, even though I've concluded that owning a vacation home probably doesn't make bottom-line sense for me, from time to time I continue to find myself online, looking at water-view building lots in southern New Hampshire. Or walk-to-the-beach bungalows on Cape Cod. Or ski condos in Vermont.

Even though the rational side of my brain has dismissed the possibility of a vacation-home purchase, the emotional side of my brain still seems to want one anyway.

This shouldn't be too surprising, perhaps. From buying supersize trophy homes to investing in Idaho duplexes, many of the behaviors I've encountered while reporting this book aren't entirely rational.

Houses are built of simple materials, and described in sterile legalese on the deeds that convey ownership. ("Said parcel containing 12,500 square feet of land, beginning at a point on the easterly side of Lot 47, a distance of 100 feet south . . .") But more than cars or jewelry, life insurance or lingerie, homes tug at emotional chords that run deep. For decades owning a house has been marketed as the American Dream—and as anyone who's woken up halfway through a surreal, incoherent subconscious narrative knows, dreams don't always make sense.

So despite all the inefficiency and expense, the missed flights to and from, and the hours spent waiting for Billy Bob the gravel guy, for a certain group of people finding that idyllic vacation getaway will remain the new American Dream.

House Lust works in mysterious ways.

EPILOGUE

In January of 2006, just days after I'd signed the contract to write this book, I visited my internist for my annual physical. He knows that I'm a little uncomfortable with just about everything that happens in a doctor's office—even checking my blood pressure. So as he pokes and prods me, he distracts me with small talk. "Anything new at work?" he'll ask. On this visit, I told him how I'd just agreed to write a book about Americans' obsession with homes during the real estate boom. Upon hearing this, my physician raised an eyebrow. "A book about the real estate boom?" he said, sounding a bit skeptical. "I hope you're writing *really* fast."

I've heard frequent variations of that sentiment while working on *House Lust*. For nearly a decade, pundits had predicted the real estate boom had become a bubble that was destined to pop. To no one's surprise, by mid-2005 the market had peaked. As I made reporting trips in 2006 and early 2007, headlines about the housing market focused on three questions: How long will the slowdown last? How far will home prices fall? And will the bust drag the rest of the economy into recession, too?

As I finish this book, late in the summer of 2007, there are no definitive answers to these questions. In recent weeks the outlook has turned particularly bleak, as rising foreclosure rates, the failure of several sub-prime mortgage companies, and spreading liquidity problems have led to a sharp pull-back by lenders. As *House Lust* goes to press, newspapers are filled with stories assessing how much blame these once-profligate lenders deserve for letting the housing market become so overheated.

Booms and busts are a recurring pattern in financial markets. But even though the depth and duration of this bust remain unknown as I write this, it's already clear that what happened to the U.S. housing market over the last decade went beyond the normal pattern. Unusually low interest rates, overaggressive lending, and an all-out frenzy by buyers to purchase a home before prices went higher combined to create extraordinary demand for houses. As in most booms, there was a chorus of Pollyannas explaining why prices would keep going up. As in most busts, these prognosticators now look foolish.

As the downturn continues, there will surely be more books examining this chapter in our recent economic history. They'll have plenty of room to maneuver: As I promised in the Introduction, I've steered far clear of any discussion of Federal Reserve policy, the evolution of housing finance, or the more serious economic forces that created the gold rush for homes. My focus—the behavior and psychology of everyday Americans whose spending drove the boom—is just one factor that led the supply-and-demand curves for homes to get so out of whack for a few glorious years.

As the market has turned, America's House Lust has receded, at least a little bit. At backyard barbecues, what the house down the street sold for is less a topic of conversation in 2007 than it was in 2004. Sales growth at Home Depot and Lowe's has slowed, too, as fewer people choose to double down on their rising home value by making improvements. The number of people buying investment properties has dropped sharply. Today few of us look enviously at real estate agents, imagining the windfalls they must be making.

The end of the boom has also made some people reexamine their dreams of getting rich off the value in their home. This may be a good thing: Yale economist Robert Shiller has analyzed home price movements going back to the 1890s, and he's convinced that over the long term, houses appreciate at a rate only slightly faster than inflation—and well below that of stocks. Likewise, the *Wall Street Journal's* Jonathan Clements notes that people's smugness about the "killing" they've made on their house usually ignores the closing costs, mortgage interest costs, annual maintenance expenses, and real estate commissions they've paid. If nothing else, the end of the boom should wipe the self-satisfied smirk off many of our faces when talk turned to the housing market in recent years.

But even as prices fall, America's fascination with homes has remained largely intact. Houses continue to define who we are and what we've achieved. Consider just a few indicators that House Lust is alive and well. Despite launching months after the housing boom ended, Zillow, the home valuation Web site, has taken root as a cultural phenomenon. Business magazines like *Fortune* and *Money* continue to garner huge newsstand sales when they put real estate on their covers. Despite the slump, sales of vacation homes hit a new record in 2006. And even as prices fall, many Americans remain optimistic—perhaps irrationally so—about the value of their homes. In a 2007 survey by the Boston Consulting Group, 55 percent of Americans said their home would sell for more money now than it would have a year ago. Nearly two years after the housing market's peak, ratings for HGTV's real estate shows remain high. "Real estate may not offer double-digit returns anymore, but it does offer an atavistic promise of security, a nest egg embodied in Sheetrock that you can touch and dirt that can't be outsourced to Mumbai," wrote *Time* magazine critic James Poniewozik in mid-2007, explaining this ratings phenomenon. "Property fever is in our blood."

In the introduction to this book, I described five forces that have fueled our House Lust. The first, which I called the High-five Effect, referred to the fact that we've been gathered in collective celebration as the values of our homes appreciated. That factor has disappeared, of course, as the boom has turned to bust.

Most of the other factors, however, remain intact. Even as home values decline, many Americans are still relying on the equity they've amassed as a key part of their financial futures. Tighter credit and stagnant home prices may reduce how often we refinance, but many of us will still seek to "play" our houses in a manner that's become similar to the way people play the stock market, refinancing and renovating to try to maximize its value. And whether home values are going up or down, many of us remain extremely nosy when it comes to other people's houses. In the last few months, two of the seventeen homes on my street have changed hands—and I'd bet the owners of nearly all the remaining fifteen know the prices the two sellers fetched. Financial planners say most Americans would be better off if they had a bigger 401(k) balance and a more modest home. But in a world in which homes are a tangible symbol of one's success, many people will continue to overinvest in the walls around them, for better or worse.

As for me, my obsession remains largely intact, too. My own home has surely dropped in value: I reckon it's worth between 10 and 15 percent less than it was at the 2005 peak. But as my work on this book winds down, I'm back to plotting new home improvement schemes. Any day now a mason will arrive to build exterior retaining walls, enhancing my home's curb appeal. I'm tinkering with ideas for redoing the downstairs bathroom. I'm tearing apart the basement to turn it into an exercise space. Three years ago I'd have justified these projects by pointing to the rising value of our home. Today I'm more likely to recognize them for what they are: not so much investments, but expenditures that give my family comfort and pleasure.

One of the more difficult tasks facing reporters is distinguishing between short-term fads and long-lived trends. In the 1920s men wore garish raccoon coats and swallowed goldfish for fun. In the 1950s homemakers made Jell-O mold desserts and cooked mushroom-soup-based casseroles. In the 1980s men wore mullets. Today, fortunately, those habits have largely disappeared.

But consider some different fads that do have an afterlife. In the 1950s Americans first went crazy for television game shows, and a half century later new iterations of this genre remain prime-time ratings bonanzas. In the 1980s Americans flocked to aerobics classes. A generation later the leg warmers have disappeared, but organized exercise remains a big part of many people's lives. In the late 1990s the nation began gorging on omelets, pork rinds, and steak, shedding pounds on the Atkins diet. A few years later that diet cooled to a slow simmer—but even today millions of Americans remain cautious about their carbohydrate intake, talking a new language of glycemic indexes and "net carbs."

Long after fads fade, some behaviors take root and become a way of life.

I believe the same will be true for House Lust. Our homes may no longer be making us rich, but living through an era when we thought they might has resulted in a permanent shift in thinking— one that will leave many of us happily obsessed with houses for years to come.

ACKNOWLEDGMENTS

Writing a first book can be daunting, and that challenge extends to the acknowledgments: I have a career's worth of people who deserve thanks, in addition to the many dozens without whom this book would not exist.

I'm fortunate to have spent nearly all my career at *Newsweek*, led by Rick Smith and Jon Meacham, and I can't imagine a more supportive professional home. Marcus Mabry and Mark Miller, my bosses while I worked on this project, each offered kind encouragement. Kathy Deveny and Alexis Gelber have edited most of my stories the last few years, and each has tolerated my inordinate fondness for writing and talking about houses.

I'm especially indebted to three of my former editors. Hank Gilman patiently edited my early stories. Ann McDaniel promoted me into a big job at a young age and has offered warm support ever since. Mark Whitaker plucked me from a pile of interns and spent more than a decade promoting me and my work. If not for these benefactors, I would likely be working in a job that's not half as much fun.

Dozens of other colleagues at *Newsweek*, past and present, helped sharpen my skills, particularly Mark Vamos and Eben Shapiro.

Several friends and colleagues played especially important supporting roles as I wrote *House Lust*.

John McCormick first taught me how to report long projects, and together we cowrote an early story on the housing boom that sparked my fascination with the topic.

Adam Bryant edited my coverage of the real estate boom and assigned me several stories that helped shape this book.

David Kaplan provided essential advice on navigating the publishing industry.

Mark Starr patiently edited my first drafts and provided countless other expressions of kindness along the way.

Robert Samuelson provided generous advice on adjusting the book's tone as the housing market weakened.

Matt Bai offered valuable suggestions for improving the introduction.

Adam Rogers read the entire manuscript and offered incisive feedback.

Joan Raymond deployed her charm and energy to fact-check the most troublesome sections of the manuscript.

Newsweek's Research Center helped me track down stray clips and facts.

Newsweek's Travel Department helped me get from Naples to Pocatello and back again.

Thanks to Jan Angilella and Mark Block for working to promote my work.

Keith Naughton, Brad Stone, Bret Begun, Steven Levy, Johnnie Roberts, Mary Carmichael, Karen Springen, Trent Gegax, Nancy Cooper, and Allan Sloan offered camaraderie and knew when *not* to ask how the book was going.

At Doubleday, Roger Scholl and Sarah Rainone took my initial proposal and helped shape it into something far more ambitious. Sarah's line editing improved the book immeasurably—anyone who believes that book editors don't have time to edit has never worked with her. I've appreciated Sarah's enthusiasm from start to finish.

Thanks to other supporting players at Doubleday, including Talia Krohn, Gretchen Koss, Kathy Trager, Meredith McGinnis, Maria

Carella, Nancy Campana, Andrea Dunlop, Alison Rich, Nora Reichard, Tiffany Yates, Ed Crane, and Vimi Santokhi.

My agent, Andrew Blauner, worked adroitly to get the book sold and offered wise counsel as a first-time author confronted a steep learning curve. I've been lucky to have him on my side.

Newsweek has an enlightened attitude toward staffers' freelancing, and I've been lucky to work with editors at other magazines who have helped me learn to write long-form stories. At the *Boston Globe Magazine*, Doug Most, Nick King, John Koch, Suzanne Althoff, and Anne Nelson have let me write fun and challenging pieces. Mike Hofman and his colleagues at *Inc.*, Keith Hammonds at Fast Company, Adam Rogers and Bob Cohn at *Wired*, and Kendall Hamilton at *Ski* have all provided me opportunities to use different journalistic muscles.

Becky Collet offered valuable ideas on marketing the book.

George Gendron and Sara Noble continue to offer sound career advice—as well as some great meals.

My reporting was assisted by many public relations people, who set up interviews, provided me access to model homes and building sites, and helped educate me about their industries. Thanks to Caroline Shaw, Dawn Christensen, Kira McCarron, Walter Moloney, Stephanie Singer, Emily Yarborough, Audrey Adlam, Melanie Hearsh, Jack Farrar, Amy Bohutinsky, Brooke Hammerling, Marie St. Hillaire, Bernard Tucker, Meredith Vellines, Rachel Neumann, Steve Zenker, Jacy Cochran, Ronna Kelly, Paula Fleming, and Matt Bushlow.

Judy Gerard, president of HGTV, arranged for me to spend an afternoon inside her company's programming division, which I especially appreciated.

Although I quote more than 100 people in *House Lust*, I interviewed many more whose comments helped me better understand my topic, even when I wasn't able to include them in the story. Special thanks to Karl Case, Nicolas Retsinas, Sara Lamia, Wade Hanson, Meredith Oliver, Katherine Salant, David Koch, Paula Sonkin, Chris Healy, Fred Cooper, and Joel Rassman.

Writing a book upsets any attempt at work-life balance, so I owe my family and friends a huge debt. My father, Howard McGinn, my mother, Judith Lasley, and my stepfather, Bob Lasley, offered constant encouragement. My sister and brother-in-law, Patty and Rob Humes, asked smart questions about the project during visits, as did Dean and Lily Streck.

My in-laws, Maureen and Phil Jutras, along with Nate and Ted, provided moral support and crucial help with child care while I was on the road or writing.

My family is lucky to have so many wonderful Westborough, Massachusetts, friends and neighbors who've been particularly supportive as I worked on the book.

My children, Abby, Jack, and Tommy, provided joyous distractions throughout this project.

Most of all, thanks to my wife, Amy, who remained patient as I devoted a year's worth of vacation days and too many weekends to reporting and writing. She has my appreciation, and my love.

NOTES

INTRODUCTION

3   **"a condition whose symptoms":** Daphne Merkin, "A Passion for Property," *KEY: New York Times Real Estate Magazine*, Fall 2006: 22.

3   **"a house or an apartment":** Eugene Robinson, "Real Estate Lust," *Washington Post*, June 7, 2005: A23.

4   **"Before the last decades":** Robert Shiller, *Irrational Exuberance*, 2nd ed. (Princeton: Princeton University Press), 26.

4   **Dinner Party Index:** Michael Kinsley, "Bye-Bye, Housing Boom," *Washington Post,* February 27, 2005: B7.

8   **she developed a bizarre habit:** Alex Kuczynski, *Beauty Junkies* (New York: Doubleday, 2006), 219.

9   **average U.S. home rose in value:** www.ofheo.gov/media/pdf/3q06hpi.pdf, p. 24.

11   **media "amplification":** Shiller, *Irrational Exuberance*, 43–44.

12   **"I always told you":** James Barron, "Rubble of Town House Yields Tubing Possibly Tied to Gas," *New York Times*, July 13, 2006: B2.

12   **value of the now-vacant lot:** Josh Barbanel, "Now That the Dust Has Settled," *New York Times*, February 11, 2007, sec. 11, p. 2.

CHAPTER 1

16   **one-third of American homes:** "Historical Census of Housing Tables: Plumbing Facilities." On the Web at www.census.gov/hhes/www/housing/census/historic/plumbing.html.

16   **among the 259 single-family homes:** This data was obtained via Realtor.com on July 31, 2006.

16   **average American home measured:** "Housing Facts, Figures and Trends." Published by the National Association of Home Builders. March 2006.

17   **the size of the plot of land:** "New Home Size Reaches All-Time High in 2005," *Nation's Building News*, June 26, 2006.

18   **extremely low interest rates:** "Freddie Mac. 30-Year Fixed-Rate Mortgages Since 1971," at www.freddiemac.com/pmms/pmms30.htm.

19   **industry-wide measure of a "small" beverage:** Christina Ianzito, "At the Coffee Shop, It's Always a Tall Order," *Washington Post*, August 7, 2002: C12.

19   **the average 155-pound American female:** Susanna Schrobsdorff, "Skinny Is the New Fat," *Newsweek*, October 30, 2006: 55.

19   **$200,000 is the new $100,000:** Alex Williams, "Six Figures? Not Enough!" *New York Times*, February 27, 2005: sec. 9, p. 1.

20   **a Washington suburb known:** Blaine Harden, "Big, Bigger, Biggest: The Supersize Suburb," *New York Times*, June 20, 2002.

20   **The first New American Home:** "Case History: The New American Home." A publication of the National Association of Home Builders.

20   Information on the 1984 New American Home comes from press materials supplied by the National Association of Home Builders and from the December 1983 issue of *Builder* magazine.

22   **The Gates home boasts:** Sara Clemence, "Homes of the Billionaires 2005," *Forbes*, March 10, 2005.

22   **it's worth $100 million:** Peter Singer, "What Should a Billionaire Give and What Should You?" *New York Times Magazine*, December 17, 2006: 58.

22   **rated New Balance the best:** Jay Finegan, "Surviving in the Nike/Reebok Jungle," *Inc.*, May 1993: 98.

22   **they're worth $1.6 billion:** Francis Storrs, "The 50 Wealthiest Bostonians," *Boston Magazine*, March 2006: 113.

25   **sixty such properties for sale:** Amir Efrati, "$65 Million: Priced to Sit," *Wall Street Journal*, January 13, 2006: W1.

26   **the next have-to-have: the mudroom:** Leslie Kaufman, "Oversize Mudrooms Tame the Clutter at the Door," *New York Times*, March 22, 2007: D8.

27   **the Kennedys entertained Franklin Roosevelt:** Ann Paterson Harris, *The Potomac Adventure* (Jantron, 1978), 73.

30   **"By 1820, parlor had come":** Jack Larkin, *Where We Lived* (Newtown, CT: Taunton Press, 2006), 24.

31   **"maximum-use imperative":** Keith Naughton, "Hybrid Nation? Nope," *Newsweek*, October 10, 2005: 46.

31   **"Neither individuals nor nations . . . being middle class"**: Robert J. Samuelson, *The Good Life and Its Discontents* (New York: Times Books, 1995), 55.

34   **"People have an image"**: I first wrote about Toll Brothers for *Newsweek*, and this quote is taken from that story: "Betting Against a Housing Bust," *Newsweek*, August 26, 2002: 28.

35   **"an ostentatiously large house"**: William Weir, "They're Looking Up 'Yankspeak' for the Oxford English Dictionary," *Hartford Courant*, July 5, 2000.

35   **"an excessively large home"**: www.dictionary.com.

35   **"It's time for a different kind"**: Sarah Susanka, *The Not So Big House* (Newtown, CT: Taunton Press, 2001), 3–5.

43   **about 1,033 square feet**: www.demographia.com/db-intlhouse.htm.

43   **more than 2,000 square feet**: www.demographia.com/db-japanhousing.htm.

43   **less than 1,000 square feet**: www.demographia.com/db-intlhouse.htm.

43   **"the old American representations of normalcy"**: Adam Gopnik, *Through the Children's Gate* (New York: Alfred A. Knopf, 2006), 33.

45   **5,000 so-called "microapartments"**: Nancy Hass, "House Proud: In Tiny Spaces, Expansive Living," *New York Times*, February 6, 2003: F4.

45   **"In my mind the apartment"**: Fred A. Bernstein, "A Studio That Refuses to Think Small," *New York Times,* March 30, 2006: D1.

46   **parents go through an annual ritual:** Jennifer Steinhauer, "Peace on Earth, but Goodwill for Toys," *New York Times*, December 24, 2005: A15.

46   **roughly 184 percent larger:** Candace Jackson, "The Really Big Sleep," *Wall Street Journal*, December 17, 2005: P4.

47   **teenagers have grown unusually squeamish:** Dirk Johnson, "Students Still Sweat, They Just Don't Shower," *New York Times*, April 22, 1996: A1.

47   **children who grow up in an overcrowded:** Dalton Conley, "A Room with a View or a Room of One's Own? Housing and Social Stratification," *Sociological Forum* 16, no. 2 (2001).

49   **"Buying a bigger house . . . price tag"**: Jonathan Clements, "Forget the Mansion: Why Buying Bigger Doesn't Guarantee a Rich Retirement," *Wall Street Journal*, August 23, 2006: D1.

54   **median U.S. home is thirty-two years old:** www.census.gov/prod/ 2006pubs/h150-05.pdf, p. 17.

56   **our fascination with luxurious bathrooms:** Clotaire Rapaille, *The Culture Code* (New York: Broadway Books, 2006), 4–5.

56   **anyone buying (or receiving):** Ibid., 41.

57   **"Tracts of pale, tile-roofed houses":** Sally Denton and Roger Morris, *The Money and the Power* (New York: Alfred A. Knopf, 2001), 8.

58   **"Six million families":** Kenneth T. Jackson, *Crabgrass Frontier* (New York: Oxford University Press, 1985), 232.

59   **1,400 families signed contracts:** Ibid., 235–37.

59   **Custom building can routinely:** Katherine Salant, *The Brand New House* (New York: Three Rivers Press, 2001), 16.

64   **some Americans worry as much:** "Whitening Is Big News in Oral Care," *Chain Drug Review*, October 2003.

67   **one in eight American families:** Clifford Edward Clark Jr., *The American Family Home 1800–1960* (Chapel Hill: University of North Carolina Press, 1986), 167.

67   **many architects believed the best kind of kitchen:** Ibid., 167.

67   **the twentieth-century living room:** Ibid., 163.

68   **a separate space apart from the living room:** Ibid., 215.

68   **"a hundred-year-long experiment":** Winifred Gallagher, *House Thinking* (New York: HarperCollins, 2006), 115.

72   **this neighborhood will soon be filled:** June Fletcher, *House Poor* (New York: HarperCollins, 2005), 73.

73   **the tactic risked coming off:** Rebecca Fairley Raney, "Model Homes and Model 'Families,'" *New York Times*, July 18, 2006, sec. 11, p. 14.

76   **"mass customization":** Julie Schlosser, "Cashing in on the New World of Me," *Fortune*, December 13, 2004: 244.

81   **reporters were able to slice through:** Matt Carroll, "Wall Sheathing Creates Headaches for Builder, Buyers," *Boston Globe*, May 5, 2001: A9.

81   **"Little boxes . . . just the same":** www.ocap.ca/songs/ littlbox.html.

83   **"Now, mister, . . . no used car again":** www.brucespringsteen.net/ songs/UsedCars.html.

87 **an idyllic place to live:** Demographic information on Newton comes from *Boston Magazine*'s lists of the Best Places to Live and Best Schools, accessed via www.bostonmagazine.com on July 6, 2006. Information was also obtained from the profile of Newton prepared by the Massachusetts Department of Housing and Community Development.

89 **home improvement expenditures were growing:** Joint Center for Housing Studies. Press release on Remodeling Activity Indicator. January 13, 2006.

89 **"is essentially a huge box filled":** David Owen, *The Walls Around Us* (New York: Villard, 1992), 7.

90 **between 1985 and 1999:** Joint Center for Housing Studies, "Remodeling Homes for Changing Households," 2001.

90 **has witnessed remodels that featured:** June Fletcher, *House Poor* (New York: HarperCollins, 2005), 88.

90 **"the visible triad":** Juliet B. Schor, *The Overspent American* (New York: HarperCollins, 1998), 59.

91 **even people who eschew materialism:** Although I've read parts of *Luxury Fever*, this material is drawn mainly from the author's interview with Robert Frank, January 5, 2006.

92 **In its 2005 study:** Sal Alfano, "Cost vs. Value Report," *Remodeling,* November 1, 2005.

93 **in order to complete a "personal project":** Diana Jean Schemo, "New Chief to Face Growing Resistance to Law," *New York Times*, November 14, 2004: A23.

93 **phenomenal rise in Home Depot:** Home Depot Annual Report, 2005.

94 Material on the decline of American handiness and the Home Depot workshop was first published in a story by the author in the *Boston Globe Sunday Magazine*: "He's Handy. You're Not. Here's Why," April 25, 2004.

95 **which chronicled how couples:** Penelope Green, "Irreconcilable Interiors: When Mates Don't Match," *New York Times*. January 11, 2007: F1.

96 **it seems inevitable:** Joyce Wadler, "The Allure of the Tool Belt," *New York Times*, July 20, 2006: F1.

96 Demographic information on Newton comes from *Boston Magazine*'s lists of the Best Places to Live and Best Schools, accessed via www.bostonmagazine.com on July 6, 2006. Information was also obtained from the profile of Newton prepared by the Massachusetts Department of Housing and Community Development.

96   **"Bathroom tile is their cocaine"**: David Brooks, *On Paradise Drive* (New York: Simon & Schuster, 2004), 30.

108   **"Renovation is a spiritual . . . to aspire to"**: Debi Warner, *Renovation Psychology* (Bloomington, IN: Author House, 2004), 24.

110   Information on Rachel Cox's practice comes from an interview conducted by the author. However, Cox was previously written about by Carol Lloyd of the *San Francisco Chronicle* (January 6, 2006) and by Karen Breslau of *Newsweek* (January 30, 2006).

CHAPTER 4

125   **"We live in an ultraopen"**: Shira Boss, *Green with Envy* (New York: Warner, 2006), 13.

125   **twice as many Americans**: Ibid., 28.

126   **comparing their own habits to a "reference group"**: Ibid., 6.

129   **wanted to do a demonstration**: Joanna Weiss, "In 25 Years on the Air, It's Built a Following," *Boston Globe*, October 3, 2004.

130   **"I was constantly griping"**: Cathy Lubensky, "Home Improvement Network Has Built Quite a Following in 10 Years," Copley News Service, May 22, 2005.

130   **each room could inspire**: Ibid.

131   **His bosses thought**: Alison Beard, "Growth from Home and Gardening: U.S. Newspaper Publisher E.W. Scripps' Move into 'Lifestyle' TV Shows Has Paid Off," *Financial Times*, October 8, 2003: 8.

131   **He thought it crucial**: Geraldine Fabrikant, "Successful Scripps Seeks Its Next Food Network," *New York Times*, August 14, 2006: C1.

131   **While networks like**: June Cooper-Hatcher, "The Cable Channel That Makes Us All More Homewise," *Chattanooga Free Press*, April 14, 1996.

131   **after Scripps committed to HGTV**: Ibid.

131   **the Three I's**: Bill Ervolino, "Addicted: For Those on the Home Front, HGTV Hits the Nail on the Head," *The Record*, May 7, 1998: H1.

132   **cable dial was cluttered**: Sarah Max, "A Makeover for Reality Television," CNN.com, October 31, 2003.

144   **"offers an intangible yet extraordinary"**: Meghan Daum, "Zillowing Hits Where You Live," *Los Angeles Times*, February 18, 2006.

144   **a postwedding party**: Kevin J. Delaney, "House Voyeurs, Click Here," *Wall Street Journal*, May 5, 2006.

CHAPTER 5

148   "Could I begin life again": Kenneth T. Jackson, *Crabgrass Frontier* (New York: Oxford University Press, 1985), 134.

149   the percentage of homes bought: Ivy Zelman, "Investors Gone Wild," Credit Suisse First Boston, July 5, 2005.

149   27.7 percent of the seven million: "Second Home Sales Hit Another Record in 2005; Market Share Rises." Press release from the National Association of Realtors, April 5, 2006.

152   investors made up the biggest percentage: Ruth Simon, "Investors Buy Homes at Record Pace," *Wall Street Journal*, June 30, 2005: A2.

152   the average home in Pocatello: I first wrote about real estate investment in *Newsweek*: "Psst. Wanna Hot Deal?" July 25, 2005.

153   read the headline: Advertisement from the *Boston Globe*, July 2, 2006: A19.

157   Carleton Sheets listed among: Richard Eisenberg, "The Beguiling Gurus of Get-Rich TV," *Money*, April 1986: 158.

157   Some went bankrupt: www.johntreed.com/Reedgururating.html.

157   Sheets remained among: Jessica Savco et al., "Top 50 Infomercials and Short-Form Spots of 2004," *Response*, December 1, 2004: 36.

157   "The Real Estate B.S. Artist Detection Checklist": www.johntreed.com/BSchecklist.html.

159   Material on Maura Hennigan is based on my interview with her; however, her experience as a Carleton Sheets investor was first reported by Scott Van Voorhis of the *Boston Herald* on October 3, 2005.

162   Information on Pocatello's history obtained at www.pocatelloidaho.com, www.pocatello.us, and en.wikipedia.org/wiki/pocatello,_idaho.

164   summarizes these benefits: Robert D. Dietz, "The Social Consequences of Homeownership." Published by the Homeownership Alliance, June 18, 2003.

169   My Pocatello property manager, home inspector, and tenants are not aware I'm a reporter who's writing a book. I have not asked their permission to describe my interactions with them in these pages. Therefore, to respect their privacy, I have changed the names of the individuals I call Jenny, Bob, James, and Chris.

172   Richard Ford, *Independence Day* (New York: Alfred A. Knopf, 1995), 24.

CHAPTER 6

179   **the height of the real estate frenzy:** Glen Justice, "Lobbying to Sell Your Home," *New York Times*, January 12, 2006: C1.

181   **looked upon as a "devious swindler":** Jeffrey M. Hornstein, *A Nation of Realtors* (Durham, NC: Duke University Press, 2005), 13.

181   **"made a concerted effort":** Ibid., 48.

181   **"a visionary artist":** Ibid., 29.

185   **General Motors commercial:** David Kiley, "Super Bowl Sunday's Hail Mary Ad," *BusinessWeek*, February 12, 2007.

192   All data on Realtors comes from the 2005 National Association of Realtors Member Profile.

196   **"Successful real estate agents":** Anna David, "The Real-Estate Stars of Hollywood," *Details*, May 2005: 84.

196   **as many as half of the brokers:** James McCown, "Out Front: Being Gay Helps Bring in Business, Realtors Say—and a Design Background Doesn't Hurt," *Boston Globe*, May 23, 2004: J1.

197   **gay men are also better able:** Ibid.

200   **"house humping":** Ken Hegan, "Have You House Humped Yet?" *GQ*, March 2006: 196.

204   **Realtors "[behave] like a cross":** Stephen J. Dubner and Steven D. Levitt, "Endangered Species," *New York Times Magazine*, March 5, 2006: 24.

204   **"Realtor Racket":** "The Realtor Racket," *Wall Street Journal*, August 12, 2005: A8.

205   **The traditional, straight . . . should be rebuilt":** Stephanie Andre, "Seizing the Opportunity, Claiming the Future," *RISMedia's Real Estate*, February 2007: 116.

207   **story featuring agents:** James R. Hagerty and Anjali Athavaley, "Amid Slump, Real-Estate Agents Hang Up Their Blazers," *Wall Street Journal*, February 7, 2007: B6.

CHAPTER 7

211   **typical vacation home owner:** "Vacation Home Sales Rise to Record." Press release by the National Association of Realtors. April 30, 2007.

211   **the average buyer spent only:** "Second Home Owner Survey Shows Solid Market." Press release by the National Association of Realtors. May 11, 2006.

212   **Twenty-first-century Americans are hardly:** Amy Willard Cross, *The Summer House* (Toronto: HarperCollins, 1992), 7.

212   **"It provides refuge":** Ibid., 4.

214 **As second homes have become more common:** Melinda Blau, "The Third Home Comes Within Reach," *New York Times*, December 23, 2005: D1.

214 **recently presented another option:** Vivian Marino, "The Allure of Buying Your Own Private Island," *New York Times*, September 25, 2005, sec. 11.

217 **sold for $10 apiece:** Lynne Howard Frazer, *Images of America: Naples* (Charleston, SC: Arcadia, 2004), 7.

218 **On Cape Cod, by long-standing tradition:** Marjorie Garber, *Sex and Real Estate* (New York: Alfred A. Knopf, 2006), 186.

218 **Within each community:** Steven Gaines, *Philistines at the Hedgerow* (New York: Little, Brown, 1998), 17.

226 The history of the time-share industry is recounted in the 2005 Timeshare Industry Resource Manual, a book provided to me by ARDA that is used by people training to become time-share salespeople.

227 **"The fact is that people":** ARDA Industry Fact Sheet.

230 I first wrote about Exclusive Resorts in *Newsweek*: "Man of Leisure," October 2, 2006. Portions of this section are drawn from the reporting in the *Newsweek* story.

232 **companies have begun offering:** Alice Park, "The Leasing Life," *Time Style & Design*, Spring 2007: 38.

EPILOGUE

241 **houses appreciate at a rate only:** Robert Shiller, *Irrational Exuberance*, 2nd ed. (Princeton: Princeton University Press, 2005), 20–23.

242 **people's smugness about the "killing":** Jonathan Clements, "How to Stop Relatives from Bragging About Their Big Profits in Real Estate," *Wall Street Journal*, August 25, 2004: D1.

242 **"Property fever is in our blood":** James Poniewozik, "Home Economics on TV," *Time*, June 25, 2007: 60.

INDEX

investing in real estate by, 197
licensing process, 188–91
networking by, 177–78, 182–83
new-home sales, 69–70, 73–74
number of, 179–80
open houses, 198–202, 203
price-setting for homes, 198–99
recreationally minded agents, 195–96
social status of, 180–81, 183–85, 196
staging of homes, 200–202
success through persistence and luck, 185–87
unsuccessful agents, 193–95
vacation-home sales, 216–19
Web sites on real estate and, 205
Real estate boom, 6, 7
Real estate media
newspaper columns, 120–22, 123
popularity of, 123–26, 146
prices, focus on, 126, 138–39
Web sites, 123, 141–45, 205, 213–14, 216
See also Television programs on real estate
Real estate slump of 2007, 240–42
Realtor.com (Web site), 143
Reed, John T., 156–57, 158, 161
Renovating of homes, 2–3, 8, 85–89, 241
architect-client relationship, 101–3, 112–16
construction-related difficulties, 112–13
contractors for, 95–96, 99
decision-making for, 92–93, 101, 104, 106–7
"discretionary" remodels, 89–90
do-it-yourself option, 93–95
financing of, 87, 104–6, 117
inspections of renovations, 96–98
"I've earned it" rationale, 91–92
marital conflict and, 107–11
neighbors and, 103–4
postrenovation depression, 111, 118
postrenovation satisfaction, 116–19

prices charged for, 97, 98
problems common to, 99–100
renovation frenzy of recent years, 89
security and privacy concerns, 104
status-seeking and, 90–91
stresses of, 88–89, 95, 98–99, 104–5, 107–11
TV shows about, 129–30
value increases and, 88, 92
"while-you're-here" syndrome, 105–6
Renovation Psychology program, 107–9
Retirement planning, 224
Ricciardelli, Enzo, 197
Robinson, Eugene, 3

Sachs, Peter, 101–3, 112–16
Samuelson, Robert J., 31–32
Sandler, Tara, 132, 133, 137
Sands, Bill, 221–23
Satter, Shalia, 233
Schmidtberger, Melissa, 69–70, 73–74
Schor, Juliet, 90
Schwartz, Barry, 77
Sex and Real Estate (Garber), 135
Sheets, Carleton H., 153, 154, 157, 159, 167
Shiller, Robert, 4, 11, 241–42
Shook, Bill, 225, 228–29
Sincock, Susie and Andy, 2
Smaller homes, 42–46, 47
Splitter lifestyle, 235–37
Spradlin, Ron, 178–79, 196, 207–8
Spring, Greg, 6
Springsteen, Bruce, 83
Square footage
larger homes and, 18–19, 28–29, 38
as prime measure of housing, 39–42
Staging of homes, 200–2
Staycations, 238
Steele, Lockhart, 142
Stocker, Edi, 147–48, 176
Strelke, Fred, 94
Susanka, Sarah, 35–38